When We Imagine Grace

When We Imagine Grace

Black Men and Subject Making

SIMONE C. DRAKE

The University of Chicago Press   Chicago and London

SIMONE C. DRAKE is associate professor of African American and African studies at Ohio State University.

The University of Chicago Press, Chicago 60637
The University of Chicago Press, Ltd., London
© 2016 by The University of Chicago
All rights reserved. Published 2016.
Printed in the United States of America

25 24 23 22 21 20 19 18 17 16   1 2 3 4 5

ISBN-13: 978-0-226-36383-7 (cloth)
ISBN-13: 978-0-226-36397-4 (paper)
ISBN-13: 978-0-226-36402-5 (e-book)
DOI: 10.7208/chicago/9780226364025.001.0001

Library of Congress Cataloging-in-Publication Data

Names: Drake, Simone C., 1975– author.
Title: When we imagine grace : black men and subject making /
    Simone C. Drake.
Description: Chicago ; London : The University of Chicago Press,
    2016. | Includes bibliographical references and index.
Identifiers: LCCN 2015046037 | ISBN 9780226363837 (cloth :
    alk. paper) | ISBN 9780226363974 (pbk. : alk. paper) | ISBN
    9780226364025 (e-book)
Subjects: LCSH: African American men—Social conditions. | African
    Americans—Social conditions.
Classification: LCC E185.86 .D73 2016 | DDC 305.38/896073—dc23
LC record available at http://lccn.loc.gov/2015046037

♾ This paper meets the requirements of ANSI/NISO Z39.48-1992
(Permanence of Paper).

Contents

When Crisis Meets Grace

On May 24, 2014, I opened my e-mail to see a Public Safety Notice from the Ohio State University Police describing three separate incidents in which OSU students were assaulted and robbed. These notices are infrequent, so it was jarring to see three incidents reported in one evening. It was disheartening to read the reports and verify what I feared: the assailants were black males. The victims of the first and third incidents identified the assailants as black males between sixteen and twenty-two years old. The victim of the second incident reported not seeing his assailant before being knocked down, kicked, and punched and having his personal property stolen. Because this incident is chronologically sandwiched between two reports that include descriptions of the assailants, many people might deduce, whether correctly or incorrectly, that the assailant in the second incident, like those in the first and third, was also a black male. Those three Public Safety Notices, like all that preceded and have come after them, almost always identify young black male suspects.

On a campus with a total African American student population of 5.33 percent or 3,630 students, in a state whose African American population is 13.7 percent or over 1.5 million people, and at a university with a total enrollment of 64,868,[1] notices that consistently identify black male suspects, in the minds of many, render all black males on campus, whether they are students,[2] staff, faculty, or guests, as suspects. This truth was evidenced later the same year on October 16, when a staff person in the College of Arts and Sciences was instructed to send the following message to faculty and staff in my department's building:

There was a stranger who had been randomly entering different offices in Bricker Hall yesterday. This morning in University Hall we believe that the same person was seen on the first floor in 143 UH, Museum Room. The stranger is an African-American male, about 5 ft. 7 in, short hair, and was carrying a black backpack.

There is a concern that he may be looking for crimes of opportunity. As always, please be very cautious about the accessibility of your purse, wallet, electronic items, etc. Please make sure that your valuables are in a secure place. Do not leave office doors open while you are away for an extended period of time.

University Police came to Bricker and spoke to several occupants who saw the individual. They are asking that if anyone see [sic] this person wandering around, you should call University Police to report his presence in the building.

I do not know who authorized the message, and after the maelstrom of e-mails from my department chair, the chair of Women's, Gender and Sexuality Studies, and a couple of faculty members, I doubt whoever authorized the e-mail would be eager to take credit for doing so. There are always students with backpacks roaming the halls of my building on weekdays. The other building, Bricker, is an administrative building adjacent to my building, but it is not uncommon to see smaller numbers of students in that building, too. Such little thought was put into the warning and its implications that the originator did not even consider that University Hall houses the Department of African American and African Studies, and, as my chair noted in his response, the description, or lack thereof, could fit most of the black men in the department. For many, then, there is a logical equation between black maleness and pathology.

When I told my husband, a patrol officer with the Columbus Police Department who is assigned to the OSU campus area, about the Public Safety Notices, he regretfully shook his head. Remembering that evening, he said, "We had to stop pretty much any black male on campus that night because they were a suspect," at least in the immediate aftermath.[3] I could not follow the logic. He attempted to clarify by explaining that, with so few black male students enrolled at OSU, any who happen to be in the campus area become suspects when a crime notice goes out identifying black male perpetrators (who match what are usually very generic descriptions). I still cannot follow the logic. I know how the logic manifests, but the way that it is publicly practiced infuriates me. As a strong debater, I pushed back against the illogical insistence that so many black men could be suspects when another spree of Public Safety Notices was released on September 27 and September 28, 2014. These notices identified "reported" and "possible" sexual assaults. The September 27 event occurred in a campus dormitory. The two events on the following evening occurred in an area that is technically off-campus but is literally across the street from university buildings; the university particularly emphasized that the location was off-campus. These reports identified white males as suspects. My immediate inquiry for my husband, then, was, "Certainly, every white male in the campus area those evenings was rounded up as a suspect, correct?" I received silence in response. He is a very intelligent man, so I am confident that silence was the best he could offer for a practice that is not just.

Legal scholar Derrick Bell recounts the violations of the civil liberties of over six hundred black men in San Francisco during the "zebra killings," when police released crude composite sketches of the black assailants who had murdered seventeen white citizens. The description read:

One or two Black males
20 to 30 years old
5 foot 8 to 6 foot
Slender to medium build
On foot or in a passenger vehicle[4]

Acknowledging that authorities would insist that the same actions would have been implemented if the zebra killer suspects had been white, Bell recalls a precedent for rampant Fourth Amendment violations,[5] which leads him to deduce:

The power of the law to protect blacks from physical abuse and deprivation of even basic rights by either governmental officials or self-appointed racial regulators is limited. At some infinitely variable point—sometimes in matters of little moment, at others when the need for protection is critical to the maintenance of dignity, property, or even life itself—the legal provisions designed and enacted to protect black rights become suddenly, and without notice, inoperable.[6]

The indifference of the law and its regulatory systems in shirking responsibility for protecting black rights is on full display when every black man in a particular age demographic at my university becomes a suspect. It is not simply because "they all look alike," as evidenced by the descriptions and subsequent mass police "stop and frisks" in both the university incidents and the zebra case. At OSU, the shirking of responsibility can be perpetuated because of the structural inequalities and prejudices that reduce black men to a miniscule minority at the university.

Such unfair parity in policing and profiling makes me woeful as a mother of three black sons. The thought that they could be, and in all likelihood will be, pulled over or stopped while minding their own business and abiding the law is infuriating. The fact that their black maleness positions them as always already suspects in the eyes of many, including the legal system and its administrators, fuels the rampant discourse around black male crisis in nearly every facet of the public and private realms. The mainstream news media, academic research-ers, private corporations, philanthropic foundations, government agen-cies, black churches, and even the president of the United States either report on or deliberate over the state of crisis that positions black men as one of the most oppressed and marginalized populations in the na-tion. Disproportionate imprisonment and conviction rates, limited and unequal job prospects, and an educational system that fails to success-fully educate black boys fuel the discourses of crisis. These discourses, in turn, support the funding of research initiatives such as the one in which I am a participant, the Scholars Network on Black Masculinity, a Ford Foundation–funded initiative. As "an assembly of scholars com-mitted to reshaping scholarly and public understandings of the lives of African American men and exposing the cultural dimensions of the Black male experience," its mission is to work "toward improving the well-being of African American men."[7] While I believe wholeheartedly in the mission and work of the Scholars Network and social science–oriented achievement programs for black boys and young men, I si-multaneously wholeheartedly believe that, as a scholar invested in social justice and the mother of three beautiful black boys, I must be wary of uncritically imbibing discourses of crisis. Put differently, I am against crisis.

When I say that I am against crisis, I am borrowing from Paul Gil-roy's book with a similar title, *Against Race: Imagining Political Culture beyond the Color Line* (2000). The basic premise of Gilroy's dense argu-ment is that humanity cannot move beyond racial codification and discrimination if we continue to accept race as a biological construct in language and codifying systems while denouncing it as socially con-structed. In a similar vein, I am against crisis because not only is the discourse often rooted in patriarchal ideologies relying, for validation of their methods and rationale, on the subordination of black women, but it also strips black men and boys, including my own boys, of any inherent ability to act for and define themselves. On the surface, discourses of black male crisis raise legitimate concerns about the well-being of black men socially, politically, economically, and psychologically; yet, psychological well-being is inherently undermined, for the language itself assigns a subordinate and limited space of victimhood to black men and boys.

When We Imagine Grace is my personal intervention to create the possibility that my sons will not understand being black and male as a state of crisis. It is also an effort to negotiate my own research agenda that draws on black feminist theories in order to analyze representations and constructions of black masculinities in the US public sphere, cultural productions, policy, and law. I aim to create a space to think about what is lost when discourse on black men is so narrowly tailored that pathology and victimhood dominate the national narrative on a *singular* black masculinity—the black masculinity that apparently haunts my university. My hope for this book is that it will serve as one example of the importance of reflecting on black men as complex, diverse, thinking subjects. The primary means by which I do this is to explicitly link the ways in which culture informs the law and public policy. This linkage will hopefully trouble the white heteropatriarchal supremacy that criminalizes hoodies, makes all black men suspects, assumes their inherent unintelligence, and ultimately, in very specific ways, makes this nation an unsafe and undemocratic space to occupy when black and male. For this reason, I believe my project fills a salient gap in black masculinity studies, where the emphasis tends toward instances when black men are unable to control their fates and act for themselves, resulting in a frequent exclusion of other narratives of black men's experiences. Whether it is Michelle Alexander's ubiquitous critique of mass incarceration in *The New Jim Crow*, John Singleton's film *Baby Boy*, or Richard Wright's novel *Native Son*, there is a propensity among scholars, activists, and cultural producers to privilege victimhood in a manner that obliterates agency and resistance. This project intervenes in addressing this disparity by not only analyzing ways in which black men have worked to control their fates and be their own agents, but also by focusing on the experiences of black men who are not positioned at what film scholar Ed Guerrero calls the "schizophrenic" poles—exceptional or pathological—where dominant culture, and many times black people themselves, often position black men.[8]

Discourses of crisis participate in producing unsafe and undemocratic spaces both rhetorically and epistemologically. Language is important, and as such, disaggregating "crisis in black masculinity" and "black men in crisis" is central to understanding my intended intervention. There is a critical difference between "maleness" and "masculinities." Maleness, as a race-neutral concept, is generally accepted as attached to biology and anatomy; masculinities, however, are constructions or performances attached to gender. "Black men in crisis" discourse, then, is just as much about black *masculinity* being in crisis as it is about black *males* being in crisis. What emerges from this discussion is something that, in a slightly different but related context, Amy Abugo Ongiri has articulated as "resistant rather than in crisis" black masculinities.[9] In the context of my argument "black men (males) in crisis discourse" is homogenous and delimiting. Not only does the discourse become exclusively about heterosexual black men, excluding black trans men (not males) and black queer males (not men), but it also produces the overdetermined equation that crisis plus black maleness equals problematic black masculinities. In other words, it is popular and widely accepted in black masculinity studies to rely on crisis as the foundational tool for conceptualizing "complex" or "multidimensional" black masculinities. The trouble is that beginning with "crisis" and "black maleness" as addends produces a sum that ultimately perpetuates static black maleness or resistant black masculinities. I propose that substituting "imagination" and "grace for black men" as addends in that equation will produce a sum neither limiting nor repetitive of the very discourses that inform narratives of dangerous black men endangering my (white) campus. While, for black nationalists, "crisis in black masculinity" discourse was a problem of black men being unable to be proper, heterosexual patriarchs, the "black men in crisis" discourse propagates the same homogenous construction of black masculinity rooted in heteropatriarchy, impossibilities, and, at times, black nationalist sensibilities—despite its admirable intentions.

When We Imagine Grace aims to challenge readers to consider an alternative equation or epistemology in order to think differently about subjectivity and agency in relationship to being black and male. Without a doubt, there is a host of systems that obstruct and limit the ability of black men to exact agency, but the fact that, in small and grand ways, black men work against those systems is no trivial matter. This narrative needs to be told alongside others that fuel discourses of crisis. This nation itself might be in a state of crisis because of its failure to extend democratic ideals to all of its citizens, but that does not mean the only way my little boys can understand their future as black men is as a future circumscribed by crisis. In other words, I want them to have stories of agency and self-definition they can wear like an armor to reassure them that they are more than suspects, more than problems.

Because seeing one's self as someone and something different than what society says you are requires a hefty dose of imagination, it is fitting that, as a theoretical tool, this book draws on a story so powerful it could be the African American Ur-narrative. Nobel Prize winner Toni Morrison's novel *Beloved* is recognized globally as a narrative of slavery and redemption. As the story of a fugitive slave woman who would rather take the life of her children than subject them to the brutality of slavery, *Beloved* calls on its readers to think critically about what constitutes freedom, as well as meditate on how the past informs and, for many, haunts the present. The past, or what sociologist Avery Gordon poignantly refers to as "endings that are not over," haunts this nation.[10] This is true, whether reflected in my own fear that my sons will be subjected to stereotypes in school, in the workforce, and simply walking down the street, or in the determination by the justice system that equality is no longer a foundational tenet, in such cases as *Shelby County v. Holder* (2013), which struck down Section 5 of the 1965 Voting Rights Act, and *Schuette v. Coalition to Defend Affirmative Action* (2014), which affirmed Michigan voters' right to ban affirmative action in college admissions. Overcoming the haunting past is at the center of *Beloved*, and the tool Morrison proposes be used is at the center of this project—imagination.

When Baby Suggs, holy, holds "service" in the Clearing behind 124 Bluestone—"a wide-open place cut deep in the woods"— it creates a space for crying, dancing, and laughter among black women, men, and children.[11] The Clearing functions as a safe space that affirms blackness. It is a space where Baby Suggs, holy, instructs her congregation of abused, tired, and disenfranchised black people to love themselves because no one else will. Without judgment, Baby Suggs tells them "that the only grace they could have [is] the grace they could imagine. That if they could not see it, they would not have it."[12] She encourages them to claim their own freedom and to join her in imagining a liminal space suspended between the realities of their racialized existence and the possibility of something else. For black men, specifically, something else is the freedom to choose a raced, gendered, and sexed identity that is not mapped onto them by mainstream culture, popular media, or the legal system. Thus, this project extracts the premise "when we imagine grace" from Baby Suggs's insistence on imagining grace in order to begin to think about black men who are *making* choices through individual self-actualization, rather than understanding themselves as the victims of others' judgments.

When We Imagine Grace is concerned with how black men actively construct black male subjectivities in direct relation to the nation and its promised democratic ideals, and in relation to the private spaces they occupy outside of the public domain. While the public sphere might continue to struggle with moving beyond a monolithic black masculinity, some areas of black masculinity studies are slowly moving beyond the notion of black men in "perennial crisis."[13] Moving beyond crisis, insisting on spaces in which black men reject identities circumscribed by crisis and, instead, define themselves and their destinies, is no simple matter given the very real structural and institutional forms of racism that affect black men's lives daily. There is power, however, in imagining grace for one's self. My intervention in black masculinity studies, then, is to analyze the vicissitudes of black men's experiences when they decide to be their own agents—when they decide to claim the authority to act on their own behalf and in their own best interests, rather than be recipients of the authority of someone else. My approach is not a popular one in an era when there are so many deficits one could measure instead. It takes a true belief in grace, however, for individuals who know firsthand the undemocratic realities of black maleness in the United States to decide that they are the men they say they are rather than the static, monolithic black man society insists they are. There is power in self-definition.

Acknowledgments

I am grateful to so many wonderful family members, friends, and colleagues who helped this project come to fruition. The place I must begin, however, is with my father, Edward E. Poindexter Jr., who has always and continues to believe in my abilities to do far more than I can imagine for myself. Parenting changes with life stages, and now that I am a mother of three sons, my father has been a secondary disciplinarian and nurturer for my sons, as well as a wise sage as I navigate all of my identities: mother, wife, daughter, sister, and scholar. He is the best! My father's father suffered a fatal heart attack when my father was only twelve years old. However, much of what made my father push me to do my best scholastically, be athletically competitive, and, as my Aunt Lady (Sheila) says, "Not take no stuff," was learned from his father, Edward "Gene" Poindexter. I am told my paternal grandfather was known to carry a knife, is said to have, with his brother, cut a white man who gave him grief, and was kicked out of secondary school in West Virginia for carrying a gun on the bus—couldn't take chances when black men were being lynched. He also instructed his only daughter not to bother fighting anyone—use a brick instead. Similarly, his children were instructed never to lose a fight—if you couldn't win on your own, get your brothers, and if you still couldn't win, get your cousins. My family certainly is not a fighting bunch of troublemakers, but my grandfather taught them how to survive and watch out for one another during a time when high vigilance was necessary. They still do this now by never failing to be willing to do *anything* they can to help me, and for that, I am grateful to the Poindexter and Deberry clan. I am also privileged to be the granddaughter of the very complicated late Major Gilbert Alexander Boothe, whose life was a tumultuous pursuit of grace and is foregrounded in this book. I am grateful to my Aunt Clara Luce Cañada for the conversations that filled in missing pieces, and for my Georgia cousins—Helen Jones, Alfeda Jenkins, and Pamela Patterson—who shared their memories of my grandfather.

I am not sure this project would have ever evolved if not for the late Jesse James Scott. Both the hours and hours of conversation and his absolute brilliance will always be cherished and forever missed. A true friend of my mind.

I have had the good fortune of gaining new mentors during the production of this book. This project was meandering along and lacking a true theoretical crux until David Ikard walked through the project with me just weeks after I gave birth to my third child, so I could make a fellowship application deadline. Mark Anthony Neal has been the epitome of an old-school scholar tradition of giving tirelessly to bring more faculty of color into the fold. In addition to remembering me from one brief encounter and later plugging me into the Ford Foundation–funded Scholars Network on Black Masculinity, he has continued to advocate for me and affirm my intellect. And, he continues to publish cutting-edge scholarship that is central to my work on black gender studies. For many, Judson Jeffries seems like an unlikely mentor. In spite of our very different personalities and disciplines of training, we meshed because we both believe in doing what we believe is right even when the repercussions can be brutal. There are also the mentors who encouraged me in my infancy as a scholar and still do today: Carol Henderson, Viola Newton, Amrit Singh, and Toni King.

This book would have been a much longer time coming if not for a conversation with Frederick Aldama, who, when I had only two chapters drafted, was adamant I could get it fully drafted that year; I came close. Townsand Price-Spratlen has encouraged me to delve into sociology, and really all of the scattered directions my interdisciplinary interests push me toward. My department chair, Ike Newsum, also was pivotal in moving my writing process along. I made the crazy decision to pursue a degree at OSU's Moritz College of Law in the middle of the tenure process. Ike wholeheartedly supported my choice, particularly through his willingness to allow me to teach during the summer in order to better juggle the law classes. This book would be a very different book if I had not completed the law program. Cinnamon Carlarnne,

Joseph Stulburg, Sharon Davies, Vincene Verdun, Guy Rub, and Stanley Laughlin allowed me an intellectual space to think about how law, culture, and social policy intersect. Marc Spindelman and Daniel Tokaji were particularly helpful with constitutional law. I love that Martha Chamallas could immediately understand why I would think about Marcus Garvey, Berry Gordy, and Jay-Z together, and then offer feedback that was so on point; she's brilliant. Jessica Richman Dworkin was the best adviser and taught me a lot more than just legal writing. I loved the academic rigor and demand for excellence Katrina Lee insisted upon in Legal Negotiations.

All work and no play is never a good way. My wellness practitioners—Daniel Pyolnim Miller, Kyron Moses, and Dr. Deryck Richardson—have helped me counter the negative energy the academy can produce. My sister friends—some old and some new—also contribute to keeping me balanced. Adrienne Dixson has no problem "keeping it real," which I love. I have had the privilege of experiencing both sides with Valerie Lee—both as her student and, now, as junior faculty mentee. Theresa Delgadillo gets me out of the house to take long hikes periodically, and both she and Lynn Itagaki have been great writing retreat companions. Lisa Woodward and I go back to kindergarten, and no matter how crazy our grownup lives are, we always stay connected; I am grateful for the steadfast optimism she brings to balance my pessimism. Stacia Jones, too, goes back to schooldays, and I am grateful for her matter-of-fact approach to navigating grown-up life. A new friend, Caryn Hederman, finds more excitement in my recent professional accomplishments than I do, and the opportunity to commiserate with another professional mother of three wild boys has been priceless. Much gratitude is owed to Captain Tiffany Cullen, whose conversation in my kitchen about a collection of army documents I inherited from my grandfather resulted in the foundation for this book. There are also the scholar friends—new and old—whom you never see often enough, but it is always good when you do: Nazera Wright, Ayesha Hardison, Kimberly N. Brown, Jeffrey McCune, and David J. Leonard. And I am grateful for those colleagues at OSU who have extended friendship and encouragement at work and outside of work: Cheikh Thiam, Monika Brodnika, Franco Barchiesi, Anthonia Kalu, Devin Fergus, Adélékè Adéẹko, Kwaku Korang, Denise Noble, and Shannon Winnubst. I am also thankful for the research assistance of Kelly Eager in the early stages of this project.

This book could not be what it became without some specific people's engaging feedback. I am, therefore, grateful to my anonymous readers, who graciously provided superb feedback and affirmation of the project. Dwan Henderson Simmons is a brilliant editor and reader who can engage ideas critically and help to challenge and strengthen arguments in ways that never cease to amaze me. Her brilliance makes me look better than I am. I cannot wait to read the work Terrance Wooten produces upon completing his dissertation. It was a privilege to advise his MA thesis, and I am grateful to call him a friend. It has been a particular privilege to have him read sections of this book and help me to reorganize and extend arguments in the final round of revising. He, too, is a brilliant scholar.

Just as I had mentors who were just right for this, I have had an editor who is fabulous! It has truly been a privilege to work with Douglas Mitchell, and I now know firsthand why he is referred to as "legendary." Interdisciplinary work is messy and complicated, and Doug was perfect for taking that road with me and both understanding and appreciating what I was trying to do. I am also grateful to the production team at the University of Chicago, including Kyle Wagner, Joel Score, Brian Chartier, Ben Balskus, and Ashley Pierce, as well as for copyediting assistance from Marian Rogers.

And, to borrow from Toni Morrison, I save "my best things" for last. Being a mother and a wife is, in my mind, far more difficult than writing books or negotiating university politics. My smart, lively, beautiful sons, Seth, Isaac, and Solon, bring exceptional joy to my life. Watching them grow (and frequently argue with one another and break things and make messes) is the best gift I could ever receive. I am thrilled to be taking this adventure with Andrew Drake, my best friend and babydaddy extraordinaire, who seems to always be thinking about my intellectual work and never holds back on adding his two cents. Thank you, Andy, and thank you, boys, for sharing me with my books.

Navigating Discourses of Crisis

Before learning my husband and I were pregnant with the first of our three sons, I had given little thought to motherhood. I experienced enough of my own challenges growing up as a black girl that any thought I had given to rearing children was singularly attuned to how to love and protect a black girl from systems designed to facilitate harm and marginalization. That was my experience—it was what I knew best. By the time I enrolled my oldest son in preschool, I was learning the systems from which I knew a daughter would need protection were the very same systems from which I would also need to protect my black sons. In fact, I remember a long, indicting letter I wrote to the director of my oldest son's first preschool when I removed him. The manner in which that preschool and, eventually, even a Montessori school, racialized his responses to a lack of intellectual and creative stimulation as a behavior problem continues to keep me on high guard; I am a fierce mama. In addition to the educational challenges that come with raising black boys, there is a host of social factors to combat, too. Thus, aside from running a loving but tight ship, I keep the realities of life in a racist, sexist, capitalist society at bay through the knowledge that my sons are not any of the negative constructions society has pinned on black boys.

I cannot close my eyes, click my heels, and make a wish for a better, more just, and equal nation and expect my wish to be granted. However, I myself can actively work toward creating a better, more just, and equal nation. This book, *When We Imagine Grace: Black Men and Subject Making*, is one effort toward creating a nation that will see black boys and men differently than the static, homogenous representations that informed how preschool staff responded to my son's intellect and age-appropriate behavior. At the center of this endeavor is *imagination*. Borrowing from Toni Morrison's *Beloved*, I propose that what I do for my sons is what many black men, in the past and present, also practice. I ultimately imagine grace for them—I imagine that in each of their unique and amazing selves exists a well-deserved exemption from the hate and ignorance that would suggest their lives do not matter, that they are a problem for this nation. The real-life and imagined black men I study in this project have also imagined grace for themselves. Imagining grace is an agentic activity that resists stereotypes and homogenous constructions of black masculinity. The narratives I weave about how the men I study work to define themselves as thinking, feeling, human subjects are equally as important as the stories we are more familiar with, like the challenges I face raising black boys. It is unavoidable, then, that the stories I tell are told against the backdrop of crisis.

There is nothing new about discourses of crisis, black men, and masculinity. When Alexander Crummell founded the American Negro Academy in 1897, he gendered black intellectuals as male only.[1] Following course, a fellow academy member, W. E. B. Du Bois, produced a seminal text on the difficulties of post-Reconstruction black life whose chapter titles alone make it clear that progress will be made through the leadership of black men. Public debates between Booker T. Washington, Du Bois, Marcus Garvey, and A. Philip Randolph emphasized black male "race men" and intellectuals as the hope for a disenfranchised black nation. The impetus for such leadership was the idea that black men occupied a state of crisis when they transitioned from slave to free due to their inability to be proper patriarchs. The pang of being denied the social and political privileges afforded white men would serve as an implicit foundation of the social movements of the second half of the twentieth century. The lifeless, grotesque corpse of Emmett Till in an open casket was published in *Jet* magazine and the *Chicago Defender*. The images were a reminder of the savage reality of life on the color line for black men and boys. The liberation rhetoric of the civil rights movement—for which Till's murder is often understood as a catalyst—was regularly gendered male. Assistant Secretary of Labor Daniel Patrick Moynihan's 1965 "report," *The Negro Family: The Case for National Action*, would inform the persistent gendering of the Black

Power Movement as one invested in recouping black manhood. Thirty years after Moynihan's controversial report, Louis Farrakhan would organize the Million Man March, which was explicit in its solitary concern with black male crisis and self-help. The discourse of black men in crisis driving efforts toward racial equality is so ingrained that, in 2014, the White House launched the My Brother's Keeper Initiative to, according to President Obama, "help more of our young people stay on track. Providing the support they need to think more broadly about their future."[2] As in previous national efforts to achieve racial equality, Obama, too, equates young (black and brown) people with being male. These prevailing suppositions that black men stand in for the nation, that having been denied the heteropatriarchal privilege of their white male counterparts, black men occupy a perpetual state of crisis, fuel such gendered discourse as the "cradle (or school)-to-prison-pipeline" and mass incarceration. These narratives consistently leave out black women and girls, who, presumably, are not in crisis.

This genealogy of crisis also fuels the recently christened Black Lives Matter movement. Almost two decades into the twenty-first century, it is heartbreaking to reflect on the state of black incorporation into the nation. The rampant lynching, beating, and maiming of black people that marked the failures of Reconstruction over one hundred years ago diminished after the civil rights era, but were never entirely eliminated; they have resurfaced today at epidemic proportions. The acquittal of white-identifying Latino George Zimmerman, who shot and killed an unarmed black teenager, Trayvon Martin, in Sanford, Florida, on February 26, 2012, left the black nation in mourning—mourning that would metamorphose into outrage and ignite a mass movement in 2014, when Michael Brown, another unarmed black teenager, was shot and killed by Ferguson, Missouri, police officer Darren Wilson, who would also be acquitted of any criminal charges. The Black Lives Matter movement was born, and its "I can't breathe" and "Hands up, don't shoot" slogans are prominent on social media and material culture (i.e., T-shirts). Just as the civil rights movement of the 1950s and 1960s gained momentum from the lifeless body of a young black man, so, too, has the Black Lives Matter movement. This contemporary movement, therefore, is also about more than the Fourth Amendment search and seizure protocols and the Fifth Amendment's due process clause. The economic, educational, political, and social realities of black life in the twenty-first century are also being laid bare. More often than not, and not without being highly problematic, the realities being laid bare are framed as a black male crisis. The remainder of this introduction, as well as the next chapter, works through the intersections of crisis and black maleness in an effort to lay a foundation for the intervention I hope to make with analyses of discourses of crisis and constructions of black masculinities within those discourses. What I hope emerges is a space for a nuanced analysis of black male humanity—an analysis that seemingly happens only when we imagine grace for black men.

When and Where She Enters, Again

My critical analysis of gender in the context of black men responds to two specific critiques of black men and gender.[3] In a 1997 interview with Evelynn Hammonds, black feminist scholar Beverly Guy-Sheftall insists that black feminist scholarship must begin to talk about black men's gender, declaring, "We race black men, but we don't gender them."[4] Guy-Sheftall does not propose what it means to gender black men or how such a task might be carried out. However, not long after Guy-Sheftall's declaration, legal and gender scholar Devon Carbado took this issue up in his 1999 edited collection, *Black Men on Race, Gender, and Sexuality*.[5] He critiques the patriarchal ways in which gender is socially constructed, and emphasizes the importance of men using their gender privilege to challenge social constructions of gender. *Progressive Black Masculinities* (2006) continues in the same vein as *Black Men on Race, Gender, and Sexuality*. In it, legal scholar Athena D. Mutua explains that, in her efforts to organize a workshop of the same name, the concept of "progressive black masculinities" ultimately became defined through an intersectional lens.[6] She notes that as discussions centered "on the gendered nature of black men's oppression as exemplified by mass incarceration," what became apparent is that certain behaviors like violence are gendered. From examining precisely how violence is gendered, the group began to think about specific ways that "black men faced suspicion and the narrowing of their life opportunities because they were *both* black *and* men." They ultimately concluded that it was not solely race, but also gender that "explain[ed] certain types of black male experiences" that could not simply be explained by poverty.[7] Although the examples of gender intersecting with race (and class) in black men's experiences reflect a crisis-victim paradigm, they do acknowledge the assertion Guy-Sheftall makes—creating a space in which the presence of both race and gender may be examined in black men's lives.

My anecdotes and analysis help to situate where I see myself entering black masculinity studies, and as I enter, I am struck by the limited scholarship by black women scholars in the field. As I completed my dissertation on contemporary black heterosexual dynamics in literature and film and considered the conclusion I drew, I determined that the tools black feminist criticism provides me are also useful for thinking about when and how black men are gendered. Yet, when I delved into the broader arena of critical race and gender studies, I could not help but notice the absence of black women scholars (or women, period) doing work in the field of black masculinity studies.[8] Michael Awkward addresses this absence through a collegial invitation in his essay "Black Feminism and the Challenge of Black Heterosexual Male Desire" (2000). In it, he proposes, "Black feminism's capacity to impact black youth may be determined, in part, by how successfully it addresses the other side of the gender divide."[9] His invitation follows a reasonable logic, noting that in order to improve black women's lived existences, black feminism might need to concern itself with the lives of those people black women overwhelmingly live alongside—black men. "Black feminism," Awkward argues, "might well come to see 'nonmonolithic black masculinity' as a crucial topic and way of encouraging potentially sympathetic men to live, work, and love in accordance with basic feminist principles."[10] Awkward defined his career as a black man who would risk asserting a place in black feminism when many black feminist women were not inclined to imagine a space for black men, and he laid out these politics well before it became obligatory for men doing "nonmonolithic black masculinity" work to offer a nod toward black feminism's influence. Thus, his issuance of the invitation makes sense.

The 1990s revival of discourses of black male crisis was a noted catalyst for Awkward's invitation to black women feminists. The revival is similarly a catalyst for bell hooks's *We Real Cool: Black Men and Masculinity* (2004). As if accepting Awkward's invitation, hooks is critical of the limited ways of imagining black masculinity in the twenty-first century, lamenting the failure of her own work and that of other advocates of feminist politics to influence "the more mainstream writing about black masculinity that continues to push the notion that all black men need to do to survive is to become better patriarchs."[11] hooks criticizes both conservatives and radicals for being more invested in "talking about the plight of the black male than they are at naming strategies of resistance that would offer hope and meaningful alternatives."[12] The seemingly incessant talk of black men and crisis in both the academic realm and the public sphere does, in fact, position this field in a precarious space—a space that could easily become more noted for platitudes than critical thought and pragmatism.

Perhaps it is the precariousness of entering yet another field of study subject to hot public discourse that has kept black women scholars and nonblack scholars at bay. Or, in the case of black women scholars specifically, perhaps the memories of backlash and denigration by black male scholars and activists during the heyday of black women's studies are still too fresh.[13] Whatever the reasons might be, the fact is that only a handful of black women scholars have done work that would be considered specifically contributory to the field of black masculinity studies (as distinct from work that happens to be on black men but with no critical gender lens). Out of those limited contributions, there are even fewer black women scholars who would actually be considered "movers and shakers" in the field. In addition to bell hooks, Hazel Carby, Beverly Guy-Sheftall, Michele Wallace, Athena Mutua, Patricia Hill Collins, Nicole Fleetwood, Candice Jenkins, and Aaronette White have also produced seminal texts engaging concepts of black masculinity and black manhood.

Carby's *Race Men* (1998) has not enjoyed the recognition and popularity of her first monograph, *Reconstructing Womanhood* (1987).[14] Whereas the latter is a must-read in black women's studies, the former is rarely noted in black masculinity studies. The differing reception could, in part, be due to exigency and structure. Although *Race Men* provides a good example of how the critical gender work of black feminist studies can be used equally as effectively when analyzing black manhood, the text lacks a clear and forceful articulation of how Carby's analysis of black male intellectuals and their experience of gender privilege offers some type of intervention in the various discourses within which her work can be situated. Where Carby offers an expository framework, Michele Wallace, arguably, is the foremother of black masculinity studies, as *Black Macho and the Myth of the Superwoman* (1979) is just as much an exposé of the raced and gendered constructions of black womanhood as it is of how those same constructions shape black manhood.[15] For both Wallace and Carby, perhaps it is the nature of exposure in their work that makes it unpalatable for the canon of black masculinity studies; as Mark Anthony Neal claims, Michele Wallace's exposé resulted in her "taking one for the team."[16]

In an effort not to have to take yet another one for the team, Guy-Sheftall, Mutua, and White situate their work as projects seeking to make black feminism and black masculinity mutually inclusive fields of study, where each complements the other. Guy-Sheftall collaborates with Rudolph Byrd on *Traps: African American Men on Gender and Sexuality* (2001),[17] a collection of writings by nineteenth- and twentieth-century race leaders, activists, and scholars that champion the rights of black women. In the edited collection that resulted from both a workshop and a conference, Mutua's *Progressive Black Masculinities* (2006) does the work of seeking to identify the "nonmonolithic black masculinities" that Awkward insists must be engaged. More recently, Aaronette White decided that in order to better understand the narratives and experiences she gathered from black women, she needed to understand why and how black men made choices to be feminists, to champion the rights of women, and to practice feminism; her resulting work is *Ain't I a Feminist? African American Men Speak Out on Fatherhood, Friendship, Forgiveness, and Freedom* (2008).[18] The growing trend of simultaneously attending to issues of race, gender, and sexuality for both black women and black men is foregrounded in Patricia Hill Collins's *Black Sexual Politics: African Americans, Gender, and the New Racism* (2005), Candice M. Jenkins's *Private Lives, Proper Relations: Regulating Black Intimacy* (2007),[19] and, to some extent, Nicole R. Fleetwood's *Troubling Vision: Performance, Visuality, and Blackness* (2011).[20]

While the way in which black male scholars have protected the field of black masculinity studies from exploitation and "an anybody-can-play pickup game," as Ann DuCille refers to the proliferation of dabbling that black women's studies experienced in the academy,[21] there is something critical to be gained by cross-gender dialogue—surely, something mutually beneficial. There is, likewise, a benefit to a concerted exploration of constructions of white masculinity in the United States for a more nuanced analysis of how black men experience and negotiate the interlocking factors of race, gender, sexuality, and class. Aside from a respectful nod toward Jackson Katz, who earns his credibility vicariously through Byron Hurt, white men and white women who theorize white masculinity, and, sometimes, black masculinity as well, often are not recognized or valued in black masculinity studies. The hegemony inherent in whiteness should not preclude critical analysis of the didactic relationship between constructions of white manhood and black manhood throughout the history of the United States. Scholars such as Gail Bederman, E. Anthony Rotundo, and Michael Kimmel offer insightful analyses of the social construction of white manhood, and, in the cases of Kimmel and Bederman, black manhood as well.[22] By situating this project at the intersections of race, gender, sexuality, cultural theory, and legal doctrine, I must necessarily examine constructions of white manhood and depictions of white masculinity, as these political, social, and cultural phenomena influence the representation and performances of the black masculinities that I explore in this book; moreover, social constructions of white masculinity bear heavily on how laws have affected black men.

Black women scholars might be underrepresented in the field of black masculinity studies, but the critical theories they have developed for engaging the "intersectional axes," Kimberlé Crenshaw's term for how identities intersect in indivisible ways, have been central to the work being done in the field. Again, Michael Awkward sits at the helm of black men working on race, gender, and sexuality who attribute their intersectional approach to black feminist theory and criticism. Awkward, however, was not doing that work in isolation. Gary L. Lemons and Greg Tate are two of Awkward's compatriots. Lemons's essays "'When and Where [We] Enter': In Search of a Feminist Forefather" and "To Be Black, Male, and 'Feminist': Making Womanist Space for Black Men" espouse a commitment to black feminism. Greg Tate's *Flyboy in the Buttermilk* (1992) is another early work that offers a popular cultural spin on pro-feminism.[23] Joining Awkward in his more recent efforts, not just to do black feminist criticism, but also to create a mutually inclusive space between black feminism and black masculinity, is a host of cultural studies scholars who register inspiration from black feminist theories and methodologies.[24]

More recently, some of the efforts by Mark Anthony Neal to create a bridge between black feminism and black masculinity studies have positioned him, arguably, as one of just a handful of scholars who are framing a field of black gender studies, a field simultaneously examining both black women's and black men's identities, representations, and experiences. His critical memoir, *New Black Man* (2005), is a foundational text, as it deconstructs the seemingly positive image of the "Strong Black Man" in order to show its potential damage to both black men and black women. Neal calls upon black people to imagine a new way of thinking about what it means to be a black man, particularly in regard to misogyny and homophobia; his New Black Man is much more vulnerable and self-reflective than most representations of celebrated historic civic leaders or Strong Black Men.

Although legal studies lag behind cultural studies in black masculinity studies, legal scholar Devon Carbado, who specializes in constitutional law, criminal procedure, and critical race theory, has been a forerunner in both interrogating a nonmonolithic masculinity and embracing black feminist theories in relationship to law and culture. *Black Men on Race, Gender, and Sexuality*, his critical reader, has remained a frequently consulted text since its publication in 1999. His introduction and epilogue complicate notions of black male victimhood and acknowledge the privilege that comes with being male, regardless of how blackness races black men; he also examines how unchecked privilege weakens antiracist efforts because the marginalization of the other half of the race—black women—is ignored or dismissed. Furthermore, along with Phillip Brian Harper, who catalyzed discourse on black masculinities in the cultural realm in *Are We Not Men? Masculine Anxiety and the Problem of African-American Identity* (1996), Carbado critiques the heterosexist nature of antiracist discourse and its ultimate and, at times, intentional exclusion of black lesbian and gay experiences.

As I have noted, in both the public sphere and, at times, the academic sphere, black heterosexual gender dynamics can play out in uncivil and hurtful manners. As a scholar who situates her work as critical gender studies, drawing on black feminist theories and theories of black masculinities, and as a mother of three young black boys, I find these gender dynamics perplexing. They are divisive and negatively affect the ability of black people to determine their collective destiny in a nation that is, by no means, postrace. I am, therefore, conscious of a need to consider this history critically as I theorize the idea of grace in the lived experiences of black men in twentieth- and twenty-first-century culture and politics.[25]

To help to situate myself as a black woman scholar doing work on black masculinities and framing my research through a black feminist lens, I would like to share two personal anecdotes that offer a history and context for how and where I enter black masculinity studies. During the 2007–8 academic year, when I was teaching at a small liberal arts university in the Midwest, a flurry of protest arose when a men's vocal group, "The Hilltoppers," posted publicity flyers featuring a border of nooses. Black students understandably reacted in an emotional fury. Not only is a noose perhaps the strongest visual symbol of racial hatred and violence, but this particular incident also occurred less than a year after the Jena 6 noose hanging and assault incidents. To compound the issue, the university, a conservative institution catering to white upper-middle- and upper-class families, had not effectively incorporated its students of color into the student body, despite successful efforts at increasing their numbers. "The Hilltoppers" responded to the African American student outrage by explaining that the nooses were used to reflect the season, autumn. And, if that explanation was not adequate enough to forgive the oversight of failing to register the racial history emblematic of nooses, the group blamed the design of the flyer on an international student who did not know the history of the symbol—a claim of historical ignorance that was also made in the Jena 6 incident. The university administration eventually registered that the issue was not going to go away quietly after the local newspaper and news stations in the neighboring big city reported the story. The administration responded with what amounted to a "speak out." Classes were canceled for a day, and everyone—students, staff, and faculty—was invited to the field house for what turned into a woeful train of students of color, LGBT students, and allies speaking about feelings of exclusion, disrespect, and pain produced during their tenure at the institution. And, then, after many, many hours, it was over. The institution, embodying a neoliberal epistemology that would posit simply allowing these students to voice their feelings as *enough*, seemed to see it as the definitive end of "the problem."[26] Yes, they also paid registration for faculty and students who wanted to attend the biannual conference of the Kirwan Institute for the Study of Race and Ethnicity at Ohio State University. But there was no understanding of the need for true dialogue—no real understanding of what building inclusion truly entails.

Although the university hoped that its goodwill gestures would do the work of mediating long-standing racial, cultural, and social frictions at that institution, black students were not satisfied. It is in how these students expressed their dissatisfaction that the importance to this study emerges. I was no longer a faculty member at this institution the following academic year, so I can only tell the remainder of the story as former students shared it with me. One of my former black male students contacted me in the fall of 2008 to inform me of a Black Men's Summit being organized by students and the Office of Multicultural Affairs. I initially thought he was contacting me to participate in the summit, since I had created and taught the first, and to my knowledge last, black masculinity course at the university. I quickly learned, however, that my presence was not needed, as black men were the desired facilitators, regardless of whether they actually did research in that area. I was not overly surprised, as the student organizers were some of the same black men who jokingly—but really kind of seriously—would insist that a woman's role is to be domestic; they liked to emphasize this when eating meals at my home and expressing their dismay at how I could be so *properly domestic* and hold so many *improper* beliefs about gender and equality.

Ultimately, I was disappointed to learn that the route to repair pursued by those harmed was just as troubling as the "image repair" work the university had done the previous academic year. These students—men and some women—determined that the way to make the wrong from the noose incident right was to try to find a way to make black men feel like men and focus on their emotional turmoil; in other words, they evoked what Paul Butler describes as a "Black male exceptionalism" metatext that proposes that "fixing Black male problems is a way to establish racial justice"; consequently, they failed to register that the pecuniary institutional response they demanded was mediated by the constructs that constrict them.[27] These students and the Office of Multicultural Affairs convinced the administration to foot a hefty, five-figure bill for a Black Men's Summit that was tantamount to the neoliberal white response to the noose event. And, yes, to propel their feelings of masculinity further, black women were asked to provide "service" to the black men. As one black woman student described how women were supposed to participate in the event, the solidarity-through-service instructions were reminiscent of the instructions given to black women during the Million Man March—stay home and take care of our children, teaching them the values of home, unity, and family. Thus, female students were invited to greet attendees and provide any other random services that would facilitate an event that they were not invited to attend. Perhaps these men's desire for servitude should not be so surprising, when I consider the one and only Black Student Union meeting I attended in the aftermath of the noose incident. At the meeting, a group of women suggested that they could support the men by offering massages. I was so grateful that the black male faculty member in attendance with me vocalized his concern about the proposed resolution. Clearly, these more recent ideas of *properly domestic* for black women would seem regressive in light of the documented work of black women during the civil rights movement.

Thus, as I revisit this situation, I remain perplexed by the fact that black women and the pain they endured during and after the noose fiasco were inconsequential, although black women are not exempt from discrimination, racial hatred, and violence, including the lynching signified by a noose. Although these young black men have experienced social changes and advancements brought about by women's social movements, they cannot imagine a repair effort inclusive of black women's experiences. Perhaps I should have expected this outcome; the same narrow focus is the solution that has often dominated mainstream black social movements since emancipation. From the Negro Academy to the Black Power Movement to the Million Man March, and most recently, President Obama's My Brother's Keeper Initiative, the goal has been to repair socially, politically, economically, and emotionally damaged black men—black men who remain in a permanent state of racial melancholia because they do not possess the same heteropatriarchal power as their white male peers. Negating black women's pain has allowed these black men focused singularity on their own victimization.

Yet, the contradiction in their notions of repair resonates personally for me. My maternal grandfather and my father have had a heavy hand in shaping the ideologies that compel me to produce scholarship theorizing black masculinities through a black feminist lens. I cannot imagine anyone ever identifying my father or my late maternal grandfather as feminists, or even as vocal champions of the rights of women; yet, these men never imagined *my* future confined to a kitchen and birthing babies (though I love the space of the kitchen and have birthed more than an average number of babies). It became clear to me some time ago that I complicate the gender role ideologies that my father embraces. He has always been critical of women who do not "look" or "behave" like women. I am guaranteed to receive a compliment on my hair if I am wearing it beyond my shoulders and flat-ironed; whereas, short cuts and naturally curly styles, whether long or short, are met with silence. I think my professional success and argumentation have eased my father's stance on gender roles somewhat, but when I was in college, he referred to women who demand equal rights as "femi-nazis"— women who do not like men and want to "be" men; Hillary Clinton was one of his favorite examples. "Being men," for my father, means not only that a woman wants to take on socially constructed male gender roles, but also that she refuses to privilege patriarchy. Yet, I recall one instance when we were debating his understanding of gender roles. At the point of utter exasperation, I asked, "So, I am just supposed to be barefoot and pregnant?" My father quickly exclaimed, "No!"

It is this complication within the larger contradiction, one that the young black men at that university fail to recognize, that informs my reading of black masculinity studies. My father has been taught, has accepted, and has found comfort in heteropatriarchal ideologies about gender roles and performances—except when it comes to me. Through me, he "imagines" differently. He has always believed I could be whatever I wanted to be, whether it is the scholar I am now or the military officer I considered being instead of pursuing my doctorate. He taught me how to throw a football, shoot a layup, pin my brother in a wrestling match, and check the oil and the tire pressure when I learned to drive. When I got married, he saw nothing wrong with my husband cooking so I would not be overwhelmed with duties; yet, until my mother had a stroke at a very young age, if she was not home by "dinnertime," my father would simply wait for her to come home to cook, regardless of how hungry he was. The gender roles that seem to shape every other aspect of my father's life were almost never applied to me.

My maternal grandfather was similarly complex. I think I can count on one, maybe two hands, the number of times my grandfather spoke to me before I went off to college, and I spent a lot of time at his house as a child. The idea that children are supposed to be seen but not heard was critical to remember when my grandfather would come home from work; when my brother and I were there waiting for my parents to come to pick us up after school, sometimes it felt like it would be even better if we were not seen as well. Although I can never remember him raising his voice *at* me, his booming voice accompanied by a stern, no-nonsense attitude made my grandfather scary to me. When I went to college, however, the scariness disappeared (though the sternness remained). I would come home from college on as many weekends as possible and visit my grandmother. At some point during those visits, my grandfather began sitting me down to listen to family stories. I would listen to the same family stories repeated for several years. At first, I thought Opa was getting old and forgetting that he had already told me these stories. But I eventually realized that he was passing on the family oral history narratives that were tremendously important to him, and he wanted to be sure his repository—me—would not forget them.

It is telling that, in spite of being older than the generation of Black Power activists who agitated for black studies programs across the country during the 1960s and 1970s, my grandfather was proud when I was admitted to the master of arts program in black studies at Ohio State University in 1997 (my politically conservative parents were vocally skeptical, my mother insisting that I add a second MA in English, and even telling people that was my field before I followed her directions). His pride in my pursuits and selection of me as receiver of family narratives compels me to address yet another gender paradox. Although my grandmother worked outside the home, my grandfather strongly adhered to defined gender roles in his own household. In fact, my grandmother was solely responsible for domestic duties and had to deposit her paycheck into the "joint" account, from which she could not withdraw. It would seem contradictory, then, that my grandfather chose me instead of my brother or male cousin, who, like his father, was phenotypically white, as his repository. But my grandfather also embodied solid racial uplift politics. He believed that black people were not receiving their equal share of the proverbial pie. Black studies programs shared his sensibility about justice, equality, and overcoming the legacy of Jim Crow. He fought Jim Crow, literally, throughout his life, whether sharecropping on a peanut plantation; climbing the ranks in a military that only desegregated during the war that he and so many other black soldiers voluntarily fought in; and fighting housing and employment discrimination after retiring from the military as an officer and earning a bachelor and master of arts. In his eyes, he finally found a suitable heir to his history, the history of which he was so proud, in me.

The fact that his narratives were imparted to me rather than to my brother or male cousin is political, just as the inscription of those narratives that I was eventually compelled to produce is political. The race politics to which my grandfather was wed trumped his subordinating gender politics. One of his sisters, Annie Cora Booth-Whitehead, is a case in point.[28] Aunt Annie Cora was a Jeanes Supervisor for the state of Georgia.[29] Jeanes Supervisors did incredible uplift work in schools and black communities; the fact that many were women did not matter to my grandfather. It did matter, however, that when arguing a political point with my grandfather, my brother snidely challenged him, "So, you want your forty acres and a mule?" My grandfather promptly responded, "You're damn right!" emphatically ending the conversation and making no effort to hide his disappointment. My brother did not have the right politics, and my cousin was not only a number of years younger than my brother and me, but his whiteness might have made him an illogical repository to my grandfather. In spite of the tradition, values, and philosophical frameworks that shape how both my father and maternal grandfather understand gender—an understanding progressive neither then nor now—they were central, nonetheless, to the development of my accomplishments and understanding of who I am as a black feminist academic.

I believe that a very scripted conception of black masculinity informed both the shortsighted logic that the noose incident only harmed or produced trauma for black men and my father's and grandfather's contradictory logic about gender roles. This book, then, is an interdisciplinary study that draws on critical race and gender studies, cultural theories, and US jurisprudence in order to rethink the popular notion of crisis in black masculinity studies with a privileging of agency. I use the notion "when we imagine grace" as a way of theorizing how black men must imagine their lives, ambitions, and desires in contrast to the narrow representations of black men's experiences in the mainstream media and both popular and academic discourses. Focusing on black men's lives in two specific spaces—civic and domestic—I analyze how black men in history, literature, film, political arenas, and popular culture have either challenged or been challenged by social constructions of race, gender, class, and sexuality. I apply this intersectional theory to explore the ways in which US law has shaped and informed the social construction of the raced, gendered, classed, and sexed experiences of some black men; the epistemological frameworks that prompt some black men either to challenge or be challenged by the law; and the homogenous and pathological social constructions of black masculinity that the law has helped to perpetuate. The chapters in this book represent a broad exploration of how some black men negotiate both the law and social constructions to imagine selves that are exempted from a scripted state of inferiority due to their blackness and maleness. I analyze a variety of laws and legislative acts in the context of real-life and imagined black men, including an African American cowboy, Nat Love; my grandfather Major Gilbert Boothe, who served in the renowned first colored military unit to fight in World War II, the 92nd Infantry; Tyron Garner, the African American petitioner in *Lawrence v. Texas*; Hwesu Murray, the African American petitioner in *Hwesu Murray v. NBC*; Marcus Garvey, Berry Gordy, and Shawn Carter, aka Jay-Z; social media sensation Antoine Dodson; Donald McKayle's dance performance "Rainbow 'Round My Shoulder"; the comedy of Richard Pryor; the artwork of Kehinde Wiley; and film and literature, which includes Cornelius Eady's *Brutal Imagination*, Charles Burnett's *Killer of Sheep*, Kasi Lemmons's *The Caveman's Valentine*, Benh Zeitlin's *Beasts of the Southern Wild*, Mel Brooks's *Blazing Saddles*, and Ridley Scott's *American Gangster*.

I begin with a chapter that employs narrative and cultural criticism to illuminate what is at stake when crisis overshadows agency. Returning to *Beloved* as theoretical framework, I propose the text is useful for both illuminating the stakes of and situating myself within black masculinity studies as a black woman. I juxtapose the vulnerability and emotiveness of Paul D and Sixo in *Beloved* with a variety of cultural phenomena and policy initiatives—including analyses of radio personality Tom Joyner, music artists Eric Benét and Chris Brown, Donald McKayle's choreographed dance "Rainbow 'Round My Shoulder," and comedian Richard Pryor. Read together, these cultural phenomena create a space to think about how imagining grace moves away from the binary constructions of masculine "strength" as "stoic" and "nonemotive." The cultural phenomena also help to analyze the (il)logic of national policy initiatives such as My Brother's Keeper. Ultimately, this chapter bridges black feminist theory and black masculinity studies, as I think critically about how we can move beyond discourses of crisis when it is so easy to use it as a filler for discussions that would otherwise call for much deeper and, perhaps, more painful dialogue.

Chapters 2 and 3, respectively, examine the real-life experiences of the African American cowboy Nat Love during Reconstruction and the Progressive Era, and the military experience of my grandfather, which is embedded in national efforts of African American men to set the record straight concerning their military service during World War II. In short, I present two historical examples of black men claiming their own authority to tell their own stories. Chapter 2 focuses on Love, who wrote his own "autobiographical" narrative and is a provocative alternative race man to the accepted race men during the Progressive Era. Reconstruction codes and various iterations of Jim Crow laws shaped Love's experiences as a cowboy and porter, but his transgressive methods of defining himself as a man made him an ideal race hero to resurrect during the 1960s and 1970s black nationalist era in black print media, children's books, and, more recently, cowboy shows. I examine Love's westward migration in the context of the law and Babs Gonzales's "Wide Open Spaces," considering the possibilities and limits of imagining grace in the postbellum West. In spite of race continuing to exist in the West, Love's negotiation of it, as it intersects with his manhood, allows his narrative to function as a canonical text for more contemporary African American literature, and even for intertextual analysis with the film *Blazing Saddles*. In similar fashion, chapter 3 weaves a narrative of resistance and invention, as I piece together the news clippings, letters, and photographs from my grandfather Major Gilbert A. Boothe that resulted in a published monograph on the 92nd Infantry during World War II (McFarland Press). I discovered my grandfather's "archive" after his death, so I juxtapose his private story produced by black men across the country circulating documents and collectively producing a historical text to "set the record straight" with the stories of family genealogy he felt compelled to tell me. The story that emerges beneath the surface of his explicit family accounts and through archival matter is a painful national narrative rooted in a dialectic between pride and shame. The realities of his dialectical existence, and the sometimes ugly way they manifested within his family circle, create challenges for me as I negotiate how to tell a personal tale that is simultaneously prideful and shameful for me, too.

The next two chapters shift from the racial and gender politics framing black men's experiences with failures of democracy in civic spaces to the challenges black men encounter defining their subjectivity in domestic and communal spaces. Chapter 4 uses *Hwesu S. Murray v. National Broadcasting Company, Inc.* (1987), the "Moynihan Report," and social policy as theoretical tools for analyzing three films: Charles Burnett's *Killer of Sheep* (1977), Kasi Lemmons's *The Caveman's Valentine* (2001), and Benh Zeitlin's *Beasts of the Southern Wild* (2012). *Murray v. NBC* is an intellectual property case pertaining to *The Cosby Show*. I use this case in order to examine an instance when culture and law intersect, resulting in a myopic construction of black manhood that, in turn, informs social policy. The myopia of the court's decision in regard to black men's subjectivity plays out in interesting ways in each of the films—films that are in dialogue with social policies designed with little consideration of the complexities and heterogenousness of black men's lives. For the men in the films, the constant state of resistance and redefinition is psychologically draining, and they are literally haunted by specters of nationalism and neoliberalism.

Chapter 5 employs the concept *twisted criminalities* to probe the complex and often invisible structures that inform intergroup dynamics and to think critically about how acts of exclusion encourage the very structures that so often oppress black people socially and politically. I consider the *twisted* way in which certain heterosexual black male criminals are deemed sympathetic or heroic, while gay black men are so often criminalized because of the perception that they have *injured* the race. Using *Lawrence v. Texas* and its co-plaintiff Tyron Garner as a theoretical framework, this chapter maps the dialectical relationship between the black thug and gay black men by performing close readings of Ridley Scott's film *American Gangster*, Cornelius Eady's poetry cycle "Running Man," and the viral video and news media spectacle Antoine Dodson. The result produces a chilling location that emphasizes the limits of imagined grace in a world where those so frequently denied grace are both intolerant and indifferent to difference.

The final chapter merges the civic and domestic, for it charts a genealogy of black men's urban business practices in relationship to citizenship and the law. Focusing on Marcus Garvey, Berry Gordy, and Jay-Z (aka Shawn Carter), I analyze the nuances of what I refer to as a hip-hop genealogy and how it infuses the ways in which these men imagine black entrepreneurship as a nationalist site of redemption enabling them to build literal empires. The self-branding that is central to how each of these men builds an empire possesses its own nuances, but each is driven by a self-actualization produced by imagining alternatives to the limited spaces open to black men. The law, custom, and intraracial conflict emerge as challenges for all three men's pursuits; the ways they negotiate and think about the obstacles challenge discourses of crisis. It is, however, difficult to separate hegemonic gender ideologies from nationalist- and capitalist-informed economic pursuits; thus, I also consider the role black women play in the empire-building legacies of these men.

I conclude by returning to one of the main impetuses for this project: my three black sons. Through an informal and somewhat unconventional process, I incorporate the voices of my sons as they have tried to make sense of race during their primary years. I believe the things they have said and the conversations my husband and I have had with them, indirectly and directly engaging race in the United States, are insightful because they give me hope that the agentic determination of their great-grandfather runs through their veins, too. What I find most fascinating about talking to my sons is their ability to think critically. Even the preschooler, who is not featured in my conclusion, thinks critically about how our household and the larger world function. Whether it is noticing when a sibling appears to have been favored or wondering out loud why I am often the last person to sit down for dinner, I love that my boys are constantly thinking and analyzing the wonders and imperfections of the world around them.

Given the centrality of my sons and their own subject making to the work I do on black masculinities, I want to be straightforward about what this book is not. This book does not purport to provide a blueprint for "fixing" the social and political systems that neglect and abuse black men and boys; it is not prescriptive in that sense. I do believe, however, that by offering a different way of seeing and "knowing" black maleness, *When We Imagine Grace* does incredibly important intervention work, because it empowers black people—male and female—to reroot themselves in a different knowledge system. This need became even clearer to me when, in August 2013, I moderated a panel at my department's Community Extension Center. The panel commemorated the 1963 March on Washington for Jobs and Freedom. During the question-and-answer period, a younger black man from the community—maybe in his late twenties—asked the panelists for a prescriptive solution for fixing the contemporary social and political ills of the black community. He clearly was frustrated, and his tone was a bit aggressive. As the session was drawing to an end, he raised his hand a second time, with an urgency mimicking the urgency prompting me to call on him earlier. My department chair, who was sitting behind him in the audience, called out to me that "this brother" has a question, pointing to the young man. I politely, but firmly, replied, "Well, I am trying to be sure this sister over here gets a chance to speak, since she hasn't had a turn." My effort at diplomacy prompted the young man to blurt out, "But they didn't answer my question!" This young man wanted a panel of academics who were offering a multiethnic perspective on the significance of the march fifty years later to be able to provide him with a concrete blueprint for repairing his community, and in all likelihood, repairing himself, too.

I appreciated that young man's passion. I believe that, if given a blueprint, he would have tried to put it into action. The fact that he wanted a prescriptive solution, however, worries me. It makes me think about the Gil Scott-Heron classic "The Revolution Will Not Be Televised," a critique of the ways the media masks the real work of a revolution. The "real revolution," according to Scott-Heron, happens in the streets and is carried out by everyday black people when cameras are not rolling. The idea that "the revolution" will be live, that it does not take commercial breaks and is not informed by the positions or allocutions of prominent black figures, is of paramount importance in the age of social media. Blogs and petitions from cyberspace are not particularly revolutionary. Laboring for freedom is never quick, simple, or self-aggrandizing, and everyone does not need the same grace. This is why imagining grace is so powerful—it is individualistic and requires knowing one's self. It seems to me, at least, to be a profoundly important starting place for changing a nation that so often fails to equate blackness with humanness.

When my sons are adults, I hope they will not feel compelled to ask anyone for an all-inclusive repair plan. If they learn anything from me, they will have their own ideas and methods for exacting change, whether small or grand. I think that, like the men I study in this book, they, too, will register themselves as empowered subjects who can work toward compelling the nation—both white and black and all other marginalized racial and ethnic groups—to see them as men. Perhaps as Justice Brown points out in *Plessy v. Ferguson* (1896), like the court, my sons will be unable to change the hearts of some elements of humankind, but, even so, they will know that they are more than what some elements of humankind say they are. As Scott-Heron poignantly asserts, the revolution only becomes real when black people decide only they can define themselves.

ONE

A Friend of My Mind, or Where I Enter

A central premise of *When We Imagine Grace* is not only that there are multidimensional masculinities, as cultural and legal studies scholars have investigated, but also that there is an inherent creativity, imaginativeness, and beauty to the ways in which many black men have negotiated identities and rights during the pursuit of equality in the United States. Therefore, I employ a creative and imaginative approach to this chapter through an arrangement of vignettes that consider the complex and sometimes paradoxical relationship between crisis, vulnerability, and agency. I begin by thinking about Paul D's story in relationship to Sethe's, and how his story, coupled with that of Sixo, provides a compelling theoretical framework for seeing what imagining grace looks like. As I do so, black feminist theory provides important tools for seeing power in vulnerability and emotiveness in the public sphere and various cultural productions. President Obama's appearance on the cover of *Ms.* and his accompanying feminist declaration, social commentary on Tom Joyner's radio show, Donald McKayle's dance performance "Rainbow 'Round My Shoulder," Richard Pryor's comedy, presidential initiated social policy, and the visual art of Kehinde Wiley all work together to illustrate how I both employ and negotiate the challenges of synthesizing black feminist and black masculinity studies. Read together, these vignettes lay out the stakes for the work I do, as well as the complicated nature of constructing complex masculine identities in an era dominated by dialogues of crisis. And, while I privilege vulnerability and emotiveness in this chapter, I also consider how what Mark Anthony Neal references as illegible masculinities— those expressing vulnerability in this case—are not always a progressive performance that fosters self-actualization and resistance to crisis metaphors.

Although Paul D does not receive as much scholarly attention as Sethe, his character is just as pivotal to telling the story of slavery, resistance, and redemption. It is obvious that there are critics who would not agree with my assertion of Paul D's significance, as Morrison's development of black male characters has often come under fire.[1] Accusations of emasculation and castration, though not acknowledged, are rooted in apprehension of representing black men as vulnerable. Ironically, the largely black male critics who shun Morrison are responding to white US constructions of masculine identities that began emerging as white anxiety grew about what manhood looked like at the dawning of the twentieth century. As historian Gail Bederman elucidates in *Manliness and Civilization*, by 1930, aggression, heterosexual sexuality, physical force, and virility were traits attributed to masculinity. These traits were inextricably linked to white supremacy and civic power, which were exemplified through Theodore Roosevelt's manhood and civilization discourse, touting Manifest Destiny and imperialism as manly duties; these were a means to avoid effeminacy and racial decadence.[2] In response to the effects of migration and immigration on urban cities, anxiety around white manhood heightened feelings of emasculation in urban spaces due to both population size and lack of land ownership, as well as fears of women feminizing boys when functioning as their primary caregivers and teachers.[3]

The early 1900s mark a point in time when manhood was no longer attached to land ownership and character, but to one's ability to prove one's manhood. In fact, the anxiety around white manhood gave rise to proving one's manhood through physical activities rooted in dominance, such as pugilism. As a result, black men also felt the anxiety around heterosexual masculinity and power dynamics. Discussions about black men, vulnerability, and general emotiveness, then, are frequently viewed as emasculating. I would argue, however, that for Paul D, those very acts represent the possibility of something else— something besides feeling emasculated by a rooster, something besides memories of chain gangs and iron bits in his mouth. They are what save him from the past. The road to salvation happens when he finds the only woman "who could have left him his manhood"[4] and whose shared pain enables him to begin to pry open "the tobacco tin lodged in his chest"[5] as he thought nothing could.

Although Paul D does not have physical scarring to mark his pain, like the chokecherry tree on Sethe's back, the narrator creates a window for readers to see his pain develop. In fact, throughout the narrative, Paul D is uncertain about his manhood and, at times, rejects particular traits of masculinity. Much ado has been made about Paul D's turn to brute-style violence when he attempts to exorcise 124 Bluestone of Beloved's ghost, but his character has greater dimension than this episode reveals. Early in the narrative, the description of Paul D sets the tone for his complexity and contradiction. He is described with "peachstone skin; straight-backed. For a man with an immobile face it was amazing how ready it was to smile, or blaze or be sorry with you. As though all you had to do was get his attention and right away he produced the feeling you were feeling."[6] The ability of Paul D to register and connect to the emotions of others reveals a great deal about him. The brutality that critics and readers have honed in on, then, is far more nuanced than acknowledged.

The brute Paul D is undercut by the empathetic Paul D, perhaps most poetically, when he and Sethe are discussing Sethe's belief that Halle, her husband, betrayed her by not showing up at the barn as planned for their escape. Paul D explains that Halle witnessed Schoolteacher's nephews steal Sethe's milk. When Sethe queries, "He saw them boys do that to me and let them keep on breathing air?" Paul D quickly retorts, "Hey! Hey! Listen up. Let me tell you something. A man ain't no goddamn ax. Chopping, hacking, busting every goddamn minute of the day. Things get to him. Things he can't chop down because they're inside."[7] While Sethe's tree marks the outside of her body, Paul D's tree grows on the inside, demanding that he suppress what stretches him to the point of feeling as though he will explode. It grows and grows, no matter how long he hacks away at it day in and day out. The tree grows, seemingly infinitely, as a marker of his psychic violation, but he registers his choice to determine if its branches will entangle and bind him to a constant state of reaction and enslavement. Acknowledging undefeatable pain is emotive and also registers vulnerability. His response pushes back against popular constructions of masculinity both now and contemporaneously with the setting of the novel. Being *willing* to throw off the pretense of invincibility, and making the choice to reject notions that real men are "strong," allow Paul D to imagine a black masculine self that is not bound by societal definitions, a self that is produced by imagining what has not been extended to him by the nation—grace. Those who would fixate on brutality without exploring this state of imagined grace actually do both Paul D and Morrison a disservice.

At the conclusion of *Beloved*, when Sethe and Paul D reconcile, Paul D remembers the poignancy of Sixo's description of the Thirty-Mile Woman; for this woman, he would walk thirty miles, miss a night's sleep to see her for only one hour, and then turn around to make his seventeen-hour journey back to Sweet Home in order to report to field call on Monday morning.[8] Sixo describes the Thirty-Mile Woman as "a friend of my mind. She gather me, man. The pieces I am, she gather them and give them back to me in all the right order. It's good, you know, when you got a woman who is a friend of your mind."[9] Sixo's description is bound up in imagining grace because certain constructions of manhood dictate hierarchical relationships between the sexes. His willingness to not only acknowledge a friendship with a woman that is healing, but also admit to being in "pieces" creates space to construct a masculine identity that is not confined by social construction. For Sixo, to be a friend of someone's mind means knowing someone with exceptional depth, knowing his or her joys and strengths, as well as his or her vulnerabilities and weaknesses. For Paul D, it means that he is attuned to Sethe's needs—insisting, "You your best thing, Sethe. You are"—and Sethe, in turn, leaves Paul D his manhood when she "never mentioned or looked at" the iron collar he wore around his neck at Sweet Home, "so he did not have to feel the shame of being collared like a beast."[10] Being a friend of your mind, then, importantly fosters a partnership that makes achieving racial justice communal, for the good of all, rather than a patriarchal project. Therefore, while I do not do this work to become a friend of black men's minds, as a black woman scholar, I understand my contributions to how black masculinities are theorized to be an act that works toward gathering the pieces of black men's lives that have been overlooked and undertheorized. Through those fragments, we can think anew about what gender means in the context of black men and their lived existences.

You Need a Man with Sensitivity; You Need a Man like Me

While this project is not intended to be yet another discussion regarding the election of President Barack Obama and its implications for perceptions of black masculinity both locally and globally, I am going to use his election to frame a discussion of black men, sentimentality, and vulnerability in the United States. The Winter 2009 issue of *Ms.*, "Visions of Change," was marketed as the "Special Inaugural Issue." President-elect Barack Hussein Obama is featured on the cover, superimposed on a distant image of the White House. In Superman fashion, with tie whisked behind him like a cape, he is ripping open his dress shirt to reveal a T-shirt with the beloved feminist T-shirt expression "This is what a feminist looks like." Rather than the bold, red *S* emblazoned on Superman's chest, *Ms.* has clothed Obama with a phrase that is the equivalent of an *F* on his chest—*F* for *feminist*. In his interview with the publisher, Eleanor Smeal, and the chair of the Feminist Majority Foundation board, Peg Yorkin, Obama declared, "I am a feminist" without solicitation. The ease with which Obama claimed the "F-word" and the subsequent depiction of him on the cover of *Ms.* as a superhero-leader who will fight for women's rights—because he believes women ought to be socially, politically, and economically equal to men—is not an image likely to appear in most mainstream popular cultural or media representations of Obama. The unlikelihood of such a depiction in black popular cultural and media representations is even greater. In order to be what cultural critic and black popular culture scholar Mark Anthony Neal has identified as a Strong Black Man,[11] black men, or at least those who strive to be considered "real" black men, are bound by codes of conduct that vehemently resist performances of sentimentality or vulnerability.

For many black men, the claim of being a feminist is the equivalent of self-emasculation. Thus, I think it is important to take a moment to analyze the significance of the four-word declarative statement Obama makes. In a firm yet simple statement, he declares, "I am a feminist." He offers no disclaimers, no conjunctions, and no adjectives. He does not foreground respect for his mother, wife, or daughters. He offers no "if," "and," or "but." More importantly, "I am a feminist" is absent of the popular adjective, "male," that often accompanies it, primarily in the circle of black male academics who want to frame their gender politics as antisexist. Instead of understanding feminism as gendered—something that women actually are and men can only be sympathetic toward—Obama suggests feminism as epistemological and divorced from sex, which is a risky move for a black man, especially a black man who is the commander in chief.

The perilousness of his position on feminism is amplified because of the always already questioning of Obama's fitness to serve as US president. The Tea Party's "birthers," for example, espouse a particularly troubling brand of racism when it comes to Obama's leadership acumen. Ironically, the same blackness that incites birthers' ire simultaneously fuels opposition from black religious leaders who condemn Obama's support of same-sex marriage; for black pastors like Rev. William Owens, president and founder of the Coalition of African American Pastors, Obama's support of same-sex marriage is tantamount to racial genocide because it is "not normal," "not natural," and defies "moral law."[12] Yet, in much the same way that his declaration of feminism recognizes the ungendered and epistemological spirit of feminism as a movement, his support of civil rights for all citizens resists the historical tendency to limit equality to certain groups and assign "difference as deviance" to others. Recently reignited rumors that, because of his support for marriage equality, Obama himself must be gay reinforce the very hierarchical systems that Obama resists. His support of women's rights, epitomized by the first law he passed upon taking office, the Lilly Ledbetter Fair Pay Act,[13] and his support of marriage equality position him as "alien" to many groups within his constituency. But their dispersions of Obama do not negate what his words and actions reveal—a conception of feminism as more than definitional—equal political, economic, and social rights for women; he conveys it as a system of knowledge not determined by one's sex, eliminating any need for adjectives.

The security that frames his declaration of being a feminist can be contrasted to two specific popular cultural demonstrations of sentimentality and vulnerability: commentary by radio talk show host Tom Joyner regarding hip-hop artist Chris Brown's 2010 BET Awards performance tribute to Michael Jackson and R&B vocalist Eric Benét's "Sometimes I Cry." The point of bringing these two texts together with the image of President Obama on the cover of *Ms.* is to think critically about how acts of sentimentality and vulnerability by black men are read and received in popular culture and, consequently, why the image of Obama "looking like" a feminist and talking like a feminist never went much farther than the cover of *Ms.* in media and popular cultural presentations. Each instance displays the limits placed on performances of black masculinities in both the public and the private domain.

Tom Joyner is a radio talk show host whose syndicated morning radio program is broadcast in over one hundred markets to over eight million listeners. Joyner is an HBCU alum (Tuskegee); he has established foundations and sponsors events that are invested in the social, economic, and political well-being of African Americans. As I was driving my children to school the day after the 2010 BET Music Awards, I was disappointed, but not terribly surprised, when I heard Tom Joyner's response to Chris Brown's emotional tribute to Michael Jackson. Joyner announced that there needed to be a ban on black men crying in public. He said he was tired that every time he turns around, another black man is on TV crying; Joyner did not note what other black men besides Brown had been crying publicly. What Brown was crying about is debatable and not the real issue. The issue is that Joyner, who had only recently lifted his ban of Chris Brown's music on his radio program— an act that purportedly demonstrated his disgust with Brown for assaulting Rihanna—would refuse black men the right to cry publicly, even though vulnerable acts like crying challenge images of black men as violent brutes. Upon hearing Joyner's rant, I immediately thought of various and largely white men's Christian organizations that embrace crying as a redemptive rite of passage to a new life. The political views of many members of these men's Christian organizations, however, are often not concerned about social issues specific to being both male and black. Whiteness makes a critical difference when it comes to stretching the bounds of masculine space because it is historically normalized through them. Black men are not afforded that flexibility and must always already be hypermasculine in order to be perceived as masculine at all. So, black men crying is emasculating rather than assuring a path to a form of redemption. Thus, it would seem that black men need a space where a new life with new images can be juxtaposed to the very images of black masculinity that Chris Brown might, in fact, have been crying about, especially given Michael Jackson's notorious crises of identity.

While Chris Brown's tears elicited condemnation from Joyner, apparently there are some tears cried by black men that are acceptable— namely, Eric Benét's "Sometimes I Cry," a single featured on his CD *Lost in Time* (2010). Presumably, the black masculine impropriety of fictively admitting tears over a lost love did not affect the ranking of this song on Billboard's "Hot Adult R&B Airplay" chart, where it reached No. 5. And, unlike Chris Brown, Benét's crying did not elicit a rant from Joyner; rather, it garnered him an invitation to Joyner's annual Black Family Reunion and a live appearance on his morning show (Sept. 2010). Not only did Joyner *not* object to a black man crying in this song, but Lil Wayne also endorsed the song, encouraging followers on his blog site, weezythanxyou.com, to stop what they were doing and listen to Benét's new song if they had not done so already. Weezy noted that, in prison, he listened to only ESPN and slow jams, and that "Sometimes I Cry" was the best song he had heard since Maxwell's

"Woman's Worth."[14] Showing his sensitive side invited joke making and speculation about his sexuality, especially considering his incarceration. Complicating Lil Wayne's endorsement was the fact that he, like many other admirers, misnamed Maxwell's song. The song's actual title is "This Woman's Work" and is a cover of British songstress Kate Bush's 1989 original work. Both the jokes that Lil Wayne unintentionally invited and the error that he made speak to why Joyner and he would not feel uncomfortable with the sentimentality and vulnerability expressed in the lyrics to both of these songs.

"Sometimes I Cry," like "This Woman's Work," had already been embraced as a lovemaking song or slow jam, in spite of the latter's lyrics not being erotic or sexual, but about complications during childbirth. Although Maxwell is, for the most part, true to the song's initial message lyrically, musically, and with his improvised asides between the lyrics in Bush's original chorus, he plays into the misreading of Lil Wayne and others (whether knowingly or unknowingly). Musically, Maxwell's cover feels sexualized or eroticized, and that brings with it some difficulties, but it could explain why Maxwell's garners acceptance from black men and sexual idolization by black women: he performs sentimentality lyrically rather than visually through crying, assumably making many black men feel his pain and want to cry for him, and because of the eroticization of the music and Maxwell himself, making many black women desire to replace his perceived lost wife. The reality of this assertion is evidenced in the YouTube Vevo comments for this music video. Unable to separate fiction—music videos—from reality, many commenters express sympathy for Maxwell about losing his wife during childbirth. The acceptance of the sentimentality assumed to be expressed in the lyrics of these songs, then, created imagined acceptable spaces for black male vulnerability because they were sexualized and confirmed heterosexual; in contrast, Chris Brown was visibly exhibiting a vulnerability that the black public domain found emasculating and ultimately threatening to perceptions of the race as a whole. The same reasoning would also explain why an image of a shirtless or basketball-playing Barack Obama is readily circulated, but an image of Obama as a feminist is relegated to the archives of *Ms.* and feminist blog sites. There would seem to be no space for black men in popular culture who wear an *F* on their chests and do not hide the tears in their eyes because ultimately the concern around vulnerable black masculinities is about visual representation. Nonvisual expressions—ones that allow admission of vulnerabilities without demonstration of them—seem acceptable within the multiple and varying levels of black masculinity occupied by Tom Joyner, Lil Wayne, and President Obama.

When Vulnerability and Crisis Meet

Even when comfortable with vulnerability—feminist Obama—or when performing vulnerability for personal gain—Eric Benét's lyrics—or when simply being unable to police one's vulnerability—Chris Brown's performance—the expression and performance of vulnerability so often return to the essence of patriarchal power. In those instances, women function as muses who either repair the men's vulnerability or justify it, as exemplified by the reception and interpretation of "This Woman's Work." I want to shift my attention, then, to a discussion about the complexity of analyzing instances of vulnerability or emotiveness that, on the surface, might resist heteropatriarchal power constructs, but are not necessarily taking one for the team. Such examples lead to a look at the intersection of culture and policy accompanied by analysis of the way in which, if not managed carefully, vulnerability can become a poster child for crisis. A brief analysis of Donald McKayle's 1959 dance performance "Rainbow 'Round My Shoulder" and a skit from *The Richard Pryor Special* (1977) serve as a cultural context for understanding the paradox of a comfortably vulnerable feminist Obama who simultaneously lacks a critical gender consciousness when embracing crisis rhetoric about black men and boys. Admittedly, "Rainbow," like *Beloved* and the skit I will analyze next, is framed by heteronormative, romantic gender relationships, and I am conflicted about offering them as examples; but heterosexual dynamics are at the heart of the challenges in bridging black feminist and black masculinities studies. For that reason, I believe these texts are useful tools when thinking about bridging and moving beyond crisis discourse to look at how black men define themselves on their own terms.

"Rainbow" is an apropos performance to analyze in the context of this chapter because of its intertextual relationship to *Beloved*. The piece is a modern dance classic that is eighteen minutes long and employs seven male dancers and one female dancer. The male dancers are imprisoned on a southern chain gang, and the female dancer is a dream vision of a remembered sweetheart, mother, wife, and ultimately, a muse for freedom. The performance premiered in New York in 1959 and is noted for its overt civil rights agenda. What is key is that "Rainbow" disallows simplistic gender readings around legibility. Critics often describe the male performances with gendered and forceful adjectives: athletic, wrenching, yearning, lyrically strong, weighted, and thrusting; yet, the men are prisoners, and their athleticism and strength are of use only as they labor, breaking rock and laying railroad tracks.[15] Their work songs express regret, love, anger, and the need to be free. The female dream character appears as a reverie and muse who encourages their desire to be free. Thus, in spite of the masculinist language used to describe the male dancers and their bodies, the language fails to truly account for the reality of their existence or the complexity of longed-for freedom being embodied in a female figure.

The performance begins with a dance sequence by the men, as the folk music is sung in syncopation and almost entirely a cappella with the periodic staggering of low chords. In the next scene, the female dream figure appears, gracefully moving to the folk tune of a solo vocalist accompanied by a guitar. The lyrics of "Dink's Blues" speak of regret: "If I had listened to what mama said, I'd still be home in mama's bed." Evoking slave spirituals, too, the lyrics reference wings and flying away.

In the third scene, the men are resting on the ground under dimmed light while the muse dances in a down light at their side. Once she exits, the men return to staccato movements that are methodical and depict the hammering and lockstep movement of a chain gang. Then, the sweetheart muse enters again and up-tempo, playful lyrics overlay the droning repetition of the work song. When she exits, the chorus sings of going home, and the muse returns as a mother chiding a respectful son about his chores. When the chiding ends, the chorus resumes its work song: "I can't read her letter for crying, huh, my time's so long, Lord, my times so long."

The climatic scene has the muse return as wife. She and her husband dance to lyrics that express the husband's regret:

Darlin', if I'd a-known my captain was blind . . . I wouldna gone to work 'til half past nine . . . I asked my captain for the time of day . . . He took out his watch and he throwed it away . . . Fightin' my captain and I land in jail . . . nobody around to go my bail . . . if I'da had my weight in line . . . I'd whip that captain 'til he gone blind.

Then, the muse leaves, the chorus sings of going home, and the tempo picks up as they sing about returning their hammers to the captain, declaring, "I don't want your cold iron shackles." As the tempo increases further, and the chorus repeats its resistance, the sound of gunshots signals the climax as a dancer falls to the ground.

Fully embracing the ideologies of the freedom movement, the men's choice to pursue nonviolent protest—turning in their hammers—is reflective of the nonviolent resistance that was the hallmark of the civil rights movement, which was contemporaneous with the inaugural production of "Rainbow." In a move similar to the "Rainbow" chain gang's negotiation of manhood, Paul D also registers the desire for freedom, and it is in that life post–Sweet Home that he begins to recognize that even though Mr. Garner insisted he "owned" men and not niggers, Paul D, as Garner's property, was no more a man at Sweet Home than he would have been imprisoned on a chain gang and forced to perform oral sex on the white guards.

Embracing the ideologies of the freedom movement seemingly has its limits in this performance. As muse and as the only female body on the stage, the black woman is needed only to bolster, nurture, and affirm black manhood.[16] From the baritone chant of the chain gang, accompanied by the constant staccato beat (until the climactic shooting), it becomes clear that the audience is supposed to interpret this performance as one concerned about the social and political status of the black man. That is complicated, however, by the fact that concerns about black men have historically been understood as synonymous with concerns about the black community writ large. The closing vocal performance makes this clear when, in chorus, all male performers somberly sing, "Another man done gone/They killed another man" as they carry his body off stage. The performance thus implies that the black man's issues are the black woman's issues, and, thus, the black woman herself has no issues unique to herself.

The brutal recognition that one was not a man, whether enslaved and imprisoned or legally free, has fueled both the antiracism movements that privilege the citizenship of black men and the ideology that black women's citizenship and well-being are subordinated to black men who are the more injured party. A skit featuring Maya Angelou on *The Richard Pryor Special* articulates this ideology. The skit begins in a neighborhood bar, where Pryor's character, Willy, is a frequent patron. Before being escorted out by the bartender and sent home to his apartment building across the street, Pryor makes light of his own alcoholism and that of the small group of male and female patrons in the bar. As he makes his way across the street to his apartment, he has a sobering reality check: "Uh-oh, I'm in trouble. I know she gonna kill me. She jus gonna kill me. Then she gonna talk me back to life. Then she gonna kill me again." Evoking images of the Sapphire caricature who berates and metaphorically castrates black male partners, Willy confronts his wife (Angelou), whose only nomenclature throughout the skit is "old lady," and does what he apparently regularly does when inebriated—passes out on the sofa.

Willy's wife sits across from him, and, through a monologue, justifies his behavior and her acceptance of it. She begins by lamenting his financial irresponsibility and describes it as "balanc[ing] the economy," since he spreads his money around all the bars (and himself, too). She tells him her social worker often asks why she stays with him, and she admits her inability to describe to the social worker how she still sees Willy as he was on their first date. Willy's wife rises and impersonates Willy when she first met him. Thrusting her shoulders back and holding her head high, she explains with admiration: "You were so sassy. Your shoulders use to rise high like the breasts of young girls. And you use to call me things that sound like I was something good to eat. Honey. Baby. Sweetie. You said marry me, and I will make you a queen." Their experience at the courthouse, however, marked a negative turning point for Willy. Willy claimed that when the judge called him by his first name, it was no different than calling him "boy." Willy's wife pays little attention to his lament and simply thinks he is being "too sensitive," but soon learns differently, "when he loses his first job, and then he lost his second job, and then he called himself a nigger, claiming it was an 'affectionate term.'" Willy then calls his wife a nigger, compelling her to concede, "and then, if there was ever any affection in it, it disappeared, because you started using it to curse me, to curse yourself, to curse the whole race, to curse life, Willy." Failing to embody what US society defines as a "man," Willy turned to "booze," or what his wife describes as something "closer than a friend, and truer than a wife." The result is Willy's wife proclaiming her hate for Willy because she is forced to fear he will make unwise choices when intoxicated and bring harm upon himself. She quickly acknowledges, however, that when he comes home, she cannot help but love him. As the stage lights dim, she emotionally explains, "I know you not, you not, what you wanted to be, Willy, and you not what I wanted you to be, but I'm yours, Willy, and you're mine, and when I forget that, there ain't nothin' else worth remembering."

This skit is set just after the 1974–78 recession, which adversely affected a disproportionate percentage of African Americans.[17] When Willy's wife notes that he lost two jobs, his job losses mirror those of African Americans, and especially African American men, when deindustrialization caused many northeastern and midwestern manufacturing plants to close or relocate to southern and western states or overseas. Since 1970, the number of manufacturing jobs in the United

States has decreased by half.[18] Compounding the job losses in the 1970s was the fact that, for many African Americans, factory wages were better than many of the other jobs available, even for many of those who were college educated. Pryor's audience surely could feel the pain of economic distress, particularly in Willy's case. I do wonder whether the audience felt as much pain for his wife and the life she also lost at the altar. She does not hate Willy for his infidelity and irresponsibility; instead, she hates him because his self-hate might result in her truly losing his corporeal self, and not just his long-gone spiritual self. Thus, while alcohol is Willy's muse and not his wife, the function of Willy's wife, similar to that of the chain gang's muse, is to serve the needs of her man; in other words, as Toni Morrison suggested about black women's communal roles when discussing *Tar Baby*, Willy's wife holds things together.[19]

The idea of black women as both selfless and subordinated to black men has not, in many ways, appeared in the public spotlight—or at least there has not been an executive declaration that black women and their well-being are issues of national concern. As a result, while feminist Obama comes across as refreshingly progressive in gender politics, his rhetoric may just be empty when it comes to black women and girls. Spurred by the killing of Trayvon Martin, in February 2014 President Obama unveiled My Brother's Keeper (MBK), a five-year, public-private sector initiative. MBK is intended to address inequalities among boys and young men of color, although most news reports identify black and Latino men specifically as the targeted groups. The government has reportedly already spent $150 million, and various private and philanthropic donors will contribute an additional $200 million, to review existing programs and determine the most effective "plan of attack." In fact, on May 28, 2014, the My Brother's Keeper Task Force submitted a ninety-day progress report commissioned by the White House.[20] On the same day, a group of what is now over two hundred black men sent a letter to the president, expressing their concern that MBK does not also address the inequalities faced by black women and girls.

The White House countered that the issues facing black women and girls are addressed through the White House Council on Women and Girls, launched in 2009.[21] It is important to note, however, that the council addresses women across racial lines. Although *Women in America*, the 2011 report in support of the council, applies racial demographics, the council itself is not tasked with specifically addressing the racial disparities of black and Latina women and girls.[22] The report, however, is more methodologically sound than the MBK Task Force Report because it addresses how each racial and ethnic group fares in each category analyzed, providing a comparative analysis that clearly elucidates inequities. The demographics in the report consistently reveal that black and Latina women and girls are disadvantaged across all areas studied. According to the report, there was, for example, a significant gap in 2009 between black (28 percent) and Latina females (27 percent) and white, non-Hispanic females (11 percent) living below the poverty line. Additionally, while black women account for the highest labor force participation among women,[23] a May 2004 data collection revealed that approximately 30 percent of white and Asian workers could vary their work hours, while only 21 percent of black and Latina workers could do so.[24] And the report demonstrated that a gender wage gap still persists across all racial groups, but "compared to the earnings of all men (of all race and ethnic groups), Black women earned 71 percent and Hispanic women earned 62 percent as much in 2009. White and Asian women earned 82 percent and 95 percent as much as all men, respectively."[25]

The MBK Task Force Report, on the other hand, begins by citing empirical data to bolster the claim that black men and boys are harmed by inequalities more than any other group, including black women and girls; in other words, the report begins with black male exceptionalism. For example, in one section of the report identified as "The Challenge," the task force offers the following statement: "Despite our advances as a country, boys and young men of color, in the aggregate, continue to face persistent challenges."[26] This statement is followed by a bulleted set of empirical data to support the preceding claim, but the first four of the seven bulleted points are group inclusive and not specific to black or Latino boys and young men:

- **23.2% of Hispanics, 25.8% of Black, and 27% of American Indians and Alaska Natives (AIAN) live in poverty,** compared to 11.6% of White Americans.
- **Black, American Indian, and Hispanic children are between six and nine times more likely than white children to live in areas of concentrated poverty.** This compounds the effects of poverty, and further limits pathways to success.
- **Roughly two-thirds of Black and one-third of Hispanic children live with only one parent.** A father's absence increases the risk of their child dropping out of school. Blacks and Hispanics raised by single moms are 75 percent and 96 percent respectively more likely to drop out of school.

· We see significant **high school dropout rates—as high as 50%** in some school districts—including among boys and young men from certain Southeast Asian and Pacific Islander populations.

This data reveals that black, Latino, and Native American *children—* both boys and girls—are disproportionately impoverished when compared to their white peers. Only the final three of the seven bulleted points specifically address boys.

The methodological errors persist in the report's "Focus Area Recommendations," which address "universal milestones": entering school ready to learn; reading at grade level by third grade; graduating from high school ready for college and career; completing postsecondary education or training; successfully entering the workforce; and reducing violence and providing a second chance. When addressing the significance of these milestones, the report, again, uses gender-inclusive language that does not account for gender differences or disparities between boys and girls. In examining reading readiness, for example, the report notes that "by the age of 3, children from low-income households have heard roughly 30 million fewer words than their higher-income peers."[27] Generalized empirical data such as this is used to support gender-specific claims consistently throughout the report. Using data about children from low-income households in an argument being made for black male exceptionalism renders the data useless, since the data is not actually or exclusively addressing black boys.

As a former constitutional law professor, surely President Obama is familiar with intersectionality, so why, then, would he commission a task force, and more recently his own nonprofit alliance,[28] to address issues among boys of color that are very often just as prevalent among girls of color?[29] Perhaps it is for the same reason that nearly fifty years ago Abbey Lincoln had to ask, "Who will revere the black woman?".[30] Black women and girls do not have political cachet or cultural capital. Yet, President Obama has positioned himself in a vulnerable space as the first black president and probably the most publicly prominent black man to claim a feminist identity. Like my grandfather's and father's gender politics, perhaps there is more grace embedded in Obama's gender politics than appears on the surface. Like my grandfather's and father's relationship with me, Obama's relationship with his wife and daughters certainly reinforces a sincerity in his policymaking around gender. I would imagine that he would readily concede his gender privilege, even as he repeats his insistence that Michelle is smarter and "the boss." Yet, it is Trayvon Martin's death that compels Obama to publicly claim Trayvon could have been his son, or even himself thirty-five years ago.[31] He did not, however, propose that seven-year-old Aiyana Stanley Jones could have been his daughter. Jones was shot and killed by a Detroit police officer during a "no knock" raid at her grandmother's house on May 16, 2010. This unbalanced, intersectional sensibility could be understood as Obama buying into the idea of black male pathology and as a historical investment in racial uplift ideologies that suggest that when black men are uplifted, so, too, are black women and children. But, to be fair, perhaps shedding black male privilege and ideologies of black male exceptionalism takes soul searching on one's own part. My father imagined grace for me at birth. My grandfather saw something in me as a means to extend grace to himself and his legacy. With time, Obama's limitations with MBK might shift beyond the current impediments to imagining that grace for black men is *entangled* with grace for black women—not that grace for black men begets grace for black women.

An Economy of Grace

I want to conclude, then, by thinking about what the soul searching that enables the shedding of black male privilege and ideologies of black male exceptionalism might look like. In the fictional realm, Paul D stands out as exemplary. In the real world, the conceptual aspects of Kehinde Wiley's visual art projects are in dialogue with discourses of crisis through a deployment of vulnerability that he has rethought with time to include both black men and black women. His recent expansion of his oeuvre to include black female subjects offers some degree of registering an entangled grace, or how the consumption (economy) of goods (race) is gendered. A California native and New York–based artist, Wiley has established a highly recognizable painting style and philosophy that have earned him the moniker "the Black Andy Warhol." In order to write African Americans largely, but also African-descended people globally, into historical, imperialist narratives as subjects rather than objects, Wiley inserts these raced figures—almost entirely male—into European visual art "masterpieces." Wiley replaces the white European aristocracy with "everyday" black and brown people whose participation he solicits on the streets, initially in Harlem and, now, globally. He allows his subjects to select a master painting or sometimes sculpture that appeals to them, and after photographing the volunteer, he uses bold colors to recreate the original pose and style against intricately patterned backdrops in grand scale. I will discuss what makes his works an example of soul searching by analyzing select portraits and recent stained-glass work.

In Jeff Dupre's documentary *Kehinde Wiley: An Economy of Grace*, Wiley insists that he is perplexed when he participates in media culture and sees representations of black people. He notes that the exotic is often thought about as something far away, "an unknown set of ideas, cultural practices." He contends, however, that the exotic can sometimes "be right in front of you": "When I watch television or participate in the media culture in America, sometimes the way that I've seen black people being portrayed in this country feels very strange and exotic because it has nothing to do with the life that I've lived or people that I've known." The unfamiliarity with the types of images and performances of black people circulating in media culture, and I would argue the public sphere more broadly, is at the heart of this project, too. Through a series of paintings of black men (and some women) and more recent productions of sculpture and stained glass, Wiley troubles the tired tropes of representation that make black men "strange and exotic." He also pushes his audience to see—both literally and symbolically—power in vulnerability.

The vulnerability Wiley showcases is probably the same vulnerability that Chris Brown put on public display during the BET Awards and incited Tom Joyner's repudiation. Joyner associated crying with weakness and, very probably, effeminacy. Wiley plays with these supposed vulnerabilities in both subtle and overt manners. He describes the process of recruiting men through his "street casting" process as laden with flirtation.[32] The homoeroticism that draws Wiley to his subjects manifests on canvas paradoxically. In the documentary, while getting his hair cut at his Brooklyn apartment, Wiley asks his black male barber what he "likes least about [a] painting" on his wall. The barber looks at the painting doubtfully and responds, "Um, it's a little rosy for a guy who looks . . . kind of hoodish." Wiley replies earnestly: "Right. Yeah, I guess that's kind of the point, in a way, it's kind of looking at black masculinity the way that we're always pictured as being so hard, and we have to always have that image. How it's impossible to see different sides of black men." Hip-hop has always been and continues to be read as a hyperheteromasculine space. Wiley disrupts that space through his representation of what Mark Anthony Neal calls *illegible* black masculinities. The hip-hop wear of Wiley's studies and very essence of urbanity that emanates through their posture, regardless of how Wiley stages them, suggest a very *legible* black masculinity in society—the black masculinity that places my white university in danger. Through his play on legible versus illegible masculinity, Neal explains, "the most 'legible' black male body is often thought to be a criminal body and/or a body in need of policing and containment—incarceration," which follows "the prevailing logics about black male bodies" that "render[s] 'legible' black male bodies—those bodies that are all too real to us—illegible, while simultaneously rendering so-called illegible black male bodies—those black male bodies we can't believe are real—legible."[33] Through his creation of large-scale and billboard-size images of urban-clothed black men on one plane of the portrait accompanied by a secondary plane of floral and soft curves of baroque and rococo patterned backdrops, Wiley renders legible black male bodies illegible, creating the opportunity to see different sides of black men. In the case of Wiley's work, illegibility is rendered through his unabashed queering of legible black masculinity and his creation of a space for black male expression and representation that is simultaneously familiar— both black urban men and classical art—and illegible—placing black men in anachronistic spaces and also queering hip-hop.

Wiley is best known for his photo-derived, grandiose images of young urban black men appropriating the stance and gestures of the subjects of classic baroque and rococo paintings. These massive portraits have displayed black men as heroic, confident, and regal, as in one of Wiley's most famous portrait paintings, *Napoleon Leading the Army over the Alps* (2005).[34] But they have also represented black men as tragically vulnerable and simultaneously beautiful, as in his *Down* series. While art critics consistently note Wiley's adoption of European conventions in the larger-than-life paintings that appropriate the originals, attention is not paid to subtle nuances. A particularly important nuance is how Wiley redirects and, therefore, empowers the gaze. The portrait *Officer of the Hussars* (2007) appropriates romantic painter Théodore Géricault's *Officer of the Imperial Guard on Horseback* (ca. 1812) (fig. 1). In this portrait Wiley, of course, adds his trademark baroque and rococo decorative patterned backdrop to his rendition, along with a black man—this time the man is wearing a white "wifebeater," relaxed-fit denim jeans worn at his hips, tan suede Timberland boots, and a purple satin jacket with rainbow-colored lining that is halfway on. With a saber in his right hand and a firm grip on the reins of the horse with his left hand, the male subject is seated on a bucking stallion that is positioned diagonally on the canvas, so that the subject must twist at his waist in order for viewers to see his face (fig. 2). Géricault's rider does the same, but with a difference. Géricault's rider's gaze

FIGURE 1   Théodore Géricault, *Officer of the Imperial Guard on Horseback,* ca. 1812.

is directed toward the ground; Wiley's rider is looking straight ahead, meeting the viewer's gaze. It is, in fact, a recurrent style in Wiley's male portraits that the subject's gaze is penetrating, even demanding. The artist's attention to light, color, and bone structure when painting faces immediately draws the viewer's eyes to the eyes of the subject, even when the subject is wearing yellow, as is the case in *Ibrahima Sacko*

(2008), where the eyes ought to be drawn first to the subject's yellow shirt.[35]

Even before their arrival on the shores of the Americas, it was firmly established that enslaved Africans were not to make eye contact with their white captors. The gaze, then, was restricted to white evaluation and observation of black bodies. After emancipation, race codes continued to prevail, forcing black citizens to avert their gaze in the presence of whites. While Wiley surely reaches a black audience—most notably through several of his portraits featured on Fox TV's *Empire*—a white audience and white consumers are surely larger than his black audience. Thus, the penetrating gaze of his subjects reflects an agency in a position that once rendered them vulnerable and subordinate. And, conversely, in *Officer of the Hussars*, for example, given the homoerotic

FIGURE 2   *Officer of the Hussars*, 2007. © Kehinde Wiley. Used by permission.

desire that both the posture of the rider's body and the prominent curvature of his exposed (yet still clothed) derriere evokes, one could also read the rider as penetrating the viewer with his own homoerotic gaze (instead of the heteropatriarchal phallus). Thus, the gaze demands that viewers critically analyze the masculinities at play when Timberlands, blackness, and rococo meet.

Wiley's persistent attention to rendering penetrating gazes and even redirecting gazes is, perhaps, best represented in the *Down* series. In it, Wiley's appropriations are oil paintings and sculptures from the European classical period to the impressionist period. *The Dead Christ in the Tomb* (2007), *Matador* (2009), *Femme piquée par un serpent* (2008), *Morpheus* (2008), and from his *World Stage: Brazil* series, *Santos Dumont— The Father of Aviation II* (2009), all redirect the gaze out toward the viewer rather than obscuring the gaze or turning it in toward the canvas, as was the case in the prototypes. Given the contemporary social realities of many urban young black men, downed (by gunshot) black men with eyes wide open seem to demand accountability from both the viewer and society at large. Depicting what, in many cases, is an honorable death—the death of Christ and bullfighters or gods sleeping—the downed men whose eyes catch the eyes of the viewer break from scripted codes, but also seem to pose a question for the viewer: can you look beyond my color, bone, hair, and genitalia and imagine innocence for bodies that have been deemed unworthy of grace?

What is immediately striking about Wiley's reconceptualization is his refusal to offer black male bodies as erotic fetish. Thus, even when the original is a nude sculpture, Wiley's subjects are clothed or at least covered. The sculpted nude in Jean-Antoine Houdon's *Morpheus* (1777) is translated as a fully clothed black male in Wiley's rendition (2008); the same is done with Auguste Clésinger's *Femme piquée par un serpent* (Woman Bitten by a Snake) (1847), as Clésinger's nude female body metamorphoses into a clothed black male body. Even when he chooses to expose flesh, the license Wiley takes continues to register a proclivity for refusing to fetishize black male bodies. Wiley's reinterpretation of Jean-Bernard Restout's *Sleep* (ca. 1771), for example, replaces the foliage covering the subject's groin in the original (fig. 3) with much fuller coverage provided by white silk chiffon wrapped around the groin and splayed out beneath his body (fig. 4). Wiley also changes the position of one of the study's hands. In the prototype, one arm hangs toward the ground while the other hand reaches across the body toward the foliage covering the groin. Wiley resists any insinuation of the infamous Michael Jacksonesque crotch grabbing, and repositions the hand

FIGURE 3   Jean-Bernard Restout, *Sleep*, ca. 1771.

FIGURE 4   *Sleep*, 2008. © Kehinde Wiley. Used by permission.

reaching across the body, raising it parallel with the navel. The repositioning, however, does not mean Wiley is performing a puritanical sanitization. There is still sexual innuendo but with a difference from the familiar black male crotch grabbing. Wiley's study has lost both the foliage and the wings from the prototype. His subject nonetheless embodies an angelic essence. Not only the fine detail to musculature, but also the soft gracefulness to the twists and bends of the prone body wrapped in silk chiffon, which are enhanced by the floral backdrop literally floating on the second plane, as well as how the body glisten accentuates skin tone, could signify the sleep brought on by postcoital ecstasy. Thus, even though his eyes are closed, the fact that Wiley's reconceptualization offers the viewer access to the subject's full facial features forces viewers to see more than his epidermal self, or the fact of his blackness and maleness—they are compelled to also see his soul. These differences compel a different interpretation of eternal sleep and temporality in the prototype versus the appropriation—the withered representation of death in the prototype suggests an inevitable finality, whereas Wiley's appropriation literally looks like the subject was taken too soon, abruptly. The vulnerability intertwined with homoeroticism, then, is always at play in Wiley's black male productions.

What critics consistently understand to be eroticized (queer) images —and Wiley quickly concurs—are nonetheless distinctively different from, for example, Robert Mapplethorpe's famously controversial athletic black male nudes in *The Black Book* (1986).[36] In an analysis of Mapplethorpe's representation of black masculinity, art history scholar Kobena Mercer asserts that even when the men are individually named, "we see only sexuality as the sum-total meaning of their black male identity."[37] Mercer's insinuation that sexuality is housed in sexual organs is probably informed by such images as Mapplethorpe's *Man in Polyester Suit*. Identifying such representation as "racial fetishism," Mercer reads a "colonial fantasy" narrative in Mapplethorpe's productions "in which the white male subject is positioned at the center of representation by a desire for mastery, power, and control over the racialized and inferiorized black other."[38]

In *Down*, all possibility of fetish is replaced with a vulnerable sensuality that reclaims the gaze, controlling both what we see and how we "look." Certainly depictions of being "down" from death, or sexuality, as in "on the down low," are inherently disempowering; yet, as was true for Paul D, and to some extent Obama, there is power in vulnerability. In the case of Wiley, being able to control how we "look," how we "see," and how we are "seen" creates a counternarrative that expands what it can mean to be a black man, as well as who gets to be read as a man as it pertains to both race and sexuality. In contrast to Mercer's troubled response to Mapplethorpe's athletic black male bodies, Mercer reads Wiley's "downed" bodies differently. Mercer argues that through his use of baroque and rococo backgrounds to create two planes in the paintings, Wiley "departs from depth models of representation" and "joins company with performative traditions in black diaspora self-fashioning in which the power to play with surface appearances was a matter of life and death wherever masking ensured survival in a hostile world."[39] The codes that Mercer registers black male figures being set loose from are greater than simply controlling sartorial style in a manner that repudiates colonial fantasy. Inserting a gaze also troubles prevailing codes.

Perhaps Wiley is unconvinced that the message is clear enough, however, as his most recent productions function as a more explicit plea for grace. His 2015 fourteen-year retrospective at the Brooklyn Museum includes new works of stained glass, gold-embossed icon panels, and bronze busts. The new material—particularly the stained glass and icons—evokes Wiley's 2006 *Mugshot Study,* which, according to Wiley, made him begin to think differently about portraiture. An actual NYPD mug-shot profile of a young black man that Wiley found on 125th Street in Harlem when he was a resident at the Studio Museum inspired *Mugshot Study.* The paper included the young man's name, address, arrest information, and physical description. It compelled Wiley to juxtapose this image, which he insists is a type of "portraiture," to that of the traditional eighteenth-century style of portraiture. Within this juxtaposition he was attuned to "how one is positioned in a way that is totally outside their [*sic*] control, shut down and relegated to those in power, whereas those in the other were positioning themselves in states of stately grace and self-possession."[40] The stained-glass images work to humanize the vulnerability captured in the mug shot—vulnerability in this case being the criminalizing fact of black maleness. Wiley pushes his audience to reimagine a type of portraiture for young black men that is illegible—that of sainthood.

When you enter the gallery, the six stained-glass images immediately draw your eye. They are inlaid in a hexagonal structure, making both the artwork and the architecture resemble a Gothic cathedral. Appropriating a Gothic style is apropos given Wiley's mission to humanize those who have lost control of their own representation. While the Byzantine period showed little interest in human form and the "underlying structure of the body,"[41] Gothic art broke from rules of classical art, embracing the imagination and producing "a believable image of a complete human being including . . . a repertory of facial expressions answering to inner emotional states."[42] In *Saint Ursula and the Virgin Martyrs* (2014), for example, Saint Ursula is replaced with a black man (fig. 5). He retains her golden halo and quiver, which is the culprit in her death, but he sheds her Renaissance regalia and, instead, is clothed

FIGURE 5   *Saint Ursula and the Virgin Martyrs*, 2014. © Kehinde Wiley. Used by permission.

in Timberlands, patterned shorts, and a clashing patterned jacket with black fur collar. He is surrounded by a handful of the eleven thousand virgin handmaidens who were also martyred with Ursula. Unlike the downed portraits, the subject in this composite does not look demanding. His head is tilted to the left, and his left shoulder is slightly hitched up, giving off an air of indifference or even deference. Rather than penetrating and directing the viewer's gaze, his eyes are obscured by shadow. We do, however, see his eyes and the eyes of some of the virgins, which is not the case in the prototype. Thus, visible eyes, even when not penetrating, still call upon the viewer to see into the soul.

Given the time period of production, one cannot help but wonder if the very explicit casting of black men as saints and martyrs is in response to the contemporary high-profile police and civilian violence directed toward black men. Many of Wiley's oil paintings have, in fact, been replicas of Christ and various saints and martyrs. Those portraits, however, often emphasized style and bravado even when vulnerably positioned against "rosy" backdrops. The stained-glass images exude the entangling of resoluteness, weariness, and, perhaps, even a hint of "shade" thrown at viewers. The facial expressions and body language suggest, perhaps, that the black models simply are tired of the gaze, are tired of the fleeting nature of grace for black men.

Just as this project is my effort to employ a black feminist theoretical framework in order to gather the pieces of black men's lives and give them back in the right order, that work is Wiley's, too. And, like me, he is working from both sides. For instance, his artistic oeuvre attending to humanizing black men took a different turn with his *Economy of Grace* series. Having often been asked why he uses only black and brown male models, and having heard some not-so-subtle suggestions that doing so was limiting or lazy, Wiley decided to create portraits of black women, too. He took his "street casting" to Brooklyn, Harlem, and Queens and put a different spin on the male portraiture that dominates his production. I end my analysis of Wiley's "soul searching" with this series because it demonstrates the possibility that a black man like Obama who claims to be a friend of black women's minds, so to speak, might one day be able to register that the lives of black and brown boys, *as well as* the lives of black and brown girls and women, are subjected to the same systems that fail to see them as human and worthy of grace.

In the documentary that shares the title of the series, the end result of Wiley's black female portraiture is strikingly different from his portraits of black men. Whereas Wiley has always depicted men as they are—meaning, quite literally, in whatever they show up wearing—with women he has considered the difference in how women, and especially black women, have figured in the history of painting. Black women have a very limited presence as subjects in fine art and popular representations. Thus, Wiley determined he wanted "to go to the heart of absolute glamour, while also letting fantasy and play come into [the] picture."[43] Turning to ballroom culture as an influence—Wiley is an avid fan of *Paris Is Burning*—Wiley chose to put the women in couture, specifically Givenchy. He enlisted the creative designer for the fashion house, Riccardo Tisci, to design the ballroom gowns for his black female subjects. For the women's portraits, everything was staged—gowns, makeup, hair, and prototypes from the Louvre. When asked why he incorporated haute couture, Wiley explains, "Couture is high culture, it's exclusion, it's class, it's about a sense of decadence as well." It is striking that Wiley chooses styles and poses for these women that emphasize the sensual but not the sexual. Appropriating images from some of the most famous portrait painters—John Singer Sargent and Jacques-Louis David in particular—Wiley selects portraits of socialites, women of high society whom it would have been taboo to depict as hypersexual or lascivious.[44] In this regard, Wiley demands that his audience see black women differently from the limited representation of what literary scholar Hortense J. Spillers calls a "marked woman"—a woman who, in spite of everyone not knowing her name, "describe[s] a locus of confounded identities."[45]

Although Wiley undeniably challenges stereotypes surrounding the black female body and femininity, the series falls flat. Wiley claims the haute couture of Givenchy, which is realistically inaccessible to these women outside of the studio, does not make them real. Rather, he insists, many of the "women carry themselves in a way that says 'I exist.'" Yet, that sentiment does not come through in the portraits. Unlike his male subjects who capture the gaze, challenge it, and then reject it, the female subjects come across as studies that Wiley truly was "experimenting" with, as he concedes in the documentary and later follows up by explaining that he is far more attracted to men than to women. It is as if, in spite of his claim and concession, he expected the high-fashion stylization to do all the work of "presenting some alternate images of African American women and femininity . . . to balance the scales."[46]

An Economy of Grace, then, seems to be more of a *study* of the black woman than a full-fledged venture into reappropriating both premodern images of white womanhood and contemporary representations of black womanhood. An interesting example is Jacques-Louis

FIGURE 6   Jacques-Louis David, *Madame Récamier*, ca. 1800.

David's *Madame Récamier* (ca. 1800). David paints Madame Récamier on a chaise lounge that was named after her, the recamier (fig. 6). She wears a white, lightweight gown with sheer capped sleeves, her left elbow is used to prop her up on pillows while her right arm is gracefully draped across her right leg, and her face is turned at nearly a forty-five-degree angle as she shyly gazes at the painter more so than an anticipated audience. Her eyes look out toward the painter, yet they do so from a slightly downcast state. She wears a black headband that contrasts with the auburn ringlets that gracefully frame her face. The soft yellows and browns enhance her femininity. The bareness of the room—David did not complete this portrait—forces full attention on a full view of Récamier. Wiley's appropriation, *Juliette Récamier*, is strikingly different (fig. 7). His subject is clothed in a navy blue sleeveless velvet gown with a chainlink shoulder strap (in spite of Wiley cautioning Tisci that chains and black people are taboo), and an oddly selected brown leather belt at her waist. She is positioned the same as the original, but her body is rigid rather than graceful. Her arm sits stiffly on her leg, and her face is not turned to a full right angle. While she does look out from the canvas, because her head is not fully turned she must strain her eyes in order to look directly out from the canvas. Just as her gaze seems strained, so, too, does her neck, which seems to match the

FIGURE 7   *Juliette Récamier,* 2012. © Kehinde Wiley. Used by permission.

tightly coiffed hairstyle. Nothing about this rendering seems graceful or soft. The shades of green and blue in the backdrop work nicely with the navy blue, but they, too, contribute to a hardness that makes the subject look angry.

As with Obama's paradoxical reverence for his wife and daughters and his inability to fully realize a critical gender consciousness, Wiley, too, demonstrates space for growth. Wiley openly acknowledges a problem with black representation and stereotyping; however, developing a complex, gendered blackness for black women, or gathering all the pieces black women are—the Sethes, the muses, Willy's "old ladies," the Michelle Obamas, and so on—and giving them back in the right order require perhaps less economy and more imagining of grace both socially and literally. To be fair, though, perhaps it is not just Wiley's brave yet flat experimenting that renders his female portraitures rigid and—with the exception of the full-busted model who is not featured in the exhibition catalog—unhappy.[47] Perhaps his models themselves felt a degree of discomfort all made-up. In the documentary, even those who were openly excited about couture and makeup and hair styling still noted that there was not a place for black women in the high-fashion industry. Even when Wiley expands his black female collection to the *World Stage* and abandons haute couture for everyday wear, images such as *Venus at Paphos*, *The Sisters Zénaïde and Charlotte Bonaparte*, *Portrait of Mary Hill*, and *Lady Killigrew* also depict women who look stiff and hard. Perhaps the trouble is that he registers that black women are victims of stereotyping, yet he does not see them as vulnerable, or as having scripted gender performances, which he laments are imposed upon black men. I believe Wiley is sincere in his pursuit of grace for black women even if it is difficult for him to figure out what it looks like. His soul searching is important because, unlike Obama, he is not saying there is no place for black women in this project. And this is the challenge for proponents of black-men-in-crisis rhetoric. Even with the best of intentions, when grace is imagined for black men first and in the absence of black women, extensions of grace toward black women will always fall flat because we never bothered to imagine what it might look like.

Imagination and its incredible power of definition as demonstrated in *Beloved*, then, are critical for any analysis of representation, race, and masculinity. The empathy that Paul D becomes known for among black women is indicative of why his vulnerability is empowering rather than disabling. Although Paul D admitted being somewhat bothered that Sethe managed to escape, pregnant and without the aid of any men, he does not hesitate to express his emotional pain to her. Likewise, she finds that the similarities of their shared past and tormented present make it safe to share her emotional pain with him. As there are two gender groups that compose the black racial demographic group, the social-justice struggles of black women and black men are difficult to separate, although the issues of each group can manifest differently. The conclusion of *Beloved* demonstrates precisely this point—that, in spite of differences in manifestation, the racial group can only be well when it is invested in the wellness of all of its members. The signatories of the MBK letter understand that. Paul D understands that when he imagines the way a partnership must work between Sethe and him if either of them hopes to be able to feel their humanity and begin to imagine the grace Baby Suggs insists they must. My grandfather, who was by no stretch of the imagination a feminist, understood the stakes of communal inclusivity in the work of uplift and resisted patriarchal practices and black male exceptionalism when he chose to pass the racial uplift birthright, so to speak, on to a granddaughter, and not a grandson or son. Wiley seems to understand, at least, the importance of engaging the entanglement of struggle. These real men and cultural references demonstrate that imagining a self that is agentic rather than acted upon is empowering, and while only fools would shirk legislation that fosters equality, perhaps in many cases the imagination is a far more powerful route for subject making.

TWO

Nat Love: A New Negro Rebel in Wide Open Spaces

Poet and scholar Elizabeth Alexander, who solidified her place in history by writing the poem read at President Barack Obama's first inauguration, coined the phrase "the black interior" as an analytic describing the space that black people occupy.[1] As Alexander explains, it is "black life and creativity behind the public face of stereotype and limited imagination"—a metaphysical space "that black people ourselves know we possess but need to be reminded of."[2] Both black women and black men throughout US history have been and continue to be subjected to the stereotypes and limited imagination of a dominant society that benefits from their social and political subordination. But women and men experience these structural and institutional mechanisms differently, in ways that are not just racialized but also gendered.[3]

In this chapter, I argue that the African American cowboy and Pullman porter, Nat Love, embodies the act of reminding black people how the black interior functions as a "metaphysical space beyond the black public everyday toward power and wild imagination."[4] More specifically, Love is an exemplar of how race, gender, sexuality, and class become intricately intertwined within the black interior. This is evidenced in his own depiction of manhood in his autobiographical dime novel, *The Life and Adventures of Nat Love* (1907).[5] But it is also evident in the narrative's construction of a black masculinity working to undo the raced and gendered ideologies of black masculinity fermenting in the US imaginary since Africans arrived on these shores. His narrative depicts an existential journey that debunks the contemporary race science prevalent during Love's western adventures; and it metaphorically challenges US legislation that asserts both African Americans' inferiority to their white counterparts and African American men's incompatibility with standards of manhood defined and embodied by white men. Alexander's "black interior" and Toni Morrison's notion of "imagining grace" work together as analytics for reading Love as an alternative to accepted forefathers of the African American literary canon as well as his contemporary "race men," who approached racial uplift much differently than Love, through their focus on direct, explicit critiques of injustice and inequalities.[6] The imaginative and signifying nature of Love's narrative, and especially the unwritten narrative I reveal that informs Love's actions, offers new and refreshing approaches to reading intertextuality in African American literature and thinking about transhistorical constructions of black masculinity that privilege agentic action over resistant reaction. Love, through his narrative, depicts a self-determination and agency that transcends injustice and inequality. Moreover, investigating his life outside the narrative offers a particularly compelling story of alternative means of battling Jim Crow and, consequently, inaugurating an alternative construction of the forefather in African American literature, history, and culture.

Simply knowing the black interior exists is not necessarily enough to free one's self from the stereotypes and limited ways of imagining blackness. A wild imagination would seemingly be born only from an understanding of one's self as worthy of the rights, citizenship, and happiness allotted to whites. Such imagining, for African Americans, necessarily had to be infused with a belief in an entitlement to *grace* during Reconstruction and the Progressive Era. I am working with the Weberian definition of *grace*—"favor or goodwill"—as that was the most fundamental need of a population supposedly transitioning from property to citizen.

Nat Love's exceptional ability to see grace for himself, and for African Americans broadly, is fascinating in a period in which others worked diligently to keep African Americans confined within the "black public everyday," deeming them inferior and unworthy of full incorporation into the nation. Together, his narrative and Love himself are, in many ways, arguably a better-suited representation of the race rebel forefather for the "I Am a Man" slogan of the striking Memphis sanitation workers, for Malcolm X's "by any means necessary," and for the "ride or die" attitude of gangster rap than are the heralded black male leaders of his time—men like W. E. B. Du Bois, Booker T. Washington, and Walter White. Furthermore, Love did not represent himself as the "invisible man" of Ralph Ellison's famed novel, and his idea of a "native son" is diametrically opposed to Richard Wright's representation of Bigger Thomas. Neither his political contemporaries, nor those we now recognize as the literary forefathers of African American literature, demonstrated the attitude, tenacity, or creativity to construct a self or fully embodied protagonist that mirrors Love.

For that reason, rather than the more popular group-level analysis, I think a more nuanced understanding of society's impact on black men's sense of manhood and construction of masculinity individually can be gained through a close analysis of the obstacles Love faced, how he surmounted them, and why his particular legacy continues to resurface during the post–Civil Rights era. After a summary of Love's narrative, my analysis begins with a discussion of the racial science that legitimated slavery and drove Love's western migration. Alongside the racial science, I offer a brief history of the ways in which ideas about manhood evolved and were being defined during Love's lifetime, as well as a consideration of how they informed Love's decisions and actions. Specifically, I focus on Love's home ownership, the history of blacks in California that helped to facilitate his home ownership, and the politics of leaving a narrative. I conclude by analyzing Love's legacy as a race man and rebel against both the racial inequalities of his time and the popular racial uplift practices for countering white supremacy. To do so, I examine his ability to imagine a self that defied racial science and to position himself in the realm of American manhood, reminding future generations of that metaphysical space of power and wild imagination that Alexander insists black people occupy, but need to be reminded of; I locate those reminders in law, literature, and media.

Race, Anthropology, and the Age of Reason

Nat Love was born into slavery in Davidson County, Tennessee, in 1854. He left his family home in 1869 for the western plains, where, according to Love, he became the roughest, toughest, and smartest cowboy on the frontier. *The Life and Adventures* is a multigenre text divided into three distinct sections. The first consists of five chapters and describes Love's life as a slave, his family's hardships as sharecroppers, and his role as head of the house when his father dies. This section echoes the standard conventions of slave narratives and, more specifically, parallels Booker T. Washington's *Up from Slavery*. The second section, which is the longest, contains twelve chapters, which record Love's life and experiences as a cowboy from 1869 to 1890. This section embodies the conventions of the dime novel and is filled with superhuman feats—being shot fourteen times, for example—and encounters and friendships with famous cowboys and outlaws. The length of this section is notable because it chronicles Love's life in the West, which was the solitary space in which he was able to construct himself as a full-bodied man, apart from raced and gendered stereotypes. The final section, which is five chapters long, chronicles Love's experiences as a Pullman porter and ends with reminiscences of the good ole days in the West.

Love's narrative stands out as a literary and social anomaly at the turn of the twentieth century. African American writers both prior and subsequent to Love's publication of his narrative rarely wrote creative narratives that did not explicitly address the injustices of race in the United States and abroad. The most noted cultural productions doing this work during Love's lifetime were slave narratives and magazine novels written by black clubwomen after Reconstruction had failed. These texts followed specific conventions and always proselytized about the evils of slavery and racial inequalities. Love's narrative does begin in this tradition, as the first section signifies on Washington's *Up from Slavery*, but Love allots only five chapters to that particular genre, spending the next twelve chapters following the conventions of a different genre—the cowboy narrative dime novel. Some might argue that because Love was only enslaved during his early childhood, his fairly quick departure from the slave narrative tradition is easily explained and reflects a lack of entrenchment in racial themes. However, Washington was also only enslaved as a young child, and both men are contemporaries. The difference is the critical reception and placement of Washington's narrative in the African American literary tradition. Washington's narrative also allots limited space to slavery, and the bulk of his narrative focuses on education and racial uplift in ways that are normalized during the period. Similarly, Paul Laurence Dunbar and Charles Chesnutt, African American writers who published novels during the same period as Love, selected race-focused themes. Because many literary critics do not register a cowboy narrative as racially focused or generically suited to the work of racial uplift, the underlying project of Love's narrative has often been overlooked. Yet, undervaluing the work illustrates a narrow logic that strips intellectualism and agency from genre selection, as well as from the unique way in which Love *battled* Jim Crow.

In previous work on Love, I have examined the narrative's eight photographs as a means of troubling how scholars have read Love and his narrative.[7] The popular critique has been that Love sought to "e-race" race in his narrative when he presented the West and life as a Pullman porter as free of racism and racial inequality.[8] I will reiterate here that the allegation that Love attempted to erase race by not attending to it in the same manner as his contemporary "race men" applies an essentialist notion of racial uplift that roots it in a particular type of performance ultimately marked by imposed notions of racial authenticity. To be a real race man, it seems, one must explicitly denounce racism and put white supremacy and racial hatred on display. While I do not want to devalue that work, there is something to be said about the decision to refuse to acknowledge that one is controlled by such mechanisms and to depict one's self, instead, as the determiner of one's destiny—a very American ideal[9] that Love sums up well when he explains leaving the range: "So I decided to quit it and try something else for a while."[10] The pervasiveness of race science within the US imaginary, as well as US social and political institutions, demonstrates both why such an emphasis was placed on refuting racial inferiority and demanding incorporation and why Love might chose a signifying route for refutation.

The racial classification system that arose out of eighteenth-century thought is rooted in a philosophical and cross-cultural anthropology that fueled Enlightenment philosophy. Emmanuel Chukwudi Eze, a philosophy scholar, points out how scholarship and treatises on the Enlightenment and its thinkers consistently and conspicuously omit any reference to their writings on race, other than to dismiss them quickly as journalistic or of no interest to philosophical inquiry.[11] This response is ironic given that social construction of race in the modern world is indebted to these very thinkers. Polygenic theories of human origin espoused by Linnaeus (Carl von Linné) and later honed by such thinkers as Comte de Buffon and Johann Friedrich Blumenbach would influence the philosophical thought of Immanuel Kant, David Hume, Thomas Jefferson, and Georg Wilhelm Friedrich Hegel, to name only a familiar few. Enlightenment thinkers began examining humanity as a species and classifying it within natural history, creating a social and cultural hierarchy distinguished by human difference. Within this hierarchy, Africans were positioned at the bottom and marked as barbarians and savages who bore little to no intellectual capacity, all of which was marked by their failure to meet Western European standards of civilization. Physiognomy, climate, moral character, and custom functioned as a rubric for classifying people and conflating popular philosophies about racial difference with science and biology.

In addition to a shift from religion to reason as the intellectual authority during the Enlightenment period, increased European global travel and exploration influenced the emergence of the concept of race as we know it. Published travel accounts depicted Europeans as civilized, and peoples inhabiting Asia, Africa, and the Americas as savages; Africa, in particular, was described as the Dark Continent, evoking notions of skin color as well as intelligence.[12] Michael Omi and Howard Winant note that geographic "discoveries" of people who not only looked different, but also possessed different social practices, mores, and religious beliefs justified human enslavement of people Europeans insisted were not "part of the same 'family of man' as themselves."[13] These ideologies would pave the way for the nineteenth-century philosopher Count Joseph Arthur de Gobineau, author of *An Essay on the Inequality of Human Races* (1853–55), a four-volume treatise on the biological inferiority of non-Europeans. His ideas were not only influential during his time, but would continue to influence racist ideologies one hundred years later—social Darwinism (the belief that superior races produce superior cultures) and eugenics (the belief that racial mixture contaminates superior racial stock).[14]

The racial science propagated during and after the Enlightenment period was the impetus for the civil rights work of race men and women during the Progressive Era; slavery and postemancipation disenfranchisement were only symptoms. Love addressed these racist ideologies through an ontological project, while his brothers in arms addressed the symptoms more than the ideologies. Addressing the ideologies gave Love the space to imagine a self that was not defined by racial science or bound by a slave past equating blackness with property. California provided Love the space to make his imaginings tangible through home ownership. Prior to Love's arrival in California, as well as during his residence there, the legal groundwork was laid for him to realistically construct a sense of manhood that could be realized tangibly through the ownership of property, rather than being property.

A Land of Milk and Honey

In the aftermath of the Revolutionary War, the concept of manhood experienced a definitional crisis. With the genteel British patriarch and his association with property ownership and patriarchal authority ideal manhood shifted to feminized manhood. This model was trumped by the Self-Made Man, who, according to sociologist Michael Kimmel, is "a model of manhood that derives identity entirely from a man's activities in the public sphere, measured by accumulated wealth and status, by geographic and social mobility."[15] Industrialization and urbanization catalyzed the redefinition of manhood, and although this new definition created opportunities for far more men to be recognized as embodying American manhood, the stakes for claiming such an identity, however, were high and, consequently, produced insecurities, competitiveness, and aggressive business practices.

One means of mitigating some of the anxiety of this newly created manhood was to be clear about who was not and could not ever become a man. Kimmel argues that language was used to emphasize the self-determination inherent in manhood, and race assisted in that project: "The term *manhood* was synonymous with 'adulthood.' Just as black slaves were 'boys,' the white colonists felt enslaved by the English father, infantilized, and thus emasculated."[16] A manipulation of social Darwinism aided the use of language, as thinkers such as Herbert Spencer in England and William Graham Sumner in the United States linked social inequality to natural inferiority. Stephen Jay Gould's *The Mismeasure of Man* debunks the pseudoscience of anthropometrics, criminal anthropology, and the theory of IQ, but it does not closely analyze how race and gender worked to produce specific narratives of inferiority.[17] Kimmel does this work when he explains that beliefs that white men represented a higher state of Darwinian evolution than women prompted a linkage between nonwhites and women and children, making "them [nonwhite men] Darwinian throwbacks, lower down the evolutionary ladder from white Anglo-Saxon or Teutonic men."[18] History and social practices, then, positioned black men as always already not men and incapable of becoming men.

Thus, a space that purported to offer black men the opportunity to become Self-Made Men had great appeal. Yet, the freedom to become Self-Made Men was not a naturally occurring dynamic for blacks in California, because of the state's distance from the South, and its rocky legal history with regard to racial equality. When the Treaty of Guadalupe Hidalgo was ratified in 1848, and the US Congress debated but adjourned without determining the fate of slavery in the new territories, explains historian Shirley Ann Wilson Moore, forty-eight delegates from these territories gathered to create a constitution to present for congressional approval as a prerequisite for statehood. In it, the one thing that was clear was a desire to extend the franchise to white males only.[19] During the antebellum period, white Californians expressed acute concerns about barring slavery, not for humane reasons, but because they did not want a competitive labor pool in the gold mines. Free blacks and white abolitionists in California, however, were relentless in fighting discriminatory laws.

A string of legal cases fighting the fugitive slave laws and public transportation would be critical for the arrival of Love in California several decades after emancipation. The Perkins case was brought to the Supreme Court when a Mississippi slave owner, C. S. Perkins, saw the passage of the Fugitive Slave Act of 1852 as an opportunity to reclaim the three slaves he had left behind in California in 1849 when he returned to Mississippi. The court held that "the residency of the former slaves in a free territory had no legal bearing on their condition of servitude under California's Fugitive Slave Act."[20] Shortly thereafter, Los Angeles abolitionists rescued Bridget "Biddy" Mason and her thirteen family members after their slave master brought them from Mississippi. This time, a Los Angeles district court ruled in favor of freedom, declaring, "All of the said persons of color are entitled to their freedom and are free forever."[21] However, the 1857 Dred Scott decision rendered California's status as a free state moot and entitled slave owners to rights of retrieval in free states, which makes Archy Lee's case notable. Archy Lee, like the Perkins slaves and the Mason family, had also been brought from Mississippi to California. His master, Charles A. Stovall, left Mississippi in 1857 for health reasons and settled in Sacramento, starting a school and hiring Archy out as a laborer for a few years before deciding to return to Mississippi. Through the aid of black and white abolitionists, Archy escaped the river steamer Stovall intended to employ to return him to Mississippi. After several court proceedings, some in Archy's favor and others favoring Stovall, Judge Thomas W. Freelon of the San Francisco County Court determined Archy was not a fugitive slave and, on April 14, 1858, discharged him. Wisely, Archy migrated to Victoria, British Columbia, after the final court decision.[22]

During the late nineteenth century, African Americans continued to wage battles with the courts. The 1863 Perkins Bill legalized black testimony in the state of California, and in 1880, six years after A. J. Ward unsuccessfully petitioned the Supreme Court of California to integrate a San Francisco public school, the state legislature abolished segregated schools, at least for African Americans.[23] In 1893, California passed an equal public accommodation law after numerous civil suits brought by African Americans, including one by Mary Ellen Pleasant, the famed San Francisco businesswoman who helped to finance John Brown's raid on Harper's Ferry and Archy Lee's court cases. The relentless struggle for freedom and equality by African Americans in California during slavery, Reconstruction, and the aftermath of failed Reconstruction created a unique social, political, and economic space for African Americans in California in the early 1900s.

In his analysis of the emergence of ghettos and slums in Los Angeles in the period 1890–1930, Lawrence de Graaf notes that the ghettos—which he identifies as areas with distinct boundaries within which African Americans resided—were not initially slums, making this distinction based upon measurements of occupational opportunities, social discrimination, and racial hostility.[24] When Love shows up in the US Census for Los Angeles, black residences were still scattered throughout the city, and the early ghettos had not begun to take shape.[25] This is evidenced by the fact that, according to census records, Love lived in Malibu and Santa Monica. De Graaf cites the desegregation and civil rights laws I have highlighted as reasons for the relative freedom blacks experienced in the public realm, but he also observes that the black population was small, which probably facilitated their acceptance and minimal racial tension, particularly in contrast to the Chinese, who were consistently treated with hostility.[26]

While migration to California increased sevenfold between 1900 and 1920—Love's heyday in California—the size of the state's population was still inconsequential and did not produce racial backlash. The legal history and migration patterns created a geography in which African Americans could believe in the American dream in spite of the fact that many of the jobs they would secure in LA were as common laborers, janitors, porters—like Love—and domestic servants (Love's wife did not work, according to the census), and that many migrants had worked previously as teachers and skilled laborers outside of California.[27] Regardless of residents' previous occupations, "commentators refer to the enterprising nature of the black population and the ability of those who came with very modest means to acquire considerable wealth."[28] This sentiment is echoed by the eminent W. E. B. Du Bois, who was very impressed on a 1913 visit to Los Angeles. Upon returning to New York City, he wrote in *Crisis*: "Los Angeles is wonderful. Nowhere in the United States is the Negro so well and beautifully housed, nor the average efficiency and intelligence in the colored population so high. . . . Out here in this matchless Southern California there would seem to be no limit to your opportunities, your possibilities.'"[29] Du Bois was not blind to racism, but he did observe a distinct difference between this region and the many other regions he visited throughout the country. The difference that Du Bois references had been explained a number of years earlier by J. B. Loving in the January–February 1904 issue of *The Liberator*: "The Negroes of this city have prudently refused to segregate themselves into any locality, but have scattered and purchased homes in sections occupied by wealthy, cultured white people, thus not only securing the best fire, water and police protection, but also the more important benefits that accrue from refined and cultural surroundings."[30]

Making a House a Home

The image of Los Angeles as a space where, for blacks at least, race was not as policed as in other areas of the nation is reflected in Love's home ownership. Love makes no mention of his home in his narrative, and I am more interested in the man who is not included in that narrative than the Love who is presented there. Love's home ownership is not included in Love's narrative because Love did not purchase his home until after 1907.[31] His home ownership is significant, however, because it not only represents an act of "self-making" that many African American men did not experience during the Progressive Era, but it also places Love's narrative within, not outside of, the African American literary tradition. The positioning of Love's narrative within the normalized African American literary tradition is significant because his self-making facilitates a new avenue of resistance in African American fiction that not only locates Love within the fold, but also serves to claim other texts whose plot or style positioned them outside of African American literature perceived as traditional during their time of production. Thus, while absent in the text itself, Love's home is a critical impetus for the production of his narrative, and for his definition of himself as a free man.

The 1920 census questionnaire records Nat and Alice Love owning a home at 1748 Twenty-Second Street in Santa Monica, California. Not only does Love own his home, but, according to the questionnaire, his ownership is "free," meaning he does not have a mortgage. This fact is meaningful, as only 22.3 percent, or 542,654 out of 2,430,828, American homeowners were African Americans in 1920. In the state of California in 1920, African Americans owned 3,523 out of 376,173 homes, and the African American population in California was 38,763, or 1.9 percent of the total population. The exact address of the Loves' home in Santa Monica no longer exists; Interstate 10 now runs through that neighborhood, and the addresses near where his home would have been are primarily industrial and office buildings. There is only one other black family listed for Love's street and the two other streets on the list. The residents of the neighborhood are identified as "white," but almost all of them possess Spanish surnames, speak Spanish, and have parents who were born in Mexico. In his previous residences, in Malibu and in Salt Lake City, Love also lived in predominantly white neighborhoods. The racial demographics of these neighborhoods are, of course, complicated by the racial formations surrounding immigration during this period.[32]

Even today, the difficulty of attaining home ownership is frustrating for many African Americans. The connection between home ownership and constructions of black manhood is a recurring theme in African American literature, and the recurrence of this theme suggests that Love has more to offer African American history and culture than simply being a symbol of virile masculinity as a cowboy. Although Love does not own a home at the time of publication of his narrative, in the narrative he does show a commitment to raising funds to purchase land for what he calls "the Porters' Home," a "Home and Hospital, with adjoining farming land, for the benefit of old and disabled porters who were not able to perform their duties as Pullman car porters."[33] According to Love, he actually proposed this idea to George Pullman in 1893, and Pullman signed a statement promising that if the porters succeeded in buying one thousand acres of land, he would erect the building on it. I am sure that Pullman knew the funds would never be raised for such a venture. However, the persistence with which Love pursues this endeavor is significant, because it not only reflects the Washingtonian principle of property ownership, but it also positions Love in the same field of activism as A. Philip Randolph, who would organize the Brotherhood of Sleeping Car Porters.

In examining this aspect of Love's life, one cannot help but think of the complex fictional incarnations of African American home ownership. Jean Toomer's Rhobert in *Cane* is one example. Rhobert migrates to the North, only to "wear a house, like a monstrous diver's helmet, on his head."[34] In Rhobert, Booker T. Washington's opposition to northern migration appears to be justified: "He is way down. Rods of the house like antennae of a dead thing, stuffed, prop up the air. He is way down. He is sinking. His house is a dead thing that weights him down."[35] Rhobert's house, and presumably the financial hardship entailed in retaining it, are his albatross—a metaphorical noose around his neck.

The burden of his home is so daunting that the image of home and the patriarchal family that girded uplift ideology offers Rhobert no redemption. As the narrator ambivalently muses, "And he cares not two straws as to whether or not he will ever see his wife and children again. Many a time he's seen them drown in his dreams and has kicked about joyously in the mud for days after."[36] What Toomer ultimately communicates is Jim Crow's ability to travel and haunt black people regardless of geography. Rhobert becomes so bogged down by his home that he literally becomes indistinguishable from the landscape around him, making race geography.

While Rhobert's home takes on anthropomorphic qualities—a dead house stuffed with stuffing that is alive, and rods that act like antennae, propped up in the air—Easy Rawlins in Walter Mosley's *Devil in a Blue Dress* ascribes different human attributes to his home:

The house itself was small. Just a living room, a bedroom, and a kitchen. The bathroom didn't even have a shower and the backyard was no larger than a child's rubber pool. But that house meant more to me than any woman I ever knew. I loved her and I was jealous of her and if the bank sent the county marshal to take her from me I might have come at him with a rifle rather than to give her up.[37]

Rawlins's commitment to keeping his home at all costs—he engages in some risky and at times criminal behavior in order to make his mortgage payments—presents home ownership as a much more pleasant burden than Rhobert's experience with home ownership and migration. But like both Rhobert and Love, Easy's battle with Jim Crow migrates to LA with him, and Mouse is quick to remind Easy of this phenomenon:[38]

That's just like you, Easy. You learn stuff and you be thinkin' like white men be thinkin'. You be thinkin' that what's right fo' them is right fo' you. She look like she white and you think like you white. But brother you don't know that you both poor niggers. And a nigger ain't never gonna be happy 'less he accept what he is.[39]

Home ownership in this incarnation is a performance of *normal* American manhood. Mouse challenges a black man's entitlement to this normalcy.

Because property has historically been a racial signifier—slaves were property, and thus blackness was a marker of property, and conversely, property ownership itself was a marker of whiteness—Easy's, Love's, and even Rhobert's fateful home ownership become symbols of racial transgression that disrupt this equation.[40] Through them, the home becomes, as in Ossie Davis's eulogistic description of Malcolm X, "our manhood, our living, black manhood." Both the physical space of the home and the domestic iconography of the home are critical determinants in achieving manhood. Thus, for a black man at the turn of the twentieth century, as in the case of Love, and in the immediate post–World War II era, as in the case of Easy, the acquisition of property is a significant, yet potentially vexing accomplishment.

It is vexing because I am not certain of the exact year Love purchased his home, although I know it was between 1910, when he rented in Malibu, and 1920, when the census reports him owning a home. It is clear, however, that he purchased his home when LA was experiencing shifts in its racial climate due to increased black migration between those years. Public resentment toward black neighbors was reflected in a growing number of race-restrictive covenants on property deeds after World War I. During the 1910s, African Americans were successful in fighting race-restrictive covenants. In several cases prior to 1919, local courts ruled against race restriction clauses in property deeds.[41] However, as a result of California Supreme Court rulings in 1919 that race-restrictive covenants were enforceable, the next decade would see the development of a restricted African American community around Central Avenue.[42] From 1919 to the present, arguably, African Americans have contended with segregated housing and other kinds of disenfranchisement and discrimination. The US Supreme Court case *Shelley v. Kraemer* (1948) made race-restrictive covenants unconstitutional, but as in the case of so many other civil rights cases, the ruling did not end discrimination. President Lyndon B. Johnson's signing of the Civil Rights Act of 1968, which included Title VIII, commonly known as the Fair Housing Act, also has not eliminated housing discrimination and intimidation toward African Americans in particular, or people of color in general. The significance of Love's home ownership, and the vexed history of African American home ownership that is recorded in law and literature, further demonstrate the significance of Love as an alternative race man to the race leaders and cultural producers who foregrounded protest over self-making.

Looking for a Hero

The growing racial tension and discrimination experienced by African Americans in Los Angeles were paralleled across the nation in the rise of lynch mobs, limited employment opportunities, and segregated housing, schools, and public facilities. These discriminatory experiences would culminate in the full-fledged launch of the civil rights movement in the mid-1950s. For many, the Civil Rights Act of 1964 and the Voting Rights Act of 1965 marked the waning of the civil rights movement, and the assassination of Malcolm X in 1965 and Rev. Martin Luther King Jr. in 1968 signaled a clear transition in black America to what cultural scholar Wahneema Lubiano calls black American common sense—an "everyday ideology" that is "articulated in everyday understandings of the world and one's place in it."[43] Lubiano insists that culture is the only thing black people can own because the reality of black experience in the United States is that they have controlled no means of production, no land masses, and until after the passage of civil rights laws, no "meaningful participation in formal, public politics."[44] Thus, the Black Power era, formally catalyzed by Stokely Carmichael's speech titled "Black Power" at the University of California, Berkeley, in 1966, had a sister movement, the Black Arts Movement (BAM). BAM produced cultural texts and, in keeping with the political arm of the movement, claimed historical and cultural icons. As a result, Nat Love quite likely experienced more public notoriety during this era than during his lifetime.

As a reclaimed cultural icon, Love initially appeared in juvenile literature and black magazines and newspapers. Harold W. Felton's *Negro Cowboy, Nat Love* (1969) and Charlotte R. Clark and Leighton Fossum's *Black Cowboy: The Story of Nat Love* (1970) were written for juvenile audiences and launched a boom in the production of juvenile literature on Nat Love during the twentieth century, with one book even being translated into Spanish. In a continuing, concerted effort to offer young black America heroes who looked like them, the January 1978 edition of *Ebony Jr.* featured an article entitled "Black Men in the Saddle" that began with an ode to "Deadwood Dick" (Love's nickname) and also covered the mustanger Bob Lemmons and Bill Pickett, who is known for his performances roping steer.[45] Also targeting youth, the January 10, 1978, issue of the *Washington Afro-American* offered an "Afro History" coloring contest featuring Nat Love (the previous historical figure was Toussaint L'Ouverture).

From the 1960s to the present, countless newspapers, especially black newspapers, have published articles on Nat Love, and other black cowboys and blacks in the West. The March 1969 issue of *Crisis* boasted that Love was the only cowboy to have written an autobiography,[46] and in 1972, *Black Enterprise* did a feature on black rodeos. Later in the

1970s, the black press became more explicit about the need to recover black heroes and write the black experience into US history. In an essay on black pioneers west of the Rocky Mountains, John Wideman included Love in a list of names that "should be commonplace in enlightened households."[47] He described Love as having known "that in the West there is wide open space, physically and mentally, where people can make a place for themselves even in urban areas like Denver."[48] Love resided in Denver with his wife upon retiring from the range, and in that space made a home. In addition, the article "The Old West Heritage Revived," in the February 22, 1977, issue of the *Washington Afro-American*, similarly speaks to a need to identify black heroes, featuring a discussion with Milwaukee hair stylist Gerald D. Coleman, who did one-man appearances portraying Love. Coleman said that when he was growing up in Milwaukee during the 1950s, his schooling did not include any history of African Americans, so he tried to tell Love's story as he believed Love would have told it—with dignity and humor.[49]

Given his growing legacy as both a black hero of the past and one who embodied a nonconforming attitude, it makes sense that Love would be at the center of a negotiation around race and representation. A news entry in the July 25, 1983, issue of *Jet* discussed decisions NBC made regarding a TV movie starring Gary Coleman.[50] The Black Anti-Defamation Coalition claimed the storyline of the film was offensive because the script centered on a black boy (Coleman) whose heroes were Tarzan and Wyatt Earp. In response, NBC placed a poster of Magic Johnson in Coleman's room and substituted Nat Love for Earp; they eliminated Tarzan. NBC was not willing, however, to insert Kunta Kinte, as requested by the coalition. The commentary of the coalition is a telling indicator of why Love received so much acclaim during the late 1960s and 1970s; for them, Coleman's character was "a Black child who has been so inundated with White heroes, and so deprived of viewing Black ones, that even in his imagination there is no reflection of self."[51] This is a particularly powerful analysis that intersects poignantly with my goal in this book—to consider how black men work to imagine a self that is diverse, complex, agentic, and, most importantly, not what society says it is.

While it has primarily been black-oriented media and cultural productions that have attended to Love, he showed up in a short 1965 article in a local Idaho newspaper, the *Lewiston Morning Tribune*. The article, "Those Early-Day Cowboys Weren't All Nordic Types," is a book review of *Negro Cowboys*, which was authored by "two white professors of English from California."[52] More recently, and exemplary of a changing social climate, Nat Love was featured in the "History" section of the April 1994 issue of *Boys' Life: The Magazine for All Boys*, notably in a section on black cowboys.[53] Love has experienced a global notoriety, too. He is featured on the cover of an album by the Canadian band Reggae Cowboys that was independently released in 1995.[54] And, in a section titled "The Negro in History," the June 30, 1970, issue of the *Virgin Islands Daily News* featured a printed biography of Love (one for Alain L. Locke is scheduled to follow).[55]

The well-established effort during the late 1960s and throughout the 1970s to frame Love as an iconic black hero makes his contemporary popularity understandable. Love's narrative was republished in 1968, and again in 1995, by the University of Nebraska Press. To meet public interest Paul W. Stewart founded what is now the Black American West Museum and Heritage Center in Denver, Colorado. Real-life black cowboys have been known to appear at the museum and answer questions. And there are many black cowboy and rodeo shows—shows that are not restricted to western states. Filmmaker and studio art professor at the University of Virginia Kevin Jerome Everson recently made the short film *Ten Five in the Grass* (2012) on African American cowboys and rodeo riders in Louisiana.

These recent cultural productions and media reports demonstrate more than just the black common sense Lubiano positions as the cultural logic of black nationalism. They reflect black people claiming ownership of a history and culture that express the black interior Alexander insists black people must be reminded of. Most importantly, Love represents a black manhood that is defined by black people for black people. Keeping with how he defined himself throughout his life, contemporary black America has chosen to remember and memorialize Love in ways quite similar to those used to honor Malcolm X: "our manhood, our living, black manhood."

Yet, to avoid risking an extremely patriarchal analysis of Love as heroic icon, I want to juxtapose those images of "living, black manhood" to a poem Elizabeth Alexander wrote to memorialize Love in a collection that broadly recognizes historical global black figures. The eight portraits in Love's narrative include one family portrait, a portrait with friends from the railroad, a portrait as a courier (his employment after Pullman), two portraits in cowboy gear, and three portraits in his Pullman porter uniform. Out of the eight portraits, only the two in cowboy attire consistently appear on book covers and in media representations. Love is known first and foremost as a black cowboy, although more of his life was spent otherwise. His notoriety as a cowboy, rather than as

FIGURE 8   Nat Love with rifle. *The Life and Adventures of Nat Love Better Known in the Cattle Country as "Deadwood Dick" by Himself; a True History of Slavery Days, Life on the Great Cattle Ranges and on the Plains of the "Wild and Woolly" West, Based on Facts, and Personal Experiences of the Author* (1907).

FIGURE 9   Nat Love with lariat. *The Life and Adventures of Nat Love Better Known in the Cattle Country as "Deadwood Dick" by Himself; a True History of Slavery Days, Life on the Great Cattle Ranges and on the Plains of the "Wild and Woolly" West, Based on Facts, and Personal Experiences of the Author* (1907).

a Pullman porter or courier, speaks apparently to black people's need, both in the United States and abroad, to have images of themselves and their accomplishments that are exceptional with regard to the manner in which such people navigated race. Ultimately, Love the cowboy who was minimally bound by racial codes of the West produces greater racial pride than does Love the Pullman porter, who, although he does not acknowledge it, was employed as a servant.

When Elizabeth Alexander memorializes Love in her poem "Deadwood Dick," she plays upon the pride a black cowboy produces by doing a little of her own "refashioning" of Love.[56] The cowboy portrait with the rifle (fig. 8) is the most reproduced image of Love (the other [fig. 9] replaces the rifle with a lariat), and it is this image in particular that Alexander responds to in her poem:

Colored cowboy named Nat Love,
They called him Deadwood Dick.
A black thatch of snakes for hair,
Close-mouthed. Bullet-hipped.

One knee bent like his rifle butt,
Just so. Rope. Saddle. Fringe.
Knock this white boy off my shoulder.
Stone-jawed, cheekboned man.

Mama, there are black cowboys.
A fistful of black crotch.
Deadwood Dick. Don't fuck with me.
Black cowboy. Leather hat.

The *Venus Hottentot* collection in which this poem is included was published in 1990, amid the waning of resurgent black nationalism, in an era marked by social consciousness and militant advocacy, especially through rap. It makes sense, then, that Alexander refashions Love's feathered, straight-haired wig with the imagery of dreaded hair that is evoked in "A black thatch of snakes for hair." It also makes sense that Alexander represents Love with a racialized hypermasculinity in the barrage of phallic language that she packs into the final stanza. After the child proclaims to her mother that black cowboys do indeed exist— the impetus for countless articles on Love in 1970s black magazines, newspapers, and journals—the speaker reveals what the existence of black cowboys means for the contemporary black psyche.

"Deadwood Dick" is not just a figure who allows black people to write themselves into the history of the West; he is also a symbol of virile, potent black masculinity that was birthed during the black nationalist era of the 1970s and propagated quite explicitly in blaxploitation film. "A fistful of black crotch," a "don't fuck with me" stance, and a name, "Dick," which, in the late twentieth century, suggests "penis" more than does its nineteenth-century British denotation "guy or fellow," surely identify Love as a New Negro rebel—the black man who not only got his dick back, so to speak, but who is also uplifting the race, read black men, as a result. Alexander is perhaps signifying on black feminist writers', activists', and scholars' critiques of black nationalism as, to use bell hooks's words, "a dick thing"—an investment in social progress that could only envision the "uplift" of the race as being bound up in the recovery of a black masculinity that slavery stripped from black men.[57] Such a masculinist investment in progress makes it worth noting that it is what African American literary scholar Marlon Ross calls the "cowboy-pose-with-an-attitude" that we are most inclined to remember when we resurrect Love, not the more passive image of him with only a rope. Ross explains that "the solitary cowboy pose—with its celebration of violence, territoriality as Manifest Destiny, sexual independence (and sometimes outright hostility to women), rugged individualism, and compulsory masculinity—accords with United States standards as the heart of manly success."[58] The racialized re-membering of Love in Alexander's poem emphasizes the hypermasculinity that resonates with ideologies of "manly success" during the black nationalist era. I propose that Alexander is, "perhaps," signifying on black feminist critiques of black nationalism, because her refashioning embeds Love's masculinity, in that by embracing the violence and hypermasculinity of the iconic image of Love, it is constructed for whiteness. It is a complicated maneuver because, at the very same time that she returns his virulence, such imagery undermines the potential intellectual agency of black men. Love, remembered solely as a cowboy, then, becomes far more complex, as it plays into certain stereotypes at the same time that it allows successful manhood. This is why I think it is important and less problematic to read Love outside of his text.

I Came Here . . .

My final reading of Love is, thus, an intertextual analysis that approaches Love's narrative as a signifying text working to establish an ethos for Love that defies the very stereotypes that have kept his memory alive. Although Mel Brooks's *Blazing Saddles* makes no reference to Love himself, the plot of the film, its narrative devices, and its deployment of political satire certainly conjure Love's narrative. I believe the comparative analysis offered demonstrates that it is much more than his feats as a cowboy or the political and social environment of Southern California in the Progressive Era that holds Love up as an exemplar of self-actualization. Obviously, Love must have possessed a degree of physical toughness to have survived life in the West as a teamster and perhaps been shot fourteen times, but what is often overlooked in celebrations of Love's physicality is his intellect.[59] He wrote a double-voiced text directed at two very different audiences—a primarily white, working-class northern readership and an African American reader-ship. When one reads between the lines, Love's narrative is more than mere slave narrative and cowboy dime novel. And in an unlikely way, Brooks captures the complexities of constructing a black manhood in the West that Love signifies on in his narrative.

Although initial literary criticism of Love's narrative expressed con-cern that he presented the West as a space where blackness could be erased and he could be whitewashed into America's favorite hero, a close reading of the visual and print narrative Love offers complicates such arguments. As already noted, in previously published work I ad-dress the photographs Love included with his narrative, and I argue that the images were one way in which he battled Jim Crow. Here, how-ever, I will focus specifically on the printed text, but I will reiterate that if Love wanted to erase or even deemphasize his blackness, then including images of himself undermined that goal. For Love, the West was indeed what jazz composer and musician Babs Gonzales called "wide open spaces," but it was a space of limitless possibility because he could negotiate black maleness there in ways he could not elsewhere in the United States at that time. In other words, it was not that race did not matter in that space, but that the social and legal structures in place at that time were not as fixed there as in the rest of the nation.

The first five chapters of *The Life and Adventures* are dedicated to Love's life as a child and newly freed slave in Tennessee. Writ-ing in a style that alludes to Booker T. Washington's slave narrative-autobiography, Love uses this first section of the text to establish an ethos that will be important for constructing a black masculinity in the West that is at once physically impressive and indicative of a sophisticated deconstruction of white US manhood. Love emphasizes, even as a child, that he embodies foundational US ideals of what makes a citizen. In the story of his first postemancipation job working for Mr. Brooks, in spite of not being the eldest son, Love takes on the du-ties of head of household because of his father's death. Working for Mr. Brooks enables Love to help his mother feed and clothe his sister's children, whose father has also died, and Love makes a point to note that it also allowed him to purchase a book for each of the children. Love's father taught him "A B Cs," and he "could read a little."[60] During Reconstruction, literacy levels were low across racial lines, as standard public educational systems did not yet exist. By the time Love is herd-ing and branding cattle in the West, however, free public education for the white working class was growing. Love's attention to literacy is reflective of a common convention of slave narratives—literacy drives a desire for freedom—but it also begins to establish his intellect. His intellectual capacity for learning will facilitate his development of the language proficiency of a native speaker of Spanish, as well as his superb skill at reading cattle brands.

In addition to taking care to establish his intelligence at a young age, Love also takes care to establish his character. Through careful language choice, Love depicts his exceptional physical abilities in ways that lend him just enough humanness to make the hyperbolic standard in cowboy dime novels believable. Love makes it clear that as a child and as a young man, he was ordinary in the sense of his ability to recognize danger and fear it. When his father and brother-in-law die, his promise to look after his mother, sister, and nieces was offered "with a bravado [he] was far from feeling."[61] His unofficial job of breaking colts also induces some trepidation, particularly when he is commissioned to break Black Highwayman—a horse with a name full of irony and with an "uncertain temper and wild disposition." Love concedes, "I can assure you it was more for the money than the fun of the thing, that I finally consented to ride him."[62] He similarly acknowledges not expecting the caliber of "pitching" when riding a horse during his initiation into a Dodge City teamster party.[63] His greatest moment of fear is during his first Indian fight shortly after he arrives, at age fifteen, in the West in 1869, when "[he] lost all courage and thought [his] time had come to die. [He] was too badly scared to run." But a reminder from his compatriots to use his gun apparently frees him of fear, as he notes, "After this engagement . . . I seemed to lose all sense of what fear was and thereafter during my whole life on the range I never experienced the least feeling of fear."[64] These moments are critical in his development during the shift in American manhood driving so much anxiety around masculinity at this time. The geography of the West and its lawlessness provide Love the space and opportunity to position himself within and outside of the emerging self-made American manhood Kimmel notes is pervasive during Love's tenure in the West.

Love thoroughly enjoyed the "rough rider" life of danger and lawlessness, and the fact that his narrative was published, and images of his iconicity have survived in the public sphere, make it likely that he was, indeed, one of the best cowboys in the West. This element of the narrative, filled with bravado and the hyperbolic braggadocio of the genre, was directed toward the white, working-class northern audience who enjoyed the relatively recent availability of affordable reading material. His narrative also confirmed the public imagination of the West as the untamed space of President Theodore Roosevelt's "manly" civilizing expeditions.[65] Yet, Love also wrote for a black audience. The low-quality paper and mass production of dime novels made them accessible to black readers, too—probably some of the same black readers who read the black newspapers that Pullman porters, like Love in his second career, bore the heavy responsibility of distributing across the nation. Both the slave narrative and the Pullman porter career are odd inclusions in a text written primarily as a cowboy narrative. I believe these two nontraditional sections were intended for Love's black audience as an uplift narrative—a narrative that would neither sell well without the cowboy narrative nor construct an enduring, iconoclastic black masculinity. Love includes these sections to demonstrate his self-made manhood and his intellect—two things not extended to black men and important to convey to a black audience.

Blazing Saddles offers little of the unbelievable physical prowess of the cowboy section of Love's narrative. It does, however, emphasize how a combination of intellectual superiority and some physical skill enables a black sheriff to "save the day" and outsmart his white opponents. Although the West was a lawless and dangerous space, and Love had to do what it took to survive, he emphasizes his remorse, rather than "pride or bravado," for the men whose lives he took. Love implores his reader to understand that "it is a terrible thing to kill a man no matter what the cause," and he assures the reader that "every man who died at my hands was either seeking my life or died in open warfare."[66] "Black Bart," the black cowboy in *Blazing Saddles,* has neither received nor delivered bullet wounds; he embodies the smooth cowboy reflected in Love's portraits of himself in his full cowboy outfit. Although the film was produced in 1974 and is full of the anachronisms from that period, it is set during 1874, a period that disallows the performances of black machismo that were rampant among black male stars of the contemporaneous blaxploitation film circuit. The film's Reconstruction-era setting offers an interesting parallel to Love's narrative. The departure from the present space and return to the "fluidity" and "wide openness" of the previous space speaks not only to the possibility in that "openness," but also to the limitations in the 1970s despite the passage of various civil rights laws in the previous decade. Masculinities not made for black men are still enveloped within the masculinities privileged, reclaimed, and "created" for black men during this time, as the success of films like *Shaft* (1971), *Super Fly* (1972),

The Mack (1973), and *Dolemite* (1974) exemplifies—to name a few films produced during the heyday of blaxploitation cinema.

When Mel Brooks was asked to direct the film, he says that he and a team of writers, including the not-yet-famous Richard Pryor, rewrote the script as a parody of all westerns. The original screenwriter, Andrew Bergman, described the end result as "Eldridge Cleaver riding into town on a pony" (with a Gucci saddlebag).[67] Originally called *Black Bart, Blazing Saddles* is a raucous parody of not just westerns, but also racial prejudice; "the hatred of blacks" is what Brooks insists drove the film. When the unscrupulous attorney general, Hedley Lamarr (Harvey Korman), learns that quicksand blocks the path of the railroad line he is spearheading, he determines the tracks must be rerouted through the town of Rock Ridge. The town of Rock Ridge is populated by white residents, so he cannot simply take the land as he does with Native Americans' land. He, therefore, devises a plan to create mayhem in the town—appointing a black man as sheriff. The plan ultimately backfires when the sheriff outwits both the townspeople and Hedley.

The film establishes Bart (Cleavon Little) as crafty and intelligent in ways similar to those used in Love's slave narrative to establish his entrepreneurial ingenuity through breaking horses. Both Love and Bart find themselves presented with difficult, if not seemingly impossible tasks, and both men privilege intellect over physical capabilities to outwit their opponents, and find social and economic success in a democratic nation that treats them unequally. In the opening scene, Bart and a crew of black and Chinese railroad workers are using pick axes to break rock when Lyle (Burton Gilliam), a white overseer, demands that the black workers sing a slave spiritual for him: "When you was slaves, you sang like birds. Come on, how 'bout a good ole nigger work song?" In response, the black workers grumble and begin grouping together. Bart, however, curtails what could become a violent response by turning the overseer's racism on him. As the leader of the group, Bart begins singing an altered version of Cole Porter's heavily covered Broadway musical song "I Get a Kick Out of You," and his crew joins in with him. Lyle interrupts them, exclaiming: "Hold it, hold it, what the hell is that shit?! I meant a song, a real song, something like, *Swing low, sweet chariot!*" Following Bart's lead, the workers shrug off knowledge of the well-known slave spiritual, so Lyle asks what about "The Camptown Lady."[68] Again, Bart and the other men feign ignorance and compel Lyle and his men to perform the song along with lively dance as the black workers watch the foolery with satisfaction.

Bart becomes available for farcical appointment as sheriff under circumstances also similar to Love's. Bart is imprisoned after he hits the boss overseer, Taggart (Slim Pickens), over the head with a shovel because the overseer had left Bart and a fellow worker to die in the quicksand, but saved the $400 handcart. Counting his life as more valuable than a cart, as well as the horses Taggart said they could not afford to lose when he said to "send niggers instead," Bart determined any consequences were worth the retribution. When Bart and his coworker save themselves from the quicksand through Bart's ingenuity, Taggart tosses them a shovel and says to put it to good use. Bart picks up the shovel, and responding to his coworker's discouragement, he explains, "Uh-uh, Baby, I have to," just before cracking Taggart over the head with the shovel. Love found himself in a similar situation when his first employer in Tennessee, Mr. Brooks, attempted to cheat him. In addition to making Love work longer than the agreed-upon month before he was paid, Mr. Brooks also shorted Love on his wages, claiming Love had drawn his wages during the month. When Love insisted upon his balance, and Brooks declined to pay, they fought, and Love says without remorse, "I hit him in the head with a rock and nearly killed him after which I felt better."[69] Both Love and Bart chose actions that were about claiming their subjectivity more than constructing a gendered identity. Although there are occasions in which both Love and Bart rely upon brute force for achieving justice, their primary modus operandi is a cunning intellect, or *taking* their manhood by force in the same vein as Frederick Douglass.

Upon arriving in Rock Ridge, Bart immediately recognizes the futility of his badge and gun in a racist environment in which he is far outnumbered. Thus, he works to outwit both the overtures of the racist townspeople, and Hedley's efforts to bring about his demise. His acts of cunning consistently position him as socially and culturally superior to his white foes. While Love reports his proficiency in Spanish, his literacy, and the privilege of mobility and seeing the nation provided by the Pullman trains, Bart exhibits similar traits and behaviors that distinguish him from white "people of the land," as Bart's alcoholic, white sidekick, Jim the Waco Kid (Gene Wilder), describes the white townspeople.

Bart's first challenge is Mongo, the oversized, mentally disabled brute commissioned by Hedley to "mutilate" the sheriff. When Mongo arrives in Rock Ridge and begins terrorizing the town, it is the sheriff's job to reestablish order. Knowing he cannot beat Mongo physically and that Mongo is impervious to bullets, Bart creates a Looney

Tunes–style solution when he dresses as a singing deliveryman and personally delivers Mongo an explosive "candygram." The candygram apparently tames Mongo and compels him to pledge his allegiance to Bart because Bart is the only man who has ever beaten him. The result leads Bart to confide in Jim, "He [Mongo] was nothin' . . . the bitch was inventin' the candygram." When brute force fails, Hedley dispatches Lili von Shtupp, the "blonde bombshell" German saloon performer, to seduce the sheriff. The lights go down when Bart spends the night in her room, and sexual activity is implied, but when Bart insists upon returning to work in the morning, rather than being entrapped by her white feminine eroticism, Lili proclaims he is too much of a gentleman to fall for the plot.

Hedley's final attempt at sabotage is to hire a band of criminals to attack Rock Ridge, but learning about his plan ahead of time, the sheriff convinces the townspeople not to flee their homes, but, instead, to stay and fight through intellect rather than might. Bart instructs them to join forces with the black, Irish, and Chinese railroad workers and give those workers a plot of land in exchange for their aid in rebuilding a fake, or Trojan Horse, Rock Ridge in one day. In this instant, Bart not only demonstrates a intellect that is superior to that of the white villains and townspeople, but he also insists upon fairness and equality when the townspeople are initially willing to allot land to the blacks, but not the Irish or Chinese. His sense of equality, problem-solving skills, and classy demeanor position Bart as civilized and intelligent, characteristics in direct opposition to Enlightenment ideologies produced by, for example, Immanuel Kant. Attacking African-descended people's sensorial and intellectual capabilities, as well as their character, Kant proclaims: "The Negroes of Africa have by nature no feeling that rises above the trifling. . . . So fundamental is the difference between these two races of man, and it appears to be as great in regard to mental capacities as in color."[70] Thus he infamously concludes, "But in short, this fellow was quite black from head to foot, a clear proof that what he said was stupid."[71]

Whether it is the air of sophistication he exudes when drinking from a brandy snifter while Jim chugs liquor straight from the bottle, or the trickery he deploys to overcome white hate and treachery, Bart redefines American manhood and civility in a way that debunks mediated depictions of black masculinity in 1874 and 1974. With his mission accomplished, Bart decides to leave Rock Ridge, because it is "dull." Having civilized and integrated Rock Ridge, Bart is determined to leave and pursue "justice" elsewhere. Love exits the West in a similar fashion. As the West is closing and the railroads are eliminating the need for cattle teamsters, Love announces, "It was with genuine regret that I left the long horn Texas cattle and the wild mustangs of the range, but the life had in great measure lost its attractions and so *I decided to quit it and try something else for a while.*"[72] Love, too, moves on to a new arena that needs demonstrations of black masculine civility in order to debunk popular depictions of black men as dangerous brutes incapable of intellectual thought. For Love, that space is the Pullman trains—a racially subjugated space in which, by mandate of George Pullman, porters were only to be black men because, according to Pullman, they were familiar with servitude as former slaves. Love uses that space to claim his citizenship as he acquires a mobility afforded to few black Americans at that time. Speaking to both black and white readers, implicitly emphasizing a nationwide racial democracy, Love invites the reader to "let your chest swell with pride that you are an American. I think you will agree with me that this grand country of ours is the peer of any in the world. . . . America, I love thee, Sweet land of Liberty, home of the brave and the free."[73] Although the legal history of race and the West would suggest that not even the West afforded blacks (or Chinese, Native Americans, or Mexicans) equal and full citizenship, Love, in an assertion similar to his decision to leave the cowboy industry, insists upon his own subjectivity and ability to claim the land he lives in. He seemingly understands Baby Suggs's articulation of grace— if you cannot imagine it, you will not have it. Love imagined a nation in which his brand of black manhood was unquestionably American.

Love owns the space of Alexander's "black interior," and the "wild imagination" he employs to claim ownership of that space is unprecedented for that time. The intertextuality of Love's narrative, Alexander's poem, Toomer's "Rhobert," Mosley's *Devil in a Blue Dress*, and Brooks's *Blazing Saddles*, coupled with Love's investment in self-making, opens a new door for critical scholarship on transhistorical constructions of black masculinity. The racial performances that Love undertakes can offer a useful genealogy when assessing constructions of black manhood in popular culture, especially in post–civil rights literature that relies heavily on satire in its response to the shifting, and as some would argue, declining significance of race. Reading Nat Love alongside Percival Everett or Paul Beatty, for example, instead of reading Ishmael Reed, Richard Wright, or James Baldwin alongside Everett or Beatty, could expand how scholars map the evolution of identity politics and racial performance in African American culture. Ultimately, a more nuanced analysis of self-making in *The Life and Adventures* will challenge scholars analyzing both this narrative and Love himself to account for Love's "self-making" in a way that offers him agency and intellect not undercut by analyses positioning his *choices* as efforts to neutralize or even erase his blackness. It will also challenge scholars working in black cultural studies and gender studies to assess more critically the relationship between race, gender, identity politics, and desire in contemporary black cultural productions—a way of thinking that ultimately positions Love's politics as postmodern instead of regressive.

THREE

Lest We Forget: Stories My Grandfather Told Me

I remember the day that my grandfather died. May 13, 1998, is etched into my memory, not only because I lost my grandfather that day, but because the ugly dissolution of my mother's family also began that day.[1] A battle royal between my mother and her sister ultimately resulted in my grandfather's estate being managed by probate court, and my grandparents' home, my beloved retreat from childhood through college, being sold. Every item in the home was tagged, either for my grandfather's heirs to subtract the value from their shares or for whatever entity the court hired to dispose of in preparation for a probate sale. There were certain items—documents and military memorabilia—that no one fought over; those items inform the story I tell in this chapter.

The majority of years that I knew my grandfather, I observed him from a distance, and until I went to college, I wholeheartedly believed he was a scary, mean old man. My most vivid childhood memory of my grandfather is my grandmother insisting we not disturb him when he arrived home from work on the days that my brother and I spent at their home after school or during summer break. My second most vivid memory is of him putting a pile of coins on the coffee table, counting them all in front of my brother and me, and then packing them away without offering us any. From a child's perspective, this was a seemingly cruel act of teasing, especially when your grandmother liked to send you home with change for your piggy bank. Consequently, when I encountered my grandfather on a kindergarten field trip to the local state history museum—I did not know he worked there—I was thoroughly shocked, confused, and uncomfortable when his response to seeing me was to hug me and plant a big kiss on my cheek.

He remained scary until I went to college, and it was in those four, too short years that I truly began to know my grandfather. I attended college less than an hour from home, and I made it a point to go home often to visit my grandmother, to whom I had been close since childhood. During those visits, however, my grandfather seemed to suddenly realize he had a granddaughter, and he began devising ways to divide my time and attention. He would instruct me to sit down and listen to what I quickly registered were the same stories, visit after visit. The stories were genealogical narratives about his family. He named his siblings and showed me a picture he took great pride in and had framed on the top of his piano (fig. 10); it showed two older sisters, a younger brother, and himself, whom he identified after asking me, "And who's that good looking fella?" While I do not recall him giving any explanation for the whereabouts of his other five siblings, my grandfather had no fear of controversy, so he also told me that his maternal grandfather was white, had his own white family, and owned the land my grandfather's family sharecropped in Richland, Georgia. When I began attending his maternal family reunions in 1997, I quickly learned that the family did not appreciate his remembrance of that particular family history; in fact, I distinctly remember a cousin remarking, "So what, he's [my great-great-grandfather's] buried in a white cemetery?" My rudimentary research on *Ancestry.com*, however, contradicts my grandfather's assertion, as both of his maternal grandparents are listed on the 1880 census questionnaire as colored and married. Census questionnaires and their recorders do not always tell the truth of the Jim Crow South. Somehow my great-grandmother, my grandfather's mother, had a fair-enough complexion to "pass" and ride in the front of trains; my grandfather told the story of his mother "getting over" on the white people with amusement and pride. The story of his mother passing was accompanied by a story of being sent with a wagon to his "white" grandfather's house on occasion to collect food provisions for his family. These stories suggest the possibility that the pages of the census questionnaire do not tell a common southern genealogical story—and yet a story not so terribly uncommon in many southern black families from slavery through the civil rights era.

FIGURE 10   Portrait of author's grandfather, Gilbert Alexander Boothe (*right*), with three siblings.

In those four, short years of genealogical tutelage, I was the receiver of an oral history that I cherish; it was, however, only after my grandfather's death that I realized his storytelling merely skimmed the surface of a far more complicated story of who he was. Perhaps the penultimate moment of my "history lessons" with my grandfather was when he told me to sit in front of his typewriter and type the biography he had penned of his mother, Talullah Belle Booth (née Gilbert).[2] I knew better than to ask the purpose of the biography, and he did not offer an explanation. After his death, I learned that he had sent it to be included in a keepsake booklet for what must have been the 1995 Gilbert Family Reunion in Baltimore. The family history my grandfather took such great pride in telling, and in ensuring through his repetition that I, too, would one day tell, was not the only history my grandfather could have told, for our family history has much in common with that of so many black families with southern roots. The history I uncovered through the items I found more valuable than the antiques, furniture, and other material goods in my grandparents' home embodies a story my grandfather never actually told—a history burdened by a dialectic of pride and shame that he apparently found unspeakable.

Even as a child, I knew my grandfather was proud of his military service. He made it a point to have his phone number listed in the white pages under his military title, Major Gilbert A. Boothe. Between his phone-book listing and frequent trips to the local military base, Rickenbacker Air Force Base, when I was a child, I was well aware that my grandfather not only served in the army, but was also a retired officer. I always liked eating in the Officers' Club. I knew little else about his military service, though. I can only recall two other facts. His eldest sister and her husband drove him to Fort Benning to enlist; he proudly told this story.[3] The other story was told somberly and only once: he was a paratrooper in World War II, and, once, he barely missed detonating a Bouncing Betty. That was all I was told about his military service until my grandmother passed, and I learned at her funeral that my grandparents had met at a Red Cross Station in Germany.

A Dialectic of Pride and Shame

It was not a story to pass on.
TONI MORRISON, *BELOVED*

Major Boothe's documents and military memorabilia paradoxically break the silence, telling the stories he chose not to share with me and, as far as I can tell, did not share with any civilian.[4] I would imagine his silence was a painful and overwhelming burden to live with, both for him and those who lived with someone so psychically wounded by a racist nation. His choice not to share those stories reminds me of the web Morrison weaves between pain, silence, and community in *Beloved*. When the narrator addresses the aftermath of the community exorcising Beloved, she states three times, "It was not a story to pass on." The first and third statements are perhaps most telling of the intertwining of memory and shame for the ancestors of US slaves. The first reads:

The girl who waited to be loved and cry shame erupts into her separate parts, to make it easy for the chewing laughter to swallow her all away. *It was not a story to pass on.* They forgot her like a bad dream. After they made up their tales . . . those that saw her that day . . . quickly and deliberately forgot her.[5]

Speaking of the corporeal rebirth of the baby girl slain by her mother, the girl, Beloved, is said by some to have exploded (by others, to have run into the woods). As the embodiment of a history of oppression and dehumanization often too painful for words or true visual representation, Beloved needed to be broken down into small pieces that could be swallowed up and then forgotten. The same can be said of the memory of a segregated military and a racist nation whose black soldiers waited to be loved; shame erupts where pride should shine, making demonstrations of valor stories not to pass on for many who never forget yet are citizens of a nation that effortlessly forgets.

The third statement speaks, perhaps more powerfully, to the dialectical relationship of pride and shame entrenched in my grandfather's memories of military service. Repeating "This is not a story to pass on" for the third time, the following passage concludes the novel:

Down by the stream in back of 124 her footprints come and go, come and go. They are so familiar. Should a child, an adult place his feet in them, they will fit. Take them out and they disappear again as though nobody ever walked there.

By and by all trace is gone, and what is forgotten is not only the footprints but the water too and what it is down there. The rest is weather. Not the breath of the disremembered and unaccounted for, but wind in the eaves, or spring ice thawing too quickly. Just weather. Certainly no clamor for a kiss. Beloved.[6]

The footprints that come and go in back of the homestead are ungendered, unsexed, and unaged, fitting every passerby and emphasizing the universal and haunting black pain that Beloved embodies. And just as the footprints fit every black body, the pain is a collective suffering. That pain and the subsequent shame render the events forgettable. It is a story not to be remembered, and, in its disremembrance, the individual story disappears like the individual footprints. My grandfather's military story, like that of the tens of thousands of black compatriots who served in a segregated and discriminatory military, was just weather. His service, his sacrifice, his sense of duty, produced no clamor for a kiss upon his enlistment, deployment, or retirement. Even now, there has been little public uproar or loud and continued protest around the erasure of black veterans in public remembrances of service and bravery.

Therein lies the paradox of my grandfather's generation of black enlistees; they sought what Chandan Reddy so brilliantly terms "freedom with violence."[7] I do not know what compelled my grandfather to enlist in a segregated military voluntarily, but I would assume it was for reasons very similar to those noted in oral narratives of other black World War II and Korean War veterans—partly the pursuit of full citizenship in the eyes and practices of their fellow white citizens, and the economic security that was difficult to find elsewhere for both educated and formally uneducated black men. Tellingly, Morrison again captures the reality of limited opportunities for black men postemancipation: "Paul D was so impressed by the idea of being paid money to fight he looked at the private with wonder and envy."[8] It did not matter that the Civil War servicemen Paul D encountered bitterly noted they were paid less than white soldiers; he got stuck on the simple fact that they earned a wage for fighting. That moment of crisis, then, when the nation was split in two, and in later wars when many nations simultaneously fought, was liberatory for many black men, despite their subordination and humiliation.

I find that the narrative of black pride and shame told through the characters in *Beloved*, combined with Reddy's concept of "freedom with violence," elucidates why my grandfather emphasized the genealogical and obscured the personal. His story was not one to pass on, yet it was. What I found in his collection of esteemed artifacts tells the tale of what I thought had been deliberately forgotten.[9] Perhaps the public sphere, especially the white one, made no clamor for a kiss and rendered black military service no more than ordinary weather, but a determined group of black men felt otherwise. Approximately one million black men served in World War II,[10] and over 600,000 served in the Korean War,[11] the two wars in which my grandfather served. In that regard, his story does not stand out as any more extraordinary than those of any of his fellow servicemen.

His story after retirement is what is extraordinary. It is a story of the determination and courage of a group of men, who, when the nation rendered them invisible, took it upon themselves to tell their own story and correct a whitewashed, national narrative. What I took from my grandparents' house while my mother and aunt argued over material goods allows me to extend that story.

I selected items I both knew about and was fascinated by as a child, and other items that I discovered while searching my grandfather's bedroom—something I surely would never have done when he was living. No one noticed. In retrospect, I cannot say with certainty why I took the items. Perhaps I did so partly because I could. My grandfather had made changes to his will shortly before his death, and the will was unsigned. Thus, initially, my mother and her siblings agreed that their cousin would serve as executor of the estate. However, when the bickering escalated, my cousin resigned, and the estate was turned over to probate court. The administration of the estate by probate court meant the house would be sold and the proceeds split between all children (including my uncle's son, whom my grandparents had legally adopted), and all appraisable items in the house would be tagged so that each heir would have to subtract that cost from their share of the selling price of the home (minus the probate attorney's fee). The other reason I took the items was that they had value to me, because, in differing ways, they were records of my grandparents' lives and, in turn, my life.

The items I took include promotional certificates, news clippings, typed letters, official military-issued photographs, army personnel rosters, and a book. The last is what gives meaning to all the other artifacts. The book, Hondon B. Hargrove's *Buffalo Soldiers in Italy* (1985), does not look much different from the other books I rescued. It was on a shelf with Robert Hemenway's biography of Zora Neale Hurston, Alex Haley's *Roots*, both of Langston Hughes's autobiographies, *Robert's Rules of Order*, and a history of the Omega Psi Phi fraternity (I took these books, too, along with photo albums and my grandmother's immigration document). The only difference was that *Buffalo Soldiers in Italy* was in pristine condition; it looked as if it had never even been opened. Through pure serendipity, I learned years after commandeering these artifacts that the random collection of papers was directly connected to the 24th Infantry, a regiment of the Buffalo Soldiers,[12] and was not so random after all.[13] Hargrove used the letters, rosters, and news clippings (along with extensive archival research and interviews) to compose a corrected "history of American arms in World War II by including the story of this unique and remarkable body of black soldiers."[14]

I find both the book and the methodology for producing it fascinating. Much ado has been made of black women writers doing similar work during the 1970s and 1980s. *Beloved*, in fact, is part of a neo-slave narrative or postmodern slave narrative genre that emerged during those two generations. The genre was dominated by black women writers like Morrison, who declared that they were "setting the record straight," as Paule Marshall, a contemporary of Morrison, described the work of giving voice to stories that could not be told during slavery. My grandfather, Mr. Hargrove, and all of the men who participated in providing information and checking facts were also working to set the record straight. There is both pain and determination in Hargrove's narrative tone as he writes in his introduction, "The hope is that an interested reader will be able to draw his own conclusions about this black division and the courage of its men."[15] While Mr. Hargrove's goal was to present a more complete, or historically accurate, story of the Buffalo Division, my goal is to tell my own story about his story. Mine unfolds in the documents my grandfather acquired during the record-gathering process. I want to think about the limits and possibilities of black men "imagining grace" through military service for a nation whose only interest in their (black men's) best interest was by way of an interest convergence.

Legal scholar Derrick Bell described the Supreme Court ruling in *Brown v. Board of Education* as an "interest convergence dilemma," meaning the president and the court were interested in creating a more just justice system through civil rights for all citizens only because it was in their own best interest. The civil rights era made the United States look hypocritical when it touted democracy and frowned upon communism, while its black citizens were being shown being beaten, attacked by dogs, and sprayed with fire hoses on televisions worldwide. An interest convergence, then, is not at all about correcting moral wrongs; it is, instead, about serving the best interest of hegemonic power. Thus, on July 26, 1948, when President Truman signed Executive Order No. 9981 Desegregating the Military, he was responding largely to protests by civil rights leaders like A. Philip Randolph and by black army veterans wishing to reenlist in positions as more than servants, and demanding equality within the armed forces.[16]

My father died,
Died fighting 'cross the sea.
Mama said his dying
Never helped her or me.
. . . .
In the land of the free

Called the home, home of the brave,
All I want is liberty,
That is what I crave.

JOSH WHITE, "DEFENSE FACTORY BLUES"

Setting the Record Straight

Decisions made by the Supreme Court, Congress, and presidents during the civil rights era were essentially responding to a period of national crisis. The idea of crisis and its multifarious modes of manifestation is at the center of both the story I discovered and the story I will tell, so I want to think first about the dialectical relationship between crisis and the extraordinary. The association of the concept of crisis with both war and black men is ironic.[17] War is typically understood as the state of being unstable and in danger (of conquest or peril). War is, thus, the state of being in crisis. Yet, men whose social, political, and educational positioning within the US nation-state has been equated with crisis understood military service to be a vehicle by which they could liberate themselves from crisis. This is no small irony. Josh White's "Defense Factory Blues" addresses how black men fought and died in vain in one line, and expresses the pursuit of freedom, citizenship, and liberty several lines later. Oral narratives from black servicemen in World War II and the Korean War consistently reveal bitter stories of segregation, discrimination, and the hard fact of unequal protection and second-class citizenship, in spite of risking one's life for the "land of the free" and "home of the brave." The 92nd Infantry Division was, indeed, repeatedly described as a defensive unit "in crisis" by the upper echelon of white commanding officers. This project is not, however, an exercise in identifying the various ways black men were defeated by a Jim Crow military. Instead, it is about reflecting on how black men have responded to disenfranchisement, marginalization, and structural inequalities in ways that debunk, resist, and ultimately are invested in self-actualization despite adversities. The documents my grandfather saved speak to a gallant, organized effort to do just that.

In a letter dated September 15, 1980, on Philander Smith College National Alumni Association letterhead, Hiram L. Tanner composed a typed request to fellow 92nd compatriots soliciting copies of printed matter regarding the 92nd (general orders, special orders, daily bulletins, award citations, 92nd newspapers, citations received, propaganda leaflets), as well as oral interviews and personal experiences (fig. 11).

PHILANDER SMITH COLLEGE

— *National Alumni Association* —

September 15, 1980
2259 Union Ave.
Columbus, OH. 43223

You may be interested to know that there are
several veterans of World War II, who are still collecting material and/or memorabillia about the 92d
Inf. Div.

A few months ago a Lt. Col. Major Clark (ret),
formerly of the 597th FA Bn. contacted me from
Tulsa, Okla. Since that time we have exchanged
some documents and information which have been very
valuable to both of us.

While Col. Clark is concentrating his study
on the 92d Division Artillery in WW II, I have been
collecting and writing stories about the outstanding performances of individuals and units within
the division. We have heard enough about the bad
and "melting away" of certain units but how about
the good deeds accomplished by some individuals
and units.

Some of my information is being secured from
indivduals, newspapers (especially the 92d Div.
newspaper, "The Buffalo"), citations received by
individuals, printed information, personal experiences, oral interviews, propaganda leaflets, etc.

If any one in the organization has any printed
matter he received while in the 92d, I would like to
have a copy of it. By that I mean such material as
general orders, special orders, daily bulletins,
award citations, 92d news paper, "The Buffalo", etc.

In the past the veterans would send me any
printed maater pertaining to themselves and/or the
92d Inf. Div. and I make copies of their material
and return the original copies back to them.

Don't give up on me, I'll make one of those
meetings some day.

Sincerely,

Hiram L. Tanner

Encl:

FIGURE 11 Hiram Tanner letter, September 15, 1980.

He noted that he was not alone in his efforts to collect material and
memorabilia of the 92nd. "A Lt. Col. Major Clark (ret) of the 597th FA
Bn."—the only all-black unit commanded by a black officer throughout World War II—contacted Mr. Tanner about his own study of the
92nd Division Artillery in World War II. Clark's study compelled Tanner to note, "We have heard enough about the bad and 'melting away'

of certain units but how about the good deeds accomplished by some individuals and units."[18] Lieutenant Colonel Clark successfully carried out his mission to chronicle the good deeds.

A May 25, 2009, online news article for a Tulsa, Oklahoma, news station addresses how his daughter, Vivian Clark Adams, was working to make sure that his story was told. Although Lieutenant Colonel Clark was awarded the Bronze Star, there were no black Medal of Honor recipients during World War II. Noting her father's insistence upon correcting that wrong, Clark Adams explains how, in 1997, President Bill Clinton (belatedly) honored seven black soldiers. For his perseverance, Lieutenant Colonel Clark was invited to the White House for the ceremony, but his health was too poor to attend; he died two years later. As the troop historian, Lieutenant Colonel Clark apparently possessed a wealth of papers and photographs, which were donated to the Oklahoma Historical Society.

True to his daughter's account, Lieutenant Colonel Clark did, indeed, actively and aggressively pursue setting the record straight, as his name is on a number of documents in my grandfather's archive. A letter dated March 5, 1982, on Office of the Assistant Secretary of Defense letterhead is addressed to Mr. Major Clark of Tulsa, Oklahoma (fig. 12). The director of Equal Opportunity Programs (Civilian), Claiborne D. Haughton Jr., addressed the letter to Clark, informing him that "concerns which [he] expressed about the incomplete references to the 92d Division during World War II have been corrected" in the Department of Defense publication "Black Americans in Defense of Our Nation." Claiborne notes the copies of newspaper articles and other material Clark shared and thanks him for his "assistance in *setting the record straight*" (emphasis mine). An additional document regarding Clark is a "Restricted" record from Headquarters 92nd Infantry Division, General Orders #39, dated June 11, 1945. It is titled "Awards of Bronze Star Medal," and third down on the list is Major Clark, who was a field artillery captain at the time of conferral.

A like set of documents attests to similar efforts Tanner and Hargrove made to set the record straight regarding overlooked or ignored citations and valorous acts by fellow combat Buffalo Soldiers in Italy during World War II. Both Clark and Tanner contacted Captain William S. M. Banks of Fort Valley, Georgia, who is cited in Hargrove's *Buffalo Soldiers*. My grandfather had a copy of a letter from Banks to Tanner dated February 2, 1981, thanking Tanner for sending him "interesting materials." Banks notes that Clark also contacted him over the previous five or six years, and he acknowledges being "the first black officer

OFFICE OF THE ASSISTANT SECRETARY OF DEFENSE

WASHINGTON, D C 20301

5 March 1982

MANPOWER
RESERVE AFFAIRS
AND LOGISTICS

qual Opportunity & Safety)

Mr. Major Clark
503 E 27th Place, North
Tulsa, Oklahoma 74106

Dear Mr. Clark:

Attached is a copy of the revised and expanded edition of the
Department of Defense publication, "Black Americans in
Defense of Our Nation".

The concerns which you expressed about the incomplete references
to the 92d Division during World War II have been corrected.
Please note the text on page 34 and the picture on page 36.

We appreciate your cooperation in providing copies of newspaper
articles and other material relating to the 92d and for your
patience in awaiting the final corrections. I am sure that you
will agree after reviewing the booklet that it was worth the
wait.

Many thanks for your assistance in setting the record straight.

Sincerely,

Claiborne D. Haughton Jr.
Director, Equal Opportunity
Programs (Civilian)

Attachment

FIGURE 12 Department of Defense letter to Mr. Major Clark, March 5, 1982.

in the division to be promoted to the rank of captain" in October 1943.
He goes on to share that he earned a PhD in sociology from the Ohio
State University in June 1949. In closing, Banks confirms that he was
awarded the Silver Star and points to enclosures attesting the fact. One
document is the citation, and a second has two newspaper clippings,
neither of which notes the newspaper name. One heralds him for being awarded the Silver Star, and the other highlights his position as the
"first negro captain." Both pieces provide a small snapshot of this New
Orleanian's life prior to joining the military: he was a Dillard University athlete; earned a master's degree at Fisk; and was a YWCA worker
and schoolteacher.

There are similar documents relating to efforts led by Hargrove to
compel the army to officially, though posthumously, recognize the
"heroic actions" of First Lieutenant John R. Fox of the 366th Infantry

Regiment for his bravery and selflessness on the battlefield of Sommocolonia, Italy, on December 26, 1944. Lieutenant Colonel James L. Hickman, chief of the Military Awards Branch, sent Mrs. Arlene Fox, First Lieutenant Fox's widow, a letter dated March 15, 1982, informing her that, although it was unusual, her husband would posthumously receive the Distinguished Service Cross, the army's second-highest award for valor in combat. The copy of the letter is accompanied by an April 5, 1982, *Army Times* article, "Posthumous DSC Ordered for WWII Hero," that describes the "proof" unearthed in order to get a recommendation approved so long after the event. There is also a declaration of the Wilberforce University Alumni Association and class of 1940 (Fox's alumni class) that attests to Fox's bravery and resolves "to authorize, encourage, and assist, in every way possible, Dr. Hondon B. Hargrove '38, to persuade the United States Military Authorities to award posthumously, the Congressional Medal of Honor, to First Lieutenant John Fox" (fig. 13). There are two additional papers, presumably from a draft of Hargrove's manuscript, that describe combat conflict, and in which the names of Fox and Banks are underlined by hand.

The need to set the record straight was no small matter. Hargrove and other historians systematically addressed the biased assessment of the 92nd in official military records, the US press, and biographies penned by white commanders. Generals Lucian K. Truscott Jr. and Mark Clark wrote inflammatory reports, describing black soldiers as unfit for combat. In a report regarding a failed operation in February 1945, Truscott concludes:

The failure of this operation is marked by the failure of the infantry and engineers of the 92nd Division. The —— [left unstated in original text] has clearly demonstrated that, in spite of excellent and long training, excellent physical condition, superior support by artillery and air, the infantry of this division lacks the emotional and mental stability necessary for combat. I do not believe that further training under present conditions will ever make this division into a unit capable of offensive action.[19]

During a time when pugilism and other muscular sports continued to be a conduit for proving manhood, combat narratives like Truscott's enabled white men to conflate male power with white supremacy. By presenting black soldiers as incompetent, unreliable, cowardly, and, ultimately, effeminate, white commanders denied black men the opportunity to gain civic power by proving their manhood on the battlefield.[20]

WHEREAS, First Lieutenant John Fox, was serving as a Forward Observer of Cannon Company, 366th Infantry, attached to 92nd Division Artillery in Sommocolonia, Italy, on 26 December, 1944, and,

WHEREAS, First Lieutenant John Fox, knowing the consequences, adjusted all available artillery fires directly on his own position; at that point, the enemy had penetrated the town's defenses and fighting was going on from door to door and in the streets, and,

WHEREAS, First Lieutenant John Fox, ordered: "That round was just where I wanted it; bring it in 60 more yards" (quoted from Journal of the 598th Field Artillery Battalion) and,

WHEREAS, First Lieutenant John Fox, was killed in the bombardment that followed upon his orders, along with many of the enemy, and,

WHEREAS, No proper recognition of First Lieutenant John Fox's brave sacrificial act, far above the call of duty, was ever approved by the military authorities, and,

WHEREAS, First Lieutenant John Fox, was a member of the class of 1940, Wilberforce University, and,

WHEREAS, The class of 1940 and the Wilberforce University National Alumni Association, hereby resolves to authorize, encourage, and assist, in every way possible, Dr. Hondon B. Hargrove '38, to persuade the United States Military Authorities to award posthumously, the Congressional Medal of Honor, to First Lieutenant John Fox, and,

WHEREAS, This resolution is proposed by Dr. Hondon B. Hargrove, formerly Captain, 597th Field Artillery, 92nd Infantry Division, and also formerly Second Lieutenant, 366th Infantry, "C" Company.

Hondon B. Hargrove

DR. HONDON B. HARGROVE '38
Member, Board of Directors
Wilberforce University Alumni Association

Motion for approval of the Resolution was made by Sidney A. Thompson '38, formerly First Lieutenant, "H" Company, 366th Infantry, and seconded by John F. Morning, Sr. '24, both members of the Board of Directors.

Done at the National Summer Conference of the Wilberforce University Alumni Association at Washington D.C. on 30 July, 1976.

James R. Tanner

JAMES R. TANNER,
President

Wyatt McDowell

WYATT MC DOWELL,
Secretary

FIGURE 13   Wilberforce University Alumni Association Resolution, July 30, 1976.

Hargrove does not reference as much pejorative commentary by General Clark as by Truscott, but Clark, too, according to Hargrove, was unwilling to lay blame for failures on anyone other than the black junior officers and enlisted men.[21] In my grandfather's collection, there are two sheets of paper produced on a typewriter with a notation that they are from a chapter of Clark's *Calculated Risk* (1950) titled "The Hard Winter in the Apennines." I will quote four paragraphs, because a handwritten note at the end of the quoted passage reads as follows:

To: Maj. Gilbert Boothe—2/14/82
Do you agree with Gen Clark's evaluation of the 92d [*sic*]. If not, how would you respond.

It is signed with three initials that look like *HLT*, for Hiram L. Tanner, who, like my grandfather, resided in Columbus, Ohio, and is noted in *Buffalo Soldiers in Italy* as editor of the black newspaper *Columbus Call and Post*. The excerpted passage from Clark's biography reads:

This performance by the 92nd—and it was a bad performance—has since been used on various occasions in an effort to argue that Negro troops cannot be depended upon to fight well in an emergency. Having commanded the only Negro infantry division in World War II, which was continuously in battle for over a period of six months, I feel I should report factually on its performance during that period. Of the ten American infantry divisions in action in the Fifth Army in Italy, the 92nd Division's accomplishments were less favorable than any of the white divisions. [A note here reads: "Colored service units (quartermaster, engineer, ordnance, etc.) and combat support units (tanks field artillery, antiaircraft, etc.) in general demonstrated a high degree of efficiency."] On the other hand, there were many instances of individual heroism and successful action by smaller units, such as a company or battalion. Shortly after the war, when asked about the effectiveness of Negro infantry troops in battle, I replied that the 92nd Division performed a useful role and its presence on Italy's west coast assisted us materially in our final drive into the Po Valley.

At the same time, it would be dishonest and unfair to future Negro soldiers to overlook the serious handicaps which they had to overcome. Leadership was one of the biggest problems. There were many illiterates among the Negro troops; hence it took longer to train them, and there was, in general, a reluctance to accept responsibility for the hard, routine discipline that is essential in wartime. This failure I view not as a reflection on the Negro soldier or officer, but as a reflection on our handling of minority problems at home. The Negro had not had the opportunity to develop qualities of leadership. Most of all, perhaps, the Negro soldier needed greater incentives; a feeling that he was fighting for his home and country and that he was fighting as an equal. Only the proper environment in his own country can provide such an incentive.

It would be a grave error, however, to assume that no suitable officer can be found for Negro combat troops. In fact, they were found in Italy. When it became necessary to reorganize the 92nd in the following weeks, we were able to select certain battle-proven officers and men who responded to special training, and to build up battalion combat teams that participated much more effectively than before. I have decorated for bravery Negro officers and men of the 92nd Division and have known of others who were killed in extremely valorous action on the field of battle.

It is unfortunate that I do not have a record of my grandfather's response to this inquiry. Although General Clark establishes an ethos that comes across as more admirable than Hargrove suggested in his historical truth-telling, the fact that Tanner wondered what my grandfather thought of Clark's evaluation suggests that Tanner certainly was not interested in taking the evaluation at face value. What I read between the lines of Clark's evaluation, and what I like to believe my grandfather saw too, is little acknowledgment of any military responsibility for the racial climate or unequal treatment of black soldiers. All responsibility is placed upon the country itself. It is reminiscent of a report fifteen years later that would begin with a condemnation of slavery and the failure of the Fourteenth Amendment as explanations for racial inequalities, but then castigate black women for dismantling patriarchal order in black households and endangering the black family. Both Clark and Daniel Patrick Moynihan shift culpability through conciliatory rhetoric. It would, nonetheless, be interesting to hear my grandfather's perspective, since he was one of the "battle-proven officers who responded to special training" (see figs. 14–16).

Commentary on white commanding officers' evaluations and depictions of black enlisted men and junior officers consistently spoke back to the recurring white narrative of black incompetence and cowardice. Most often, this commentary offered a counternarrative, like the one requested of my grandfather, but, sometimes, the commentary provided its own assessment of the competence of white commanding officers. One page containing four news clippings tells an interesting story through the perspective of the individual who compiled the collection. Two of the four clippings remark on the illogic of General Lesley J. McNair's (commander of the ground forces) decision to restrict overseas combat to colonels forty-eight years old and under. A newspaper clipping published December 31, 1944, explains that the rule

FIGURE 14 35th FA Officers in Germany, 1956; *back row, sixth from left,* Gilbert Alexander Boothe.

FIGURE 15 Officers' Refresher Course, Kitzingen, Germany, ca. 1948; *third row (standing), third from right,* Gilbert Alexander Boothe.

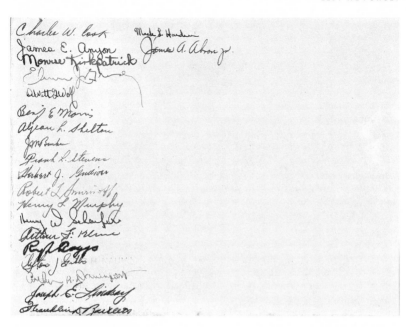

FIGURE 16   Officers' Refresher Course, ca. 1948 (*reverse of photo*); autographs of fellow officers.

resulted in "youngsters, who were only lieutenants or captains in 1941, [taking] their places. These youngsters had all the courage and vigor in the world, but they lacked one thing so all-important in battle—experience under fire." My grandfather was one of those youngsters. Born in 1922, he was still a teenager when he was promoted from private to sergeant in Company L, 24th Infantry (Fort Benning) (fig. 17). Given that his first promotion occurred before the United States had declared war on Japan and Germany and begun deploying troops overseas, his promotion was based solely on performance in training. He was again promoted in June 1942 to staff sergeant (Roses Island) (fig. 18).[22] It is difficult to fathom how these men negotiated the psychological trauma of war in addition to the prevailing and often blatant racism at home and abroad. The commentary on the illogical choices made by General McNair imply that his decisions compounded the already unavoidable trauma of war.

The other two clippings talk back to white commanders, the press, and news media—more so through the textual underlining and marginal notes added by a Buffalo Soldier during the circulation of the assemblage of clippings than in the content of the articles themselves.

Army of the United States

To all who shall see these presents, greeting:

Know ye, that reposing special trust and confidence in the fidelity and abilities of Private Gilbert Boothe, 14015047, Co. L 24th Infantry, I do hereby appoint him Sergeant, Company L, 24th Infantry, ARMY OF THE UNITED STATES, to rank as such from the Fourth day of February one thousand nine hundred and Forty-one. He is therefore carefully and diligently to discharge the duty of Sergeant by doing and performing all manner of things thereunto belonging. And I do strictly charge and require all Noncommissioned Officers and Soldiers under his command to be obedient to his orders as Sergeant. And he is to observe and follow such orders and directions from time to time, as he shall receive from his Superior Officers and Noncommissioned Officers set over him, according to the rules and discipline of War.

Given under my hand at Fort Benning, Georgia this Fourth day of February in the year of our Lord one thousand nine hundred and Forty

James M. Ogle
Colonel, 24th Infantry

W. D., A. G. O. Form No. 58
March 25, 1924

FIGURE 17 Fort Benning promotion, dated February 4, 1941 (in the body of the order) or 1940 (above the signature).

Army of the United States

To all who shall see these presents, greeting:

Know ye, that reposing special trust and confidence in the fidelity and abilities of Sergeant GILBERT BOOTHE, 14015047, Company L, 9156-A, , I do hereby appoint him Staff Sergeant (Temporary) Company L, 9156-A, ARMY OF THE UNITED STATES, to rank as such from the fourth day of June one thousand nine hundred and forty-two. He is therefore carefully and diligently to discharge the duty of Staff Sergeant by doing and performing all manner of things thereunto belonging. And I do strictly charge and require all Noncommissioned Officers and Soldiers under his command to be obedient to his orders as Staff Sergeant. And he is to observe and follow such orders and directions from time to time, as he shall receive from his Superior Officers and Noncommissioned Officers set over him, according to the rules and discipline of War.

Given under my hand at Roses Island this fourth day of June in the year of our Lord one thousand nine hundred and forty-two.

HAMILTON THORN,
Colonel, 9156-A, Commanding

FIGURE 18 Roses Island promotion, June 4, 1942.

The first was published in Rome on December 28; the year 1944 is handwritten above the text. The headline runs: "Yanks Forced Back in Italy: Strong Allied Air Defense Hinders Nazi Drive Toward Livorno." Although the article emphasizes the forced withdrawal of the 92nd and allied troops, someone has underlined "road town of Barga in two days of fierce fighting," with "fierce fighting" boxed for emphasis. The paragraph immediately following is also boxed, and a marginal note simply states, "Black Soldiers." So, even though the blocked paragraph and the overall article discuss the challenges the 92nd Division and allied troops experienced in holding ground, the point of the interpolator was to emphasize the division's determination and fortitude under fire. Juxtaposed to this 1944 article is one without date or location, but entitled "106th Division Caved First." The entire first paragraph is underlined, as is the last sentence of the second. A hand-drawn box circumscribes these two paragraphs, with the marginal note "white soldiers." The underlined passages read:

Military experts point out that the division reported to have caved in first when the Germans counterattacked was the 106th. It had just gone into the line and not one hostile shot had ever been fired over its head. This division gave way like straws before a tornado. . . . Had the 106th Division held for only a few hours it would have made all the difference in the world to the rest of the army and to the length of the war.

Both articles are about retreat, but the interpolator has emphasized the fact that the black division fought fiercely and the white division "caved." These interpolations challenge white commanding officers' favored descriptions of black soldiers "melting away" and "straggling"— descriptions that seemed intentionally to overlook the phenomenon of poorly trained troops in both white and nonwhite units during World War II. The anger and pain evident in Hargrove's description of the distinctions made between white and black soldiers through the language choices of Generals Truscott, Almond, and Clark offer an understanding of the interpolator's sentiments: "The point is that General Truscott, General Clark and General Almond were unable to bring themselves to extend the same compassion and objectivity in evaluating the black Buffalo Soldiers, as they did when analyzing white soldiers." He notes General Clark's "careful, generous, and compassionate . . . references to the infantry soldiers of the 36th Division [white] during the Rapido River 'Fiasco.'"[23] Hargrove insists that if the 875 soldiers Clark describes as "missing" from that conflict were black, they surely would have been described instead as "stragglers"—a term used to define black soldiers as unreliable deserters and cowardly under fire.

Beyond Setting the Record Straight

It is fairly simple to deduce why many of the documents in my grandfather's archive were circulated. The citations for commendation and passages from Clark's biography make a significant contribution to Hargrove's intent that his monograph "dispel many myths and stories" of black soldiers' performance in combat.[24] Other material, however, has circulated but is not mentioned in *Buffalo Soldiers*. I do not think this was simply a matter of the limits on what could be included or the trajectory of the history being told. Instead, I believe the men who sent documents to archivists like Tanner and Major Clark were sending them in an effort to share their stories with one another. Setting the record straight, undoubtedly, was imperative for many of the men, but the audience of counternarratives is not always a hegemonic one. As much as the black women writers of the black women's literary renaissance were writing to set a white record straight, they were also writing those narratives to help repair black pain. The final set of documents I will discuss, then, seems to be more attuned to doing the work of creating a private, intimate dialogue between black compatriots than to setting a (white) public record straight.

My favorite document is what appears to be the cover of sheet music. Scaling down the left side of the cover, at a slant, are the words "We're Division 92," with the Buffalo Soldier insignia—a black buffalo encapsulated by a circle—directly in front of the number 92. Scaling down the right side linearly are photographic reproductions of active-duty Buffalo Soldiers. Music bars and notes ribbon around the images. At the bottom of the page in script is the phrase *Words + Music by*. The rest of the page is cut off, but Helen Osborne composed the music and wrote the lyrics. Documents at the US Army Military History Institute in Brigadier General Benjamin O. Davis Jr.'s (the army's first black officer holding the rank of general) personal collection include a copy of the sheet music, noting Osborne's contribution and dating it in 1943. Tanner sent the reproduction I have to my grandfather. On the bottom of the legal-size paper, Tanner wrote in red ink, "This is the face that should have been on the cover page instead of Gen. Almond." The face he is referencing is his or someone else's superimposed image of a young and very pretty Lena Horne in the middle of the cover page. Above her photograph are the typewritten words: "Dedicated to the 92d [sic] 'Sweetheart.'" This seemingly small act of superimposing Horne's image—an image that is widely accepted as beautiful, but also represents a dedicated activist—is, in fact, a noteworthy act of resistance. Surely, it defies logic that a segregated black infantry unit would be expected to place the image of a racist white commanding officer on the cover of its sheet music.

An alternative explanation for why the image of General Almond was covered over by Horne's image is the change in black enlistees' attitude toward him over time. Lieutenant General Edward E. Almond initially impressed black enlistees at the October 15, 1942, activation ceremony at Fort McClellan, Alabama, when he promised fairness, the best leadership, and the production of a "first class battlefield unit."[25] By June 1943, however, when Brigadier General Davis composed his inspector general report, he reported a decidedly different attitude about Almond—a belief by black enlisted men and officers "that General Almond had been unduly influenced by some of his officers, and that his attitude had changed." These beliefs resulted in Davis concluding: "General Almond had overlooked the human element in the training of the 92nd Division. Great stress has been placed upon the mechanical perfection in execution of training missions . . . and not enough consideration given to . . . maintenance of a racial understanding between white and colored officers and men."[26] Hargrove points out that, unlike in other divisions, there was no effort to produce an esprit de corps in the Buffalo unit. Their history, accomplishments, and traditions were not extolled.[27] Thus, in spite of someone circulating a document featuring an October 4, 1943, memo signed by Almond inviting parents of sons in the 92nd Infantry Division to the first anniversary of its reactivation on the top half of the page, and a June 12, 1979, newspaper obituary of his death on the bottom half, it is clear why Tanner—and I feel confident many other men of the 92nd—preferred the face of Lena Horne on the cover of their sheet music to that of a white commanding officer who deemed black soldiers unfit for combat.

Oral history narratives collected by the Howard University Moorland-Spingarn Black Military Oral History Project support my presumption. The narratives were collected between 1981 and 1990, with the majority collected in 1981 and 1982—the same period as the record-correcting campaign initiated by men like Tanner and Clark. Colonel John Thomas Martin (ret.), a member of the Howard University Moorland-Spingarn Oral History Project team, collected most of the military oral histories. The histories he collected focus on the 366th Infantry Regiment, a regiment consistently described as an all-black unit, from commanding officer down. The men in this unit consistently express disdain for General Almond, with every man who mentions Almond describing a racist statement he made when he introduced himself as their commanding officer. Lloyd French sums it up when he describes Almond as "speaking out of the side of his mouth like a typical southern white 'cracker,' saying, 'your folks wanted you in combat, and you're going in combat tonight.'"[28] Statements to this effect or referencing this exact statement appear frequently in the archived oral histories.

Other documents in my grandfather's collection, seemingly more for division archival purposes and sustaining a black male confraternity, include several laudatory news articles. It would appear that my grandfather circulated one about himself. It is not dated but is most certainly post–World War II and Korean War, because the location is Columbus, Ohio, and his rank is captain. In this article, titled "Defense against Air Attacks; Battery 'D' Stands Prepared," the journalist foregrounds a question: "Have you ever stopped to wonder, what would happen to you in case of an actual enemy air attack? Probably not, not many of us have. Clear your mind for a moment and think it over. Would you be safe?—Battery D of the 32nd Battalion, commanded by Capt. Gilbert Boothe, Columbus, Ohio, has the answer." The accompanying photograph shows my grandfather sitting behind a desk going over the week's activities with his subordinate white officer (standing), First Lieutenant Edward V. Ryan, Executive Officer (fig. 19). The text of the article itself is brief and offers nothing more about my grandfather. The image, however, depicts what was a highly unusual reversed racial dichotomy, even for that postwar period, in which a black commanding officer gave orders to a white junior officer. I cannot be certain what orders they were reviewing, but I can conjecture that, as a commanding officer—which means he did not train troops or perform equipment maintenance himself—my grandfather was probably instructing his subordinate on what needed to happen during the training cycle.

Two additional images, which must also have been included in the news feature, show my grandfather standing behind a large machine gun armory—in the middle five white enlisted men (figs. 20 and 21). In the second of the two images (fig. 21), he is shown with one arm stiffly at his side, and the other arm raised, and he is pointing with his index finger toward one of the men. The caption again lists him as commander of "D" Battery. Here, my grandfather is probably both participating in a certain degree of staging for the journalist and doing what

FIGURE 19   Capt. Gilbert A. Boothe, commander, Battery D, 32nd Battalion, reviewing
schedule with First Lieutenant Edward V. Ryan, Rickenbacker Air Force Base, 1960s.

FIGURE 20   Capt. Gilbert A. Boothe with enlisted men, Rickenbacker Air Force Base, 1960s.

FIGURE 21   Capt. Gilbert A. Boothe instructing enlisted men, Rickenbacker Air Force Base, 1960s.

good officers did—getting out of the office to talk to soldiers, ask questions, troubleshoot, and, generally, demonstrate his investment in the morale, health, and welfare of his troops. In contrast to the countless verdicts from senior white commanding officers during World War II, declaring black men unfit for battle and incompetent to lead, these images compel viewers to imagine a new military and a new black man. Surely the hearts of men did not change simply because President Truman desegregated the military; men like Major Boothe defied stereotypes, and it had to be a victory for men of the 92nd Division to see a black man *giving* rather than *taking* orders.

Similarly, another news clipping circulated among my grandfather's comrades, the Black History Edition of the *Post* (Oakland, California), February 10, 1982, features an image of General Clark presenting Charles J. Patterson a Silver Star for gallantry. The presentation was made October 29, 1944, in Italy, but the article serves as a proud remembrance during "Black History Month." The notation points out that at that time Patterson was vice president of World Airways, lauding both his military and his professional accomplishments. Below that image is one of a group of Buffalo Soldiers in Pisa, Italy, July

1945, with a specific individual identified. Technician Fourth Grade Norvel L. Smith is distinguished as having received a commendation for "outstanding performance of duty," as well as being the current vice chancellor of student services at the University of California, Berkeley. Again, there is a recognition of both military service and professional success. Recognizing the dual successes was probably about more than just praising the patriotism and progress of the race—it would seem that it would also be important to recognize that in none of his manifestations could Jim Crow beat these men, who both physically and, at least to some degree, psychically survived racism and war.

A final article is from the most mainstream of all the identifiable newspapers, the *Washington Post*. The February 5, 1969, article "First Negro Joins Va. School Board" highlights Hilary H. Jones Jr.'s appointment by Governor Mills E. Godwin to the Virginia State Board of Education. Jones is identified as a (Negro) lawyer and local school board member in Norfolk. The article also gives his age as forty-five, reveals he was the first Negro member of the Norfolk School Board, and identifies him as a former member of the mayor's biracial advisory committee and youth commission. The article does not address Jones as a military veteran, but a different document in my grandfather's file does. Records from the headquarters of the 92nd Infantry Division in Fort Huachuca, Arizona—the location where "assigned enlisted personnel" of the 92nd convened to complete training together—list Hilary H. Jones as a Tec 3 along with Hiram Tanner. Collectively, these images and articles encourage both the men featured and circulating them, as well as those receiving them, to recognize and claim a manhood that the military was invested in denying them.

In addition to the historical narratives, letters, and various journalistic records, my grandfather's archive also includes two personal narratives. The human element that Brigadier General Davis determines General Almond overlooked in training the 92nd Division emerges, perhaps most acutely, in these stories. One is by Hargrove and is published in *Michigan History*. "Il Corsaro: A Story of War and Friendship" is Hargrove's heartwarming story about his endearing friendship with an Italian partisan commander who went by the name Il Corsaro. Hargrove explains that once the war ended, he met Il Corsaro's family and "made vows never to forget our love and respect for one another." The two exchanged letters for a while, but eventually lost contact. When Hargrove began working on the history of the 92nd in earnest, his wife found a picture of Il Corsaro while sorting Hargrove's memorabilia.[29] Unlike many veterans, especially combat veterans, Hargrove talked to his wife about his time in the military and his friendship with Il Corsaro. Some time later, in the fall of 1976, his wife told him they would be going to Italy in June 1977 to find Il Corsaro. They did, indeed, find Il Corsaro's sister, and then Il Corsaro himself, after an adventurous escapade through different regions of Italy. During the emotional reunion, Hargrove recounts, "Il Corsaro and I sat close to each other and often as we talked, he would embrace me and we would clasp hands." And Il Corsaro showed Hargrove recently written Italian books "recount[ing] the true stories of those men who fought so bravely for Italy."[30]

I see in this story more than a sentimental account of friendship lost and found. The story lends humanness to one of the most inhumane human actions—war. Hargrove's narrative takes a moment of crisis—both war as a state of crisis and the segregation Hargrove begins the narrative describing as a secondary battle for black men—and makes it intimate. The human touch—embraces, clasped hands, hugs, and kisses—are not typical elements of stories men tell, at least not men in the United States. Hargrove, however, unabashedly includes such details, and though he makes no such assertions, his narrative redefines American manhood. When Hargrove recounts what friendship means, toughness, authority, and power construct—what Gail Bederman describes as "gender system" or "the process of manhood"—look significantly different. For Hargrove, in particular, to publish a story about emotion, vulnerability, and love at a time when black men were supposed to be "strong" is important work toward deconstructing static constructions of black masculinity.

The process of manhood also takes a different turn in the final document I will discuss. It is two pages photocopied from the book *Journey to Washington*. No other details are provided. Someone has printed across the top of the first page, "Who is this man?" *Journey to Washington* was an autobiography written by Senator Daniel K. Inouye (Hawaii) and published in 1967. Senator Inouye served as a lieutenant in World War II in the renowned 442nd Regimental Combat Team. He was one of four thousand Nisei, who, when allowed, voluntarily enlisted in an effort to prove their loyalty to a nation that had shown no loyalty to them. The two pages describe the first of eight operations he would endure on his arm (amputation) and side. At one point during his hospitalization, prior to blood being rigged for transfusion, he was shown a bottle of blood with the name Thomas Jefferson Smith, 92nd Division, inscribed on it. He initially thought it an odd thing to be shown this information, but he had seventeen transfusions that week, and half of them were whole blood transfusions, which seemed to help him shape a perspective:

A lot of that blood was collected from the 92nd Division itself, and it was shown to the recipient, without comment, as silent evidence that fighting men did more than fight, that they cared enough about each other and the men assigned to their sector to donate their blood against that time when somebody, maybe the guy in the next foxhole, would need it to sustain life. And as I thought about the all-Negro 92nd Division and looked at those names—Washington, Woodrow, Wilson, Peterson—it dawned on me that I was being pumped full of Negro blood. I am very, very grateful for it, and wish I could personally thank every man who donated it for me.[31]

Senator Inouye's revelation and subsequent celebration of those who sustained his life offers a much-needed disruption of black-white binaries in discussions of race and inequalities, especially given the similarly despicable treatment of Asian American enlisted men during WWII. Most likely, Inouye was shown the blood in the event that he was opposed to using Negro blood in his transfusion. He, however, flips that racism and celebrates the origins of the blood that saved his life. And, as in Hargrove's narrative, Inouye, too, determines that war—a state of crisis—is no place for a crisis of masculinity, when he freely expresses his gratitude.

From Rage to Grace

Two hours later I was in the army.
CHESTER HIMES, *IF HE HOLLERS LET HIM GO*

Considering the complexity of the dialectic of pride and shame resonating from my grandfather's archive, I cannot help but wonder how men like my grandfather contained the rage that surely was boiling over inside many of them. I recall my mother frequently referring to my grandfather as mean when I was a child. A conversation with my aunt as I was writing this chapter revealed just how mean he was when she was a child. I never personally experienced his meanness; in fact, there were moments when he let a little love toward me show: a prideful photo taken at my first (and last) ballet recital (I was pretty bad); a gift of money to go to the state fair when I left him a note saying my parents had said they could not afford it, and asking if he would subsidize it; a Cabbage Patch doll (purchased at the Wright-Patterson PX) that I had not requested but was all the rage at the time; and multiple, unsolicited automobile repairs when I was in college. Those acts were tempered by the sense that he was naturally grouchy and disagreeable, and prone to explode at any moment. That is how I felt about him despite being unable to ever recall him actually "exploding." I believe it is fair, however, to say that expressing love for his immediate family and being loved by them was quite difficult for my grandfather. Share-cropping in the Jim Crow South undoubtedly contributed to these challenges with regard to love. I would venture to say that the military probably had even more to do with the challenges he faced. Leaving Jim Crow to serve his nation, in theory, ought to have opened the door for my grandfather to pursue the American dream unfettered by race. The fact that neither patriotism nor formal education gave him the same access to the American dream as his fellow white citizens seems to have compelled him to spend decades trying to temper his rage.

Bob Jones, the protagonist in Chester Himes's World War II–era novel, *If He Hollers Let Him Go* (1945), offers a cultural example of the challenges I imagine my grandfather faced. Bob succumbs to what Ellis Cose describes as "black rage" when he is the leaderman in the sheet-metal department at the Atlas shipyard during World War II. Involved in a conflict and falsely accused of rape by a white migrant employee from Texas, Madge Perkins, Bob is presented with a proposition by the judge: "Suppose I give you a break, boy. If I let you join the armed forces—any branch you want—will you give me your word you'll stay away from white women and keep out of trouble?"[32] Bob thinks to himself, "I wanted to just break out and laugh like the Marine in my dream, laugh and keep on laughing. 'Cause all I ever wanted was just a little thing—just to be a man."[33] The judge in the novel, like Moynihan in his report, proposes military service as a disciplining device for un-controllable black male bodies when all Bob wants, like the Memphis sanitation workers would want a couple of decades after the novel, is to be recognized as a man by his nation. It was that seemingly small act of grace—the extension of manhood—that would have made all the difference for Bob.

In conclusion, then, I want to think about how rage shapes the possibilities and limitations of imagining grace. The book Hargrove wrote and the small archive of circulating records my grandfather pos-sessed reflect determination and confraternity, along with simultane-ous shame and pride. It is the latter that can produce rage. The 92nd has been my focus thus far, but they were not the only all-black unit considered incompetent and unreliable. The 24th Infantry Regiment was so defamed during and after the Korean War that an investigation and official army report was released in April 1996 that vindicated the regiment and resulted in President Clinton awarding seven Medals of Honor to black soldiers who fought in World War II (six were posthumous).[34] By the Korean War, the 24th already had an established reputation as troubled. In what has been touted as the largest murder trial in US history, sixty-three soldiers in the 24th who were assigned to Camp Logan, just outside of Houston, were "charged with disobeying a lawful order (to remain in the camp), assault, mutiny, and murder arising out of the Houston riots" in 1917.[35] The Houston riots and subsequent court-martial occurred because of racial tensions and white police brutality inflicted upon two black soldiers. Fed up with the injustice, nearly one hundred enlisted men took up arms and stormed into Houston on the night of August 23, 1917. The riots lasted for nearly two hours, and at their culmination, fifteen white citizens were dead, four of whom were police officers, and four black soldiers were dead. Of the sixty-three men tried, five were acquitted, thirteen were sentenced to death, forty-one were sentenced to life imprisonment, and four received lesser terms of imprisonment.[36]

The Houston riots is a rare instance in history in which black men collectively reacted in rage. It is also an instance that does not seem to be resurrected during Black History Month, a time when black heroes who were far more passive are remembered. I wonder if a little rage, not necessarily a heaping bowl of it, but just a little rage, might be in order. I am not proposing regular recurrences of the Houston riots. But I think members of the 92nd shared records for a greater purpose than setting the record straight and advancing confraternity—they were not free to express public rage. The silencing of the rage of these men, like Bob's rage when he is offered enlisting in the military and staying away from white women as an alternative to imprisonment, is further troubled by an interview Henry Louis Gates Jr. conducted with film director Quentin Tarantino on *Django Unchained*. Gates begins by asking Tarantino, "What's next on the list of oppressors to off?" Not surprisingly, Tarantino offers a bizarre response, explaining how he sees *Django* being part of a trilogy that includes another film he directed and wrote, *Inglourious Basterds*. *Inglourious Basterds*, according to Tarantino, was originally suppose to be

a huge story that included the [smaller] story that you saw in the film, but also followed a bunch of black troops, and they had been f—ked over by the American military and kind of go apes—t. . . . They basically . . . go on an Apache warpath and kill a bunch of white soldiers and white officers on a military base and are just making a warpath to Switzerland.[37]

Gates's only response is to affirm the possibility of a trilogy—"That might very well be the third of the trilogy"—and to ask some mundane questions regarding setting.

There is always controversy surrounding Tarantino's films; here I will only address two problems that are specific to this particular revenge fantasy. The first is that it is problematic that enraged, violent retribution can so freely and openly be imagined by a white man. What does it mean when a white man imagines retribution for black men? Later in the interview, Tarantino recounts a discussion he had with one of the producers of the film, Reggie Hudlin, a black man. About eight years ago, the two had a conversation regarding a film about slavery. Tarantino had not seen the film; Hudlin had seen it and insisted that it was not the empowering film it hoped to be. Hudlin finally declared, "Look, this is a movie obviously made with the best intentions, yet at the end of the day for black folks watching it, it's not half as empowering as *The Legend of Nigger Charley*" (1972). When *Django* opened, Hudlin did an interview on the Tom Joyner Morning Show and explained, "I didn't want symbolic victories; I wanted victory victories." I wonder what a "victory victory" looks like for people who are silenced and marginalized. Does it look like the production of *Buffalo Soldiers in Italy*, or a national coalition of black men circulating documents to set the record straight?

The other problem with Tarantino's revenge fantasy is that he explains how *Inglorious Basterds* was originally intended to be a miniseries, and he acknowledges, "When I decided to try to turn it into a movie, that was a section I had to take out to help tame my material."[38] Although he proposes the removed content will be expanded into a trilogy, there is something to be said for the fact that it was removed, similarly to how the stories of my grandfather and his compatriots were simply removed from the history they participated in making. It is problematic that Tarantino registers neither the implications of his cutting the black troops' story nor what it means that a white man is ultimately empowered to imagine and portray black rage. Hudlin offers *The Legend of Nigger Charley*, a high-grossing blaxploitation film, as an example of black empowerment. *Legend*, like its predecessor one year earlier, Melvin Van Peebles's *Sweet Sweetback's Baadasssss Song*, depicts black men taking their freedom (not being given it by a liberal,

foreign white man, as is the case in *Django*) and making their own justice. But only *Sweetback* was written, produced, directed, and, therefore, imagined by a black man; *Sweetback*'s success can be traced to its
endorsement by the Black Panther Party and the requirement that all
party members view it. Black rage has been contained and packaged in
peculiar ways by this nation. Emotional suppression, however, is not
healthy for the suppressor or others.

The Story Not to Pass On

If my grandfather were still living, there are, of course, many things I
would like to discuss with him. There is obviously much more to the
story about the setting the record straight campaign, but what I really
want to know is whether it was, indeed, empowering: did it help squelch
internal and eternal rage? In my mind, it is a fascinating example of extraordinary ordinary black men creating a public subjectivity. I wanted
more details about that effort, as well as about my grandfather's military career, so I loaded my family into the minivan in the summer of
2013 and drove to Atlanta to talk to my second cousins and see what
they remember and what photographs, letters, and postcards they
might have. These cousins are my grandfather's oldest sister's children,
so they were younger than my grandfather but older than my mother.
Once there, I realized no one knew much more about my grandfather's
military career than I did. My relatives produced one typewritten letter, dated April 6, 1996, that was so congenial and happy that if he
had not signed it (using his nickname, Nick, a name only his extended
family used) I could not imagine my grandfather having written it. My
grandfather extended only backhanded compliments to his immediate
family—such as when I was in high school, and he announced when I
walked into the room, "I see you finally did something with your hair."
Instead, when mentioning high school photographs he had found
of the cousins to whom he wrote, he noted their beauty and promised more details of their "pulchritude" later. When I spoke to these
cousins, whom he seemed to love and admire more than his immediate family, they only remembered how much fun they had when he
would come to visit. Fun and my grandfather definitely did not seem
appropriate together, yet they all remembered him that way. They even
recalled going to the movie theater with him. One specific memory
surfaced for each of two sisters—his undeniable anger after watching
A Time to Kill.[39] I wonder what was greater, his anger about the racial

violence or his anger about the Hollywood ending of the film? *A Time to Kill* is yet another iteration of a white man imagining retribution for a black man. I wonder, then, if maybe my grandfather's anger after viewing that film extended beyond the repeated failures of the US justice system and dug much deeper—it dug into the reality that racial trauma is not so easily repaired, and moving on is not as simple as a defense lawyer asking the jury to imagine a raped and beaten black girl was white. Perhaps for my grandfather, the jury's acquittal and the film's nonjudgmental conclusion foregrounding interracial confraternity did an injustice to the cause of eradicating racism because he knew the real-life consequences of a black man taking vengeance upon white rapists. The film's "happily-ever-after ending" is available only in the pulp fiction of Quentin Tarantino and the unrealistic legal fictions of John Grisham.[40]

How does a man like my grandfather imagine grace? He served his country, repeatedly risking his life for US freedom and democracy, yet his service was ignored, and his uniform denigrated by a US public that continued to view him as a second-class citizen. He eventually earned a masters in psychology, after retiring from the military; yet when my mother was young, the best employment he could find initially was managing a convenience store. Military service and higher education were the logical routes to living the American dream for my grandfather's white male contemporaries, and few of his white male peers could compete with his military experience and educational achievements. Knowing that reality is probably why I primarily remember my grandfather as scary and mean. Borrowing from Dr. King's famous imagery, my grandfather was tired of the nation writing him bad checks.

My grandfather did not like clutter and was apt to discard items that were not necessary for daily life, so the fact that he carefully stored his collection of military memorabilia and documents that would set the record straight means he had some level of faith that his service and the service of his brothers in arms was the ultimate act of grace—the ultimate act of grace in the sense that these men would give to a nation what the nation did not deserve. Now that I am all grown-up, there are so many things I would ask my grandfather if he were still living. There is one question, however, that I believe I already know the answer to: do you regret your military service? I believe my grandfather would answer similarly to Officer French, who noted in his oral interview that, in spite of being "treated as second class citizens," his military service invokes a sense of pride in him. In his comments at the 366th Infantry Veterans' 41st Reunion at Fort Devens, Massachusetts, for the presentation of the Distinguished Service Cross to Lieutenant John R. Fox's widow, Mrs. Arlene Fox, French asserted:

And I still believe, and still think, and I still feel with great pride at having been a member of this organization, because it was an all-black organization from a full-bird Colonel on down to the lowest private. And today as I saw the parade, as I saw the integration that exists in the Army that I've seen throughout the years, we've gone a long ways from the days of 1942, 1943, 1944, and 1945. And, again, I am proud to have been of member of the 366th Infantry.[41]

Robert A. Brown, an officer in the 366th, also says he does not regret his service, even after describing the racism perpetrated by General Almond toward black soldiers.[42] While these men did not regret their service to their nation, the experience of being a uniformed soldier and being treated worse than the white enemy by white comrades in arms surely had a different effect on them than the discrimination experienced by black men who never enlisted in the armed forces. In other words, there is a logical equation between military service, patriotism, and citizenship. I imagine it must have been a particularly hard blow when the ultimate act of patriotism—risking one's life for the nation—did not make black soldiers citizens or men in the eyes of most of their white compatriots and the nation as a whole.

There is one specific question I would not ask my grandfather if he were still alive, and that question is about his acts of private rage. To my knowledge, my grandfather never engaged in a public expression of rage of the kind that drove the 24th Infantry soldiers during the Houston riots. He did, however, release his rage in private on his wife and children frequently and with an unimaginable cruelty. As a child, and even as an adult, I remember my mother making comments about her father's meanness. The moment that stands out to me most was when he beat my grandmother and then forced her to go shopping at the military commissary with a black eye; my mother always noted how embarrassing it was for her (my mother). The reality of his domestic violence, however, did not truly sink in until I had a conversation with my aunt. After my grandmother, grandfather, and uncle all died within an eighteen-month period, my aunt and her Spanish husband moved to a small, provincial island, Isla Mujeres, off the coast of Mexico.[43] Her husband has passed on, and my aunt only comes home for important doctor visits now. I often miss seeing her on these visits, but we did manage to get together on one of her returns to Columbus. There was a lot I wanted to know, and I am grateful that she was open to telling stories that I know were hard for her to revisit. Her stories were painful—not stories to pass on, although she quickly agreed that I must include them in this narrative. My aunt only alluded to the physical, and I suspect sexual, violence inflicted upon my grandmother by my grandfather, and I did not request details about it; my grandmother endured so much emotional pain being married to my grandfather and separated from her family by an ocean that I could not bear to add more burden to the pain I continuously feel for her.

My aunt did speak of one of her own encounters with my grandfather. She had recently graduated from high school and was working at a local hospital. When she returned home one morning after spending the night at her girlfriend's house, my grandfather confronted her, asking where had she been. She identified the friend with whom she spent the night, but my mother responded, "No, she wasn't."[44] My grandfather then began to beat my aunt, ripping her blouse, punching her with his fist, and kicking her and stomping on her. My uncle jumped on his back and was quickly thrown off. As she retold the story, my aunt kept repeating how she was on the floor in the closet (presumably trying to find an escape), and he just kept kicking her. To this day, she remembers the blouse she was wearing. After the beating, she said, she left and never lived in my grandfather's home again.

I was haunted for days by that story. The phone cord getting pulled out of the wall and things thrown around when my mother did not get off the phone (talking to my father) when my grandfather told her to get off so he could go to sleep without "a bunch of noise" was not as chilling. My uncle being elated about finding a one-dollar bill on the front lawn, and my grandfather chastising him for taking something that was not his and beating him was not as chilling. But the idea that someone could use their bare fists and punch someone in the face, body, wherever the blows landed, and kick and stomp on them mercilessly is chilling. I never witnessed the violent side of my grandfather. He seemed scary to me only because of his grumpiness.

I did, however, witness his meanness during my senior year of college, when my grandmother was diagnosed with cancer. Although the cancer had spread to her lymph nodes, she decided to fight it and receive chemotherapy. A number of months into the treatments, and no longer having a servant to cook and clean for him, my grandfather berated her for trying to beat the cancer. I do not remember exactly what I said to him, but I told him very directly he had better not have anything more to say that was not supportive; it was, in fact, the last time I ever spoke to him. My aunt similarly told him she would hurt him if he was mean to her mother. Our words were of little consequence when it came to modifying his behavior. During my grandmother's last hospital visit, she (or maybe my mother) informed the social workers that my grandfather would leave my grandmother locked in her room all day with no food. Thus, my grandmother had a choice: move in with my family and receive hospice care there, or go to a hospice facility. Going home would result in neglect charges against my grandfather. The morning my grandmother passed on, my grandfather's response to my mother's call was, "Finally!"

I remain conflicted about telling about the "Mr. Hyde" side of my grandfather, as my father calls it, in a story about determination and valor. When I talked to my father about the things my aunt told me, he reiterated what he has always told me, "That's where your mother gets her meanness from." His analysis, however, was not uneven. Noting my grandfather's dislike of him when my father was a teenager and admitting he was not the best boyfriend (although my grandfather respected my father once he was honorably discharged from the US Navy), my father went on to discuss how significant my grandfather's accomplishments were for a black man of his era. His military service and rank and his educational achievements my father readily extolled as something quite remarkable. He explained it was particularly remarkable that my grandfather could fight on the battlefield in two wars and return home, finish his bachelor's degree, earn a master's degree, and then go on to be successful in the professional world. Many men, my father, explained were not functional after World War II. Forgetting history, I said, "I thought PTSD issues were experienced by Vietnam veterans, not World War II veterans." My father reminded me PTSD just had a different name—shell shock. My father probably knew of lots of men who were violent, but he knew very few men, when he was growing up, who had achieved as much as my grandfather.

The simultaneous repulsion and awe that my father expresses about his late father-in-law is a complex set of emotions. The conclusion my aunt drew was similar. She said she forgave her father, and after my grandmother died, he was simply a pitiful old man who could not take care of himself and insisted my grandmother was in the house making noise at night. For my aunt, it took decades of counseling therapy, but she finally got to the point of not forgetting the past, but rather letting the past be the past. Perhaps the stories she said my grandfather "opened up" and told her about the military helped her get to that place. She says they were unbelievably horrific. I am not sure if I want to know more. Maybe getting a glimpse of his pain helped her to proudly tell me about a history section of the US Army website that includes a picture of my grandfather.[45] Ultimately, my aunt extended my grandfather grace because she did not simply forgive him—that is, cease resenting him—but extended to him something that he had not seemed able to fully imagine for himself: unmerited favor. And that could have been the crux of my grandfather's problem. His rage was directed at his family—a family whose "white" phenotype reminded him of the white perpetrators who drove him to become enraged—because he could not direct it at the true white perpetrators.[46] And, of course, his rage was learned—probably from his own father, about whom my grandfather never spoke, and whose funeral, according to my mother, he made no effort to attend. The story of his father was one my grandfather chose not to pass on. Like many black men of his generation (and now), who subscribed to a paradigm of masculinity that was not open to them in the public sphere, he, instead, exercised that dominance in domestic space—making a traditionally feminized space a space of his power. Therefore, he created an environment of fear and silencing, which reenacted what he felt either psychically or physically outside the home to some extent.

In the end, it is the story that is in fact passed on that enabled French and my grandfather to imagine grace. French describes trying to talk to his fifteen- and seventeen-year-old sons about his war experiences in order to help them visualize what it meant to be a World War II officer. He does not comment on whether he perceived himself as failing or succeeding, but he apparently thought it important that his story be told to his sons, as well as to Martin, so it could be preserved in the Moorland-Spingarn archive. When my grandfather began teaching me family history, he decided I would be an archive; his documents, records, and I would be his grace. I believe he saw me as a small yet mighty form of repair for both his grievances against this nation and the nation's own need for atonement. As I noted above, my grandfather was proud when I enrolled in a black studies master's program. And I will never forget his argument about reparations with my brother. A granddaughter in graduate school who showed promise of remembering and preserving a family history of determination and pride just might have been his 1990s variation on forty acres and a mule.

Thus, Morrison's omniscient narrator's suggestion that the inhumane story of US slavery is not a story to pass on, and act of passing it on anyway, resonate with my story here—my grandfather did not and, perhaps, could not speak it, but I think he would be full of pride and joy knowing that his story and those of his compatriots are much more than just weather; that they are, without a doubt, a clamor for a kiss—a kiss of grace. Yet, his full story, I feel confident, would return me to his "offenders list," a list I found with his treasured documents.[47] Written on a yellow legal pad, the list recorded "infractions" his wife, children, and I, the only grandchild represented on the list, committed against him. For me, that list is not much more than weather. That is all I can let it be if I want to imagine grace for myself and for my very complicated grandfather.

FOUR

Deliver Us from Evil: Black Family Hauntings in a Neoliberal State

My parents heavily policed my television viewing as a child.[1] My brother and I were largely restricted to Public Broadcasting Station programs during our primary years. My mother, in particular, believed that "wholesome" television was the black-and-white movies she grew up watching, and during a brief period when we had cable, television series like *Donna Reed* and *Leave It to Beaver* were added to *Happy Days* and *I Love Lucy* on the local syndicated stations. These restrictions all changed when I was in fourth grade; *The Cosby Show* was introduced and served as the anchor for an evening lineup that would make Thursday nights on NBC top-rated. *The Cosby Show, Family Ties, Cheers*, and eventually *The Cosby Show* spin-off, *A Different World*, became ritual family viewing on Thursday evenings in my home. I was too young throughout the eight seasons that *The Cosby Show* aired to be aware of the novelty of seeing an affluent black family on television. Besides, I was far more intrigued with HBCU[2] life on *A Different World*—especially the snobby southern belle, Whitley Gilbert (Jasmine Guy).[3]

Looking back and thinking about other televisual representations of black people encountered during my childhood, I realize that, in spite of not growing up upper middle class, I could relate to *The Cosby Show* far better than to any other shows with black people. This might have been because the other shows embarrassed me in ways that I had no language at the time to express. George Jefferson on *The Jeffersons*, which I watched at my grandparents, and Buckwheat on *Spanky and Our Gang*, for example, made me feel embarrassed for them and for myself, since people might think that I, too, was loud and rude, like George Jefferson, or could not speak articulately, like Buckwheat. I did not talk or behave like any of those characters, and most of the black people I knew did not either. *The Cosby Show*, however, had relatable characters and plots. I liked school, my parents were present and engaged, I appreciated the arts and participated in them, and even though my parents did not finish college, they made it clear that I would. In spite of not experiencing the economic privilege intrinsic to the Cosby family, the middle-class values my parents chose to emphasize inevitably produced social and cultural advantages many African American children during the late 1970s and 1980s lacked. The 1970s and 1980s were, thus, a complicated period—a postsegregation era when racial stereotypes still proliferated, and, when at times, some acts of resistance, such as *The Jeffersons* and the "movin' on up" theme, blended resistance with stereotype to create new spaces for identity recognition. Perhaps what distinguished *The Cosby Show* most from the numerous televisual representations of black families before and contemporaneous with it was its insistence upon rejecting stereotypes and, instead, offering an image of black family life that had never been represented in the mainstream public sphere.

I offer this brief personal narrative because it provides a context for how I will respond to a decision by a US district court regarding *The Cosby Show* and its originality. I will frame this chapter by analyzing *Hwesu S. Murray v. National Broadcasting Company, Inc.* (1987)[4] as a theoretical tool for examining three films: Charles Burnett's *Killer of Sheep* (1977), Kasi Lemmons's *The Caveman's Valentine* (2001), and Benh Zeitlin's *Beasts of the Southern Wild* (2012). The judgment of the court in *Murray v. NBC* aligns the case with others that define blackness in restrictive ways, denying black people rights not only to their ideas, but also to the essence of their lives.

This chapter begins with an analysis of the *Murray* case read through the 1965 report *The Negro Family: The Case for National Action*, commissioned by the Department of Labor, prepared by Assistant Secretary of Labor Daniel Patrick Moynihan, and better known as the "Moynihan Report." Alongside the infamous report, the chapter includes analysis of the case through President Obama's recent fatherhood initiative, a program known as the President's Fatherhood and Mentoring Initiative.[5] Read together, the court's ruling in *Murray*, the Moynihan Report, and the President's Fatherhood and Mentoring Initiative demonstrate the insidious effects of the court's ruling and the federal government's questionable efforts to eliminate poverty and build economically and morally strong families. For instance, while *Murray* raises a variety of legal issues, the case is rooted in a conception of culture firmly embedded in the visual economy of race. This location of culture has been (and continues to be) a precarious space for black people as a racialized group, with black men, black women, and black children experiencing the space differently. For them all, culture has been a site where images of black people and the production of knowledge around the meaning of those images have directly affected the social and political lives of black people since European Enlightenment. Culture becomes the site in which hegemonic efforts have been made to represent black people as intellectually inferior, inherently violent, and immoral; and those representations then infiltrate the political systems that control black people's lives. Thus, rather than empirical data, I use film to demonstrate the troubling ways in which the government and society view black men's relationship to black families. A useful medium for cultural study, film creates spaces for both the reproduction of hegemonic knowledge and, so to speak, the subalterns' production of counternarratives and alternative epistemologies.

Like the black men studied in the previous chapters, the legal case *Murray v. NBC* provides a theoretical framework, in this instance for reading films that depict black male protagonists who see themselves differently. The failure of the nation to imagine black men and black families that are "functional" literally has the ability to produce a haunting effect. Sociologist Avery Gordon observes precisely what haunting means in this instance: "It is *waiting for you*. We were *expected*. And therein lies the frightening aspect of haunting: you can be grasped and hurtled into the maelstrom of the powerful and material forces that lay claim to you whether you claim them as yours or not."[6] I would venture to say safely that most black men do not want to claim subjectivities that are in crisis and always already facing imminent doom; yet, the material forces of which Gordon speaks are indeed present.

As films produced and/or set in the post–civil rights era, *Killer of Sheep, The Caveman's Valentine,* and *Beasts of the Southern Wild* provide an opportunity to think about new and emerging challenges black men encounter when they have the courage to imagine selves that are invisible—that do not occupy a space in the national imagination. Within the films, the haunting is compounded by nationalism, patriarchy, and neoliberalism. Thus, I propose that the Moynihan Report and legal activity function as mediums of trauma for black men in these films, as they produce the specters that haunt black men and trouble self-imagination even in the private, domestic spaces of home. In addition to examining how these black men struggle to imagine grace manifested in a way that can deliver them from a public sphere that makes even home unprotected and vulnerable, I also consider another element that is common in all three films and deepens the links between *Murray*, Moynihan, and the president's Fatherhood Initiative— the father-daughter relationship. Each of these films depicts a concerted effort by black fathers to protect their black daughters, though only *Beasts* invites audiences to understand that as an explicit theme of the film. It could be argued that the fathers have imbibed the rhetoric of Moynihan and want to prevent their daughters from becoming castrating matriarchs. But an alternative reading emerges when one considers that the fathers in all of these films occupy precarious spaces entrenched in a melancholia that threatens their corporeal existence. From that perspective, the father-daughter relationship serves as a manifestation of the black fathers' desire that their daughters be able to navigate nationalism, patriarchy, and neoliberalism in the event that they are no longer there to protect them.

Although there is a father-daughter relationship in all three films, and that relationship is challenged by nationalism, patriarchy, and neoliberalism, all three films do not center the father-daughter relationship. In fact, only *Beasts* directly invites an analysis of the relationship, which is why it is important to recognize the relationships in the other two films that also cast a daughter and represent the black male protagonists as fathers. Both the Moynihan Report and the President's Fatherhood Initiative speak to a grim, historical narrative of black fathering, a history of "haunting." The explicit referent in the Moynihan Report and the implicit referent of the President's Fatherhood Initiative is the absent black father—the black father who, during slavery, as literary scholar Hortense Spillers elucidates, could not claim the name of the father.[7] Gordon describes haunting as something that is *waiting* for you, something that you cannot avoid no matter how much you anticipate it or work to avoid it. Haunting, then, complicates what constitutes "functionality," or what is and what is not "functional," in black families. The self that the filmic black fathers desire to imagine is not only invisible in the national consciousness, but historically that self is truly a void, lacking the semblance of corporeal shape to be imagined.

Considering how complicit the US judicial system was in producing "dysfunction" in the black family during slavery, it is ironic that in 1987 a US district court would produce a decision that ignores its own history, while continuing to disallow black men to own their own names. To examine this incongruity, this chapter is divided into three sections. The first section lays out and analyzes *Murray v. NBC*, arguing it is a critical framework for understanding various policies that work to thwart efforts of black men to imagine selves that defy stereotypes; it also serves as a useful analytic for reading how black men negotiate nationalism, patriarchy, and neoliberalism in domestic spaces. The second section considers the relationship between neoliberalism—a prevailing force in all three films—and policy, specifically the foundation the Moynihan Report laid for post–civil rights neoliberal policies that diminish black men's subjectivities and work to thwart their efforts to imagine selves that are not socially defined. The final section analyzes the three films, considering how *Murray* and social policy can be applied as analytics for reading black men's efforts to construct subjectivities that are free from the evils of the nationalism, patriarchy, and neoliberalism that suffocate their lives.

Contradictory Logic

On September 30, 1985, Hwesu S. Murray brought a lawsuit against the National Broadcasting Company (NBC), Brandon Tartikoff, the president of NBC, the Carsey-Werner Company, a California corporation, and Marcia Carsey and Thomas Werner, the principals of Carsey-Werner. Murray claimed that the defendants based the highly successful and lucrative television series *The Cosby Show* on a proposal he submitted in confidence to NBC. Murray, who held a master of arts degree in broadcast journalism and a law degree, worked as a unit manager for NBC Sports in 1980, when he submitted proposals to NBC for five television programs. One of the programs was titled *Father's Day* and featured a black middle-class family based on Murray's own family. Murray outlined specific details in his one-page proposal, and later, upon the request of William Dannhauser, the NBC official who encouraged him to submit the initial proposals, Murray developed the initial proposal into a two-page proposal and submitted it to Josh Kane, a vice president and one of the top two entertainment programming officials at NBC. The expanded proposal was submitted to Kane on November 1, 1980, and included details such as casting Bill Cosby as the father and Diahann Carroll as the mother. Following submission of the proposal, Murray made an oral presentation to Kane and provided additional details. Twenty days after Murray had submitted the proposal to Kane, Kane notified him that NBC was not interested in pursuing the series.

In the fall of 1984, however, *The Cosby Show* began airing on NBC, starring Bill Cosby. Murray sued, claiming NBC misappropriated his ideas and citing

the similarity of such details as the number of children in the family, the fact that the eldest child is away at college and appears only periodically, and the fact that both parents are working professionals. Most importantly, plaintiff contends that *The Cosby Show*, like his proposal, is the first television series to portray an intact black family in a color-blind, nonstereotypical manner.[8]

In response to Murray's claims of appropriation of ideas, racial discrimination, false designation of origin, misappropriation and conversion, breach of implied contract, and unjust enrichment and fraud, the defendants asserted that Murray had no legally protected right to an idea that was not new: "Defendants contend that because plaintiff's proposal lacked novelty, all of the plaintiff's claims must be dismissed."[9] The sole issue before the court ended up being "whether the idea contained in plaintiff's 'Father's Day' proposal was sufficiently novel to support a claim for its unlawful use,"[10] because existing New York case law dictates that "the lack of novelty of an idea is fatal to any cause of action based on the use of that idea."[11]

Murray's first proposal describes *Father's Day* as resembling *Father Knows Best* and *The Dick Van Dyke Show*, but with a black cast. He distinguishes *Father's Day* from other sitcoms with black casts, noting:

It will be radically different from "The Jeffersons," "Good Times," "Different Strokes," and "That's My Mama." The father will not be a buffoon, a supermasculine menial, or a phantom. Children will not engage in eyerolling "sassiness," or abusive antisocial behavior. The mother will be neither a heavy-set cleaning woman, nor a struggling person without purpose or direction. In short, the characters will present various human personalities. The program will show how a black father can respond with love to something as mundane as a Father's Day card, and will present a closely-knit family and . . . how much they care for and support one another (which was the strong quality of "Roots").[12]

The expanded proposal includes a discussion about an element of social consciousness fostered by the father and accompanying the humor: "With tongue-in-cheek humor, he re-evaluates middle-class American life, with a Black perspective, and adjusts his perception of the American dream in light of new realities."[13]

The court identified two factors that precluded Murray's proposal from being novel and worthy of property rights. It claimed that Murray simply fused two existing ideas—the family situation comedy and the casting of black actors in nonstereotypical roles—in order to produce a hybrid idea—a sitcom framed around a black middle-class family.[14] The other problems the court identified were a belief that *The Cosby Show* was too similar to other television shows associated with Bill Cosby and the fact that, in a 1965 interview, Cosby noted a desire to see a black middle-class family show.[15] While legal scholars have addressed the legal standing of this decision, and more recent case law has abrogated the court's decision, my intention in examining this case is cultural.

My goal is to consider the ways in which the 1987 ruling in this case makes a cultural statement about black property rights, on the one hand, and the heterogeneity of black families, on the other. In support of his case, Murray called J. Fred MacDonald, a professor of history at Northeastern Illinois University in Chicago, as an expert witness. It is my opinion that MacDonald's testimony harmed Murray's case far more than it helped it, as the court clearly had no critical lens with which it could understand how media and visual culture have been long-standing tools for reproducing and perpetuating racism. MacDonald's book *Blacks on White TV: Afro-Americans in Television since 1948* describes television shows featuring black actors in an encyclopedic manner: *I Spy* featuring Bill Cosby, *Julia* featuring Diahann Carroll, *Room 222* featuring Lloyd Haynes and Denise Nicholas, the *Bill Cosby Show* featuring Bill Cosby, and Cosby's animated Saturday morning program, *Fat Albert and the Gang*. Unfortunately, the court used MacDonald's text and its references as proof that blacks had already been portrayed in nonstereotypical roles on television. In doing so, the court failed to address the fact that not one of the cited shows focused on a black family; while the shows included a character or two who happened to be black, there was no attention to family life, which was a theme extensively covered in white television programming.

In addition to being unable to actually cite any previous or current television programs featuring an intact black middle-class family, the court insisted that Murray's idea was nothing more than a bastard form of ideas already existing in the public domain—even though Tartikoff and Cosby himself testified to the uniqueness of the series, and NBC sought a contract with Carsey-Werner that explicitly protected its property rights. When addressing the additional causes of action, the court proclaimed: "Defendants cannot have enriched themselves at the expense of the plaintiff since plaintiff had nothing of value to confer"; "Plaintiff cannot be defrauded of property that he does not own."[16] The court claimed that Murray had nothing of value to confer; yet *The Cosby Show*, which the court accepted as Murray's idea for the purposes of the hearing, was exceptionally successful and highly lucrative. It is clear that there is a contradiction here.

Furthermore, Murray insisted that his *Father's Day* proposal was more than an idea; he said it was based on his own family.[17] If Murray was arguing that his proposal mirrored his own family, and the defendants were arguing that *The Cosby Show* ended up mirroring the kinds of middle-class-family ideas that Cosby incorporated into his stand-up comedy, then perhaps the issue was not novelty, but rather invisibility: the invisibility of respectable black families on television, since that is what Murray and Cosby mean by middle class; and the invisibility of Cosby and Murray as black fathers and husbands in the public sphere. Aside from telling Murray he could not own his own personal story, then, when the court failed to see the representational novelty of a socially functional black family adhering to the patriarchal norm of US society, it was also perpetuating an understanding of the black family as a homogenous, tangled pathology produced by absent, irresponsible black men.[18]

Fear of a Neoliberal State

The "trickle-down" theory of Reaganomics birthed a phenomenon of upward redistribution and a pro-business activism. The local and global upward redistribution of goods has, according to Lisa Duggan, "shifted toward greater concentration among fewer hands at the very top of an increasingly steep pyramid."[19] Neoliberalism is the cause of upward redistribution, what Duggan defines as "a vision of competition, inequality, market 'discipline,' public austerity, and 'law and order.'"[20] The last three decades mark a significant turn away from the policies inaugurated by President Franklin Roosevelt's New Deal—policies that created possibilities for more equal distribution of wealth and opportunities, and that ultimately ushered in the post–World War II decades of shared prosperity. In fact, beginning in the 1960s, the United States began moving away from the social democracy that had framed political culture since the 1930s, and in the 1970s, neoliberal economic policies began undoing social progress. Growing conservative attacks on the New Deal social-welfare programs manifested in a pro-business activism that developed in the United States, spread to Europe, and worked toward raising profits by redistributing money allocated to social welfare. Ultimately, Reaganomics catalyzed a period when the distribution of wealth and income would become dramatically unequal.

According to a 2011 study by Anthony B. Atkinson and others, the top decile share of total income "has surged (a rise of more than 10 percentage points) since the 1970s and reached almost 50 percent by 2007, the highest level on record."[21] The top percentile within the top decile has been the overwhelming benefactor of these changes, as the top percentile's share rose from 8.9 percent in 1976 to 23.5 percent in 2007. The share of the top 0.1 percent has grown even more, quadrupling from 2.6 percent to 12.3 percent over the same period.[22] Economics scholar Tim Koechlin insists that economic inequalities cannot simply be explained as the result of the market, because conscious policy choices undeniably determine the market.[23] Although workers are producing much more per hour, Koechlin points out that they are not earning more, and he contrasts this to the rate of increase in CEO salaries between 1973 and 2011.[24] The economic disparities have been particularly damaging for black men, whose earnings in 1975 were 74.3 percent of white men's earnings and in 2010 were 74.5 percent, showing virtually no change.[25] Disparities in the growth of wealth along with the real value of the minimum wage falling by more than one-third, the reduction of the tax burden for the wealthiest of the wealthy by Reagan and Bush, low taxes on capital gains, and the cut in the inheritance tax rate from 50 percent to 0 percent are all indicators of the significant divide in distribution of income and wealth created by US government policy in the last three decades. Reaganomics did not make us all rich or even comfortable, and while neoliberal economics is a global phenomenon, of the richest countries in the world, the United States often has the most unequal distribution of wealth and income.[26] Examining the United States' "90–10 ratio," "which compares the income of a household in the 90th income percentile to that of a household in the 10th percentile," Koechlin points out that the United States is ranked number one with a 90–10 ratio of 5.9, meaning "a family in the 90th percentile earns 5.9 times the income of a family in the 10th percentile," with Japan following the United States with a 90–10 ratio of 4.8, and Denmark and Sweden tied with the lowest ratio of 2.8.[27] This is an instance in which being number one is not admirable.

Rising to the rank of number one in wealth distribution disparities among industrialized nations was a calculated process. Duggan notes that the development of neoliberal hegemony happened in phases, and every phase has relied on identity and cultural politics, as "the politics of race, both overt and covert, have been particularly central to the entire project. But the politics of gender and sexuality have intersected with race and class politics at each stage as well."[28] Thus, the duplicity of the "trickle-down" theory within neoliberalism can be seen in other realms of 1980s television. *Dallas* and *Dynasty* (and to lesser degrees *Falcon Crest* and *Knots Landing*) were as monumental in US cultural history as *The Cosby Show*. They were award-winning 1980s primetime soap operas, with *Dallas* airing from 1978 to 1991 on CBS, and its competitor on ABC, *Dynasty*, airing from 1981 to 1989. While *The Cosby Show* became ritual viewing in my home, *Dallas* and *Dynasty* were ritual viewing for my grandmother. If you happened to be at my grandparents' house when these shows aired, you had better be quiet and not interrupt one of the few pleasures my grandmother indulged in besides bingo. Daytime soap operas were still in their heyday during the 1980s, and these primetime soap operas shared the standard conventions of deception, drama, and repetition with the daytime programs, but there was something different about the primetime shows. Both *Dallas* and *Dynasty* embodied the "trickle-down" theory of Reaganomics. The focus of both television series on corporate wealth generated through the oil industry, as well as the display of conspicuous and excessive consumption, reflected the upward redistribution of wealth at the dawning of a neoliberal economy. The story lines of the primetime shows operated in stark contrast to the undermined state of black men during this period; most black men could not realistically imagine an empowered space for themselves in the world of *Dallas* and *Dynasty*, or really, during any postindustrial period in the United States.

Before the policy changes of the 1970s, the Moynihan Report had demonstrated how intersectional identity politics of marginalized populations were bound up in neoliberal policy development. Though not immediately, Moynihan and his report were eventually vilified for what came to be understood as racist dogma, in spite of Moynihan's heavy reliance on the work of black sociologists, such as E. Franklin Frazier, to support his claims. The problem was not with what Moynihan said, but how he said it. He repeatedly noted the root of the problem was a three-century history of racial subordination and the fact that black people were given liberty but not equality at emancipation. These sentiments were not contested. In his analysis, however, the symptoms produced by inequality were framed as pathological. Thus, the racial inequalities inflicted by a racist government were attributed instead to a black matriarchy that inherited the fault of undereducated black men and boys, disparities in black men's employment opportunities versus those of black women, black children's low IQ scores in Harlem, crime and delinquency, narcotic use, and black men's failure rate on the armed forces mental test. As Moynihan notes, "A fundamental fact of Negro American family life is the often reversed roles of husband and wife,"[29] which, he concluded, when combined with the distribution of liberty without equality, resulted in "these events work[ing] against the emergence of a strong father figure. The very essence of the male animal, from the bantam rooster to the four-star general, is to strut."[30]

If, indeed, the expectation is for the "male species" to strut, then black men who desire to understand themselves as something other than both victims of crisis and patriarchal tyrants really must rely upon an imagination that, though embattled, can conjure possibilities for grace—the opportunity to experience life and shape one's identity in a manner that is aware of but divorced from Moynihan's bantam rooster. In fact, Moynihan's definition of the black family as a "tangle of pathology"[31] informed the political rhetoric that supported policies a decade later—policies that reversed social incorporation and economic progress for many black people, and had specific negative outcomes for black men. Therefore, the 1980s *Dynast(ic)* portrayals relate directly to the economics of black manhood described by Moynihan. Blackness is just as absent in *Dynasty* and *Dallas* as in the Gilded Age and the nation's postindustrial history. The whitewashing affluent imagery of the 1980s, then, plays into the ruling in *Murray v. NBC* when the court ultimately declares that black professional men like Hwesu Murray do not exist. In this way, culture both reflects and reinforces elements of policy.

Ironically, the black home space became a site for conservative and aggressive policy that was indirectly, but more often directly, targeting black men. Legal scholar Jessica Dixon Weaver insists that there is a close relationship between Moynihan's 1965 report and the President's Fatherhood Initiative, taking issue with both.[32] President Bill Clinton and Vice President Al Gore launched the first federal Fatherhood Initiative in 1995, and President George W. Bush emphasized responsible fatherhood in his 2000 campaign literature, "pledging to provide $200 million in competitive grants over five years to community and faith-based organizations for initiatives that both worked to deal with the crisis of father absence and to conduct marriage education courses." During his second term, Bush escalated efforts by more than tripling the funding allocated in his first term to promoting marriage and responsible fathering.[33] President Barack Obama has sustained this project, and even makes periodic radio announcements for www .fatherhood.gov on black radio stations.[34]

Weaver maintains, however, that both the Moynihan Report in 1965 and the President's Fatherhood Initiative catalyzed in the 1990s "re-emphasize patriarchal, classist solutions to 'America's family crisis,' and ignore how underlying racist criminal policy and systemic employment discrimination impacts minority fathers."[35] She supports her contentions by pointing to the disjuncture between social science and policy:

Similar to the 1960s, unemployment among black men is double that among white men, particularly in urban cities. One of the reasons that the reiteration of the Moynihan Report fails is because of the emphasis within the responsible fatherhood programs on marriage and the maintenance of a relationship with the mother of the children. While this tracks the best means to establish paternity and custody through the legal system, there is a loose connection between black male employment and black male commitment to marriage or serious relationships. . . . The Pew Research Center found that a biological father's level of education is closely linked with the likelihood that he will be married to the mother of his children. If this is the case, perhaps it would be better to focus on ensuring that every black male graduates from high school AND college.[36]

Political scientist Stephen Baskerville echoes Weaver when he notes, "There is evidence that the critical dimensions it [the fatherhood 'crisis'] has assumed in the last decade proceed at least in part from public policy, and that the problem should be seen less as sociological or psychological and more as political."[37] Weaver's and Baskerville's logical deductions highlight where Moynihan's well-intended work went afoul, demonstrating that his "tangle of pathology" language obscured inherent policy problems and, instead, emphasized pathology, or labeling the essential nature of what he considered a disease rather than its root causes.

Patriarchal and classist solutions to "America's family crisis" abounded during the 1990s. For instance, in keeping his campaign promise to "end welfare as we know it," President Bill Clinton signed the Personal Responsibility and Work Opportunity Reconciliation Act (PRWORA) in 1996. This legislation, like the fathering initiatives, failed to see the politics and instead embraced pathology. Liberal scholars,

127

activists, and policy analysts have made much of this act and its purported negative effects on low-income families, for whom marriage would not or has not attended to the complex nexus of social ills that produced and perpetuates their poverty. The manner in which neoliberal hegemony, as Duggan calls it, has relied on identity and cultural politics to sustain its reign is evidenced by social policies during the 1990s such as Clinton's, which shifted attention from poverty and racial and gender inequality to a morality platform. This shift, as legal scholar Kaaryn Gustafson bluntly states, "signified the rejection of commitment to material inequality and gender equality as public values, and the rejection of egalitarianism."[38]

Marriage promotion through social policy and legal reform became a hallmark of George W. Bush's presidency. The President's Fatherhood Initiative laid the groundwork for policy, legislation, and, ultimately, a movement that touted "responsible fatherhood." Yet, these new social policies and legislation that influence government spending, Gustafson insists, are part of "a new patriarchy" that works to "stabilize the now unstable notions of masculinity and empower men."[39] Wade Horn, former US Assistant Secretary for Children and Families from 2001 to 2007, articulates the logic of the new patriarchy when he links marriage promotion and welfare policies: "[Moving] welfare-dependent single mothers into the paid labor force and putting their kids in subsidized child care is not enough."[40] Horn advocates a two-parent married household (understood as heterosexual) as the ideal world for children, and declares, "An increase in the earnings of single mothers [may] decrease the probability that they will marry."[41] Marriage, then, bespeaks a normalcy that blacks, in particular, but also Latino/as and poor whites have failed to achieve. In the context of the new patriarchy, marriage is ultimately defined as a space of white middle- and upper-class normalcy that is being threatened by deviant racial groups, and though not the point of this particular argument, one must also note that the new patriarchy also expresses absolute resistance to perceptions of feminizing masculine space through same-sex marriage. The new patriarchy, then, is perhaps not so new, but is doing what patriarchy has always done: embodying the implicit goal of gender subordination, making women economically dependent upon men.[42]

The policies within which race, gender, sexuality, and class intersect might seem tangential to *Murray v. NBC*. However, in fact, they are at the heart of the exigency that compelled Murray to imagine a black middle-class family sitcom that mirrored his own black middle-class family. Almost presciently, Hwesu Murray responded to the forthcoming government policies that would work tirelessly both to patholo-gize black families and to erase black middle-class families from the public sphere, policies that ultimately sought to privatize dependency and halt black incorporation into the nation by constructing the family as a private institution.[43] Economics are, therefore, an obscured but central factor in *Murray v. NBC.* The impetus for Murray's lawsuit was theft of intellectual property, and that stolen property was extremely valuable. By declaring that Murray's proposal expressed no ideas that did not already exist in the public domain, the court assured the redistribution of wealth corporately and participated in a pro-business activism that is antagonistic to the upward mobility of racial minorities and the poor. The message the court ultimately sent to Murray, and by extension to black America, was that there was no place for him in the marketplace of capitalism. In this way, the court, like Moynihan, removed the power of self-definition from the black family—in this case, Murray's ideation of his own family—and gave that power to the domain of US neoliberal capitalism. In other words, the court advanced the specific interests of NBC and Carsey-Werner, transferring potential wealth from the public interest to the private interest of a corporate marketplace, thereby raising corporate profits.

In this regard, *Murray v. NBC* is linked to the films I will analyze; even though the films do not focus on black middle-class families, they do attend to the ways in which a neoliberal agenda and policies affect black families, and specifically how black families are defined and policed by the state. The black middle-class family Murray sought to see portrayed in popular media is becoming common in "black film," but not necessarily in films that are not marketed specifically as black films for the black community. Marriage is a common theme in many of these "black films." *Something New* (2006), *Just Wright* (2010), *Jumping the Broom* (2011), *Think like a Man* (2012), and any number of Tyler Perry films feature weddings, and inaugurating these films, *The Best Man* (1999) and its long-awaited sequel, *The Best Man Holiday* (2013). As if in response to not only the Moynihan Report but also government programs like the President's Fatherhood Initiative, black film directors are choosing to focus on the marriage plot and families. Although the proliferation of this repeating narrative along with representations of black people as entertainers might be more desirable than black male criminals and welfare queens, film scholar Ed Guerrero's "empty space of representation" remains. Murray proposes that *Father's Day* would portray black characters as "'real people in real life situations, striving for personal achievement."[44] Yet, neoliberalism suffocates opportunities for the individual to depict real black people in ways that are diverse and complex. Efforts to "fill representation's empty space," as Guerrero describes the representational absence, "with many more black dramas, family films, films with black men in loving relationships, but also with science fiction and horror films and dramatic transcriptions from black intellectual and political culture and African American history" are also often thwarted by neoliberalism.[45] And neoliberalism is deceptive because the popular marriage plot in millennial black film is a cultural response to the merging of what Duggan refers to as the new liberal centrism of the 1990s and 1980s conservatism, which resulted in "a state-supported but 'privatized' economy, an invigorated and socially responsible civil society, and a *moralized family with gendered marriage at its center.*"[46]

The focus on marriage in black films has not, by extension, focused on families, perhaps with the exception of Tyler Perry films, but his focus raises troubling concerns that fall outside the scope of this project. The marriage plot films are generally carefree and almost exclusively framed by middle- to upper-middle-class realities and sensibilities. Thus, while the films represent a representational void in black film, as did Murray's proposal for 1980s television, the social consciousness Murray intended to work into his sitcom has largely been absent from those films. A socially conscious thread has, however, had a presence in a number of independent, millennial films that focus on black families and the dynamics within those families rather than a marriage plot. The three films I will analyze have been selected because they demonstrate ways in which the law—not just in *Murray v. NBC*, but in broad social policy—and racialized social theories work concomitantly in attempts to police and exclude black families from political power and are invested only in a certain type of mainstream visibility of black families—the type controlled by and literally indebted to a capitalist market. The films also foreground father figures, and these men are far more complex characters than the wealthy, benevolent black fathers who "give away" their daughters to respectable black, and sometimes white, men in the marriage films. These black male characters are the "real people in real life situations, striving for personal achievement"[47] that Murray hoped to depict in *Father's Day* and that Guerrero, in his 1995 essay, identifies as being absent from film that tends to depict black men in a "schizophrenic way . . . at the poles of celebrity and pathology."[48] The men in these films are both real and complicated.

Troubling Nationalism

The same year that the Moynihan Report was leaked to the public, riots erupted in the Watts neighborhood of Los Angeles and lasted for six days. Ironically, it was also the same year that Bill Cosby expressed the desire to see a black middle-class family on television. Race riots broke out in cities throughout the United States during the second half of the 1960s through the 1970s. Watts and cities like Detroit and Newark were never rebuilt, and after the riots, the residents continued to suffer from lack of jobs, poor educational systems, police brutality, and inferior living conditions.

Killer of Sheep (1977) reflects the 1970s aftermath of the Watts riots and is set contemporaneously with its production. Charles Burnett produced *Killer of Sheep* as his master's thesis in UCLA's film program in 1977. As part of what is known as the "LA School of Filmmakers," Burnett is at the center of a "first wave" of film students whose work is noted for a political agenda that trumped material profit. Because of costly music copyrights, the film was only screened sporadically at film festivals and museums until its theater debut and video release thirty years later, in 2007. The film is shot in black and white and was restored from its original 16 mm print to 35 mm for its debut. The protagonist, Stan, who works in a sheep abattoir and suffers from insomnia, is presented as the soul of everyday black folk in Watts who are trying to survive. I begin with *Killer* partly because, chronologically, it is the earliest produced of the three films, but also because the politics of its production and reception are so clearly in conversation with the wedding of the patriarchal dilemmas espoused by Moynihan and the masculinist, black nationalism of the period. *Killer* is consistently read as a lament for the "black everyman" who must embrace nationalist ideologies in order to survive during the unprecedented birth of neoliberal politics.

Probably because of its limited availability to a large audience until 2007, there is limited scholarship on *Killer*. The current scholarship privileges a nationalist lens for viewing the film, lamenting Stan's inability to be a man, to be the patriarch Moynihan insisted was absent in black families. In these analyses, Stan is the embodiment of a failed civil rights movement, and he truly represents the "black everyman" of Watts and disempowered black communities throughout the nation. Paula Massood and Armond White, for example, read nothing but despair. Massood contends, "The space itself resembles a war zone, with empty lots and abandoned buildings dotting the urbanscape."[49] And

White echoes her sense of danger: "The deeper one looks, the more complex and tragic common things appear—like the playtime image of a boy's head under a train wheel; folly that mimics decapitation."[50]

The tragedy, danger, and ultimate despair that Massood and White identify in the film is understandable, but what Massood and White seem to have overlooked is the incredible and fascinating ability of children to imagine even amid racialization and poverty, whether they are conscious of such realities or not. The children have turned the empty lots, abandoned buildings, and defunct railroad into play spaces. While they are indeed surrounded by the bleak and desperate landscape of post-riots Watts, their play itself does not have to be understood as bleak and despairing; instead, it can be read as a celebration of life that stands in contrast to Stan's social death—a form of death that produces a profound inability to feel. It is important to view the children's play and leisure in contrast to the bleak adulthood represented through the adult characters, particularly Stan, for children are not born despairing.

The perceived despair reflected in the children's play correlates with an understanding that Stan's insomnia and general malaise are symptoms of his emasculation at the hands of a castrating wife and economic oppression. The nationalist lens with which critics have read Stan, then, is also a lens informed by neoliberalism. Stan is precluded from participating in a capitalist economy, making him the representation of one of many victims of not just the riots, but also pro-business activism and the upward redistribution of goods. The problem with reading Stan this way is that it overlooks his dogged efforts to escape nationalist and patriarchal dicta by trying to reclaim the feeling that nationalism and patriarchy stripped from him. The most compelling example in the film is, perhaps, the scene where Stan is sitting across from his friend, Bracy, at his kitchen table, playing dominos and drinking tea before he goes to work. There is silence as each man blows on his tea to cool it. Finally, Stan asks, "What does it remind you of when you hold it next to your cheek?" Bracy looks at Stan doubtfully, but takes the cup and puts it next to his cheek, then places it on the table, and replies, "Not a damn thing but hot air." Stan is not discouraged by Bracy's response. Instead, Stan smiles and proposes the cup's warmth feels like making love. Bracy begins to laugh, and he exclaims, "Myself, I don't go for women who got malaria," and he laughs even harder. Bracy ridicules Stan through his laughter and quickly rejects any ability to relate to the intimate memory that has slipped past Stan's almost permanent malaise. His reaction is crafted to imply that Stan is not being a man. For just a moment, however, Stan has forgotten the emotionless and violent construction of manhood presented to him as a young boy when he failed to assist his brother in a fight that his brother started—his failed manhood was reinforced when his father lectured and threatened him and his mother emphasized both parents' disappointment by slapping Stan across the face; this is the opening scene of the film.

This kitchen scene is compelling because it challenges both gender and sexual constructs that foreclose spaces for black men to be emotive, and it speaks to why it is important to view the children's play against the bleakness of adulthood. As adults, both Stan and Bracy have experienced the socialization and exposure to impossibility within the normalized frame that the children are oblivious to. The fact that this scene takes place in the kitchen and is a discussion between two men drinking tea is significant. Kitchens are feminized spaces where "women's work" takes place. Aside from the sheep abattoir, however, a significant amount of Stan's time is spent in the kitchen doing handiwork, eating, having conversations, and spending time with his daughter, Angie. If interpreted through the nationalist lens that critics have used to analyze this film, Stan's relationship to the kitchen and his actions in that space (drinking tea, something gendered as feminine) are indicative of how racial despair has pathologized him, made him forget how to be a "real" man. Such a lens would also question Stan's sexuality. An intersectional and postnationalist reading, though, offers an alternative interpretation. Stan, his feelings, and the space of the kitchen all work together to debunk the nationalist and heteropatriarchal order outside of which Stan is being situated. I use the term *heteropatriarchal*, and not simply *patriarchal*, because race, gender, and sexuality are all deconstructed and bound together in this scene. Bracy's response—a stand-in for the nationalist critique—makes it clear that heterosexual black men do not sit around in the kitchen drinking tea and drawing parallels between making love and the warm touch of a teacup against their cheek, even if the lovemaking is with a woman. Heterosexuality and patriarchy are inherently linked—a patriarch must be heterosexual; he must be able to rule the nation while controlling the reproduction of the nation, too. This is an ideology Stan seemingly failed to register as a child, and, as an adult, resists embracing.

The peculiar irony here is that while they are in the kitchen, the kitchen is indeed a space that men occupy. Although women might traditionally order and manage kitchens, men often act as spectators and voyeurs in the space. Whether waiting for or eating a meal or watching a mother or wife do a female relative's hair, men become circumscribed in that feminine space. The fact that the pleasant memory of intimacy that the teacup conjures for Stan is recalled in the kitchen, an intimate space, speaks to the way the kitchen becomes an intimate space for many African American men, who have observed and sometimes participated in the conversations and hair styling that has traditionally occurred in African American kitchens.[51] The kitchen is not only an intimate space, but also a safe space for letting emotions run free—that is, if you are a woman. The intimacy and safety of the kitchen, combined with the memories evoked by the warmth of the teacup against his cheek, create a brief moment in which Stan can feel.

Bracy's laughter and ridicule of Stan also foretell the way that Scooter and Smoke, two neighborhood thugs, feminize Stan when he is unresponsive to their murder-for-hire proposition—when he refuses to perform black masculinity as violence. Scooter and Smoke approach Stan when he is sitting on his front porch steps one afternoon. They propose that Stan join them in the murder of another neighborhood man. Stan quickly declines the offer before his wife joins him on the porch and chastises the men. This scene is well noted by scholars, but when it is noted, it serves as evidence of how the socioeconomics of post-riots Watts disallows Stan to be a true man through his material possessions. Massood notes that there are two definitions of manhood operating in this scene. Smoke and Scooter define manhood through economics and violence, whereas Stan's Wife defines manhood through intelligence.[52]

I find it troubling that Massood quotes Scooter's assertion that Stan "can be a man if [he] can," as well as a couple of other lines critiquing Stan's "questionable" manhood, but she does not quote how Stan's Wife defines manhood when she confronts these thugs. The only comment that Massood makes about Stan's Wife's confrontation with Scooter and Smoke is that when she first appears on the porch and is standing behind Stan, she makes a triangle with Scooter and Smoke that entraps Stan. Massood further states that once Stan's Wife moves from the porch and positions her body in front of Stan, she removes "him from the conversation and literally eras[es] him from the onscreen action. . . . Stan's static and submissive position symbolizes his paralysis in the face of both Scooter's rather tautological demand . . . and his wife's definition of manliness."[53] But Massood does not include Stan's Wife's definition of manliness, which is not only troubling because of the salience of that definition, but also because it is the only time that she is granted that many lines in the film. Instead, when Massood interprets Stan's Wife's one opportunity to speak, she characterizes her as a castrating bitch—the black matriarch getting in the way of Stan being a man.

It is important to reflect upon Stan's Wife's definition of manliness, because it challenges the social constructions that Scooter and Smoke are invested in and Stan and his wife resist:

Stan's Wife: Why you always wanna hurt somebody?

Scooter: Who me? That's the way nature is. I mean an animal has his teeth and a man has his fist. That's the way I was brought up goddamn me. I mean when a man's got scars on his mug from dealing with son-of-bitches everyday of his natural life. Ain't nobody goin over this nigga. Just drylongso. Now me and Smoke here we takin' our issue. *Pause.* You be a man if you can, Stan.

Stan's wife steps off of the porch and gets in Scooter's face.

Stan's Wife: Wait. You wait just one minute. You talkin' about be a man. Stand-up. Don't you know there's more to it than just your fists. With scars on your mug you talkin' about an animal. You think you still in the bush some damn where? You here? You use your brain. That's what you use. Both of you nothing-ass niggas got a lot of nerve comin' over here doin' some shit. . . .

What is also overlooked here is that before Stan's Wife arrived as his *partner*, who is invested in their household and its well-being, Stan had already swiftly dismissed the proposition and expressed irritation with being presented with it. Nothing in Stan's verbal response or gestures suggests he would be moved from his decision. Stan's being a man is not a "struggle with self-definition" that "is linked to a larger community dilemma of self-definition."[54] He knows who he is. He is not a criminal. In his mind, he also is not "poor," as he makes clear when he declares in a different scene: "Man, I ain't po'. I give away things to the Salvation Army. You can't give away nothin' to the Salvation Army if you po'." Stan has defined himself quite well in the film, but he has not defined himself squarely within a black nationalist patriarchy, and he is consciously unwilling to perform some of the prescribed acts of manhood as the larger community defines them. Stan, therefore, is not as tragic as the space around him; he is actually resisting those spaces and the values that define them, which has a lot more to do with his sleeplessness than with being trapped and feeling claustrophobic as Massood suggests.[55] This is yet another instance when a nationalist reading denies Stan the ability to make a concerted effort to define himself and control his circumstances.

The children and their play, then, represent an innocence that exists only in a brief utopian space of childhood, when race, gender, sexuality, and class have no meaning. The children are content to play and create play objects out of the natural environment and relics of a past industrial economy because they do not yet know what they do not have access to. The inability to possess this innocence and occupy that utopian space creates a far greater malaise for Stan than not owning "a decent pair of pants," as the neighborhood thugs taunt. Perhaps this is why so much of Stan's time is spent in the kitchen—a warm and reassuring space—with his daughter. Whether she is watching her father repair the kitchen sink or floor, riding with him on errands, or being a dog-mask-wearing observer of her father's conversations with friends, Angie provides hopefulness that life is manageable. It is ironic, then, that Stan finds *grace* in a space—the kitchen—that a patriarchal society says is not manly, and he is content in a social system that values communalism. The normalcy of neoliberal politics informs how scholars and viewers read Stan's character, readings that disallow the grace he has identified as simply being able to spend time in *his* kitchen with *his* daughter.

Murray had a clear focus on black middle-class representation in his proposed television sitcom, but as I have noted, the films I am analyzing intersect with the political conundrums Murray encountered, because the films feature black men, who regardless of class status are subjected to government policies that work tirelessly to pathologize black families. Having imbibed the neoliberal rhetoric of the state, critics and scholars have removed the power of self-definition from Stan, and in this case, by extension, the black family. Those critics and scholars who give the power to define Stan to the state ignore Stan's ideation of himself as a father and husband who provides for his family and possesses well-defined moral codes. Thus, as viewers and scholars consider "how . . . we watch *Killer of Sheep* in the context of today's cinema,"[56] I would propose that the primary thing we need to do is to imagine a grace for Stan, a self that is not scripted by nationalist, patriarchal, neoliberal politics. We should recognize the possibility that, in spite of his insomnia and working-class lifestyle, he can indeed be a "real" man. This is not to say that the very clearly depicted social inequalities rampant in Watts are not a problem. Rather, it is to say that if Stan can only be a man through either performances of hypermasculinity—murder for hire—or capitalist consumption, then black manhood is being defined in a manner equally as troubling as the social inequalities inherent in post-riots Watts.

When There Is More to Fear than Fear Itself

The Caveman's Valentine, based on George Dawes Green's novel of the same title, was not a box-office hit. Because the film was not widely seen, a brief plot summary is in order. The film's protagonist, Romulus Ledbetter (Samuel L. Jackson), was once a music performance student at Juilliard, and presumably dropped out of school and left his wife and daughter to live in a cave in Central Park when he manifested symptoms of paranoid schizophrenia. From this location, he delivers regular public rants that draw crowds. Rom insists that Cornelius Gould Stuyvesant is an evil corporate demigod who controls Manhattan through y-rays and z-rays. Rom feels compelled to abandon cave dwelling temporarily when he wakes one morning to discover a frozen body in a tree outside his cave. The body is Scotty Gates, a grifter and model for David Leppenraub, a world-renowned photographer, whose sadistic themes make his work both popular and controversial. A young homeless man informs Rom that Scotty was one of Rom's fans and that Leppenraub tortured and killed Scotty. Rom feels obliged to investigate the story and find evidence that will prove Leppenraub guilty. After doing research on Leppenraub at the library, Rom realizes that an old friend from Julliard, Arnold, is a close friend of Leppenraub. Rom convinces a wealthy bankruptcy attorney with whom he has had exchanges on the street to give him a suit so that he can pursue an invitation Arnold has secured to attend a party at Leppenraub's farmhouse. After a couple of close calls with masked henchmen, Rom discovers that Leppenraub is actually innocent and that Leppenraub's video cameraman killed Scotty out of jealousy. Throughout Rom's investigation, his wife, Sheila, from whom he is estranged, appears and warns him of trouble and encourages him to keep it together. She also pushes him to acknowledge that he is playing detective to impress their daughter, who is a police officer and involved in the investigation of Scotty's death.

As in *Killer*, there is a theme of fatherhood in this film—Rom needs to return to being a responsible husband and father—but reviewers consistently describe the film as being about a homeless paranoid schizophrenic, featuring the theme of "madness" framed within a neonoir detective story. Just as I propose reading nationalism differently in *Killer*, I propose that reading madness differently in *Caveman* will elucidate a black masculinity that is not bound by a mental illness, but freed from the mechanisms of the state that work to control him politically, economically, and socially. Reading madness differently also redirects attention to the impetus for Rom's detective work. He has a moral conscience that wants to see justice served, but he also wants his daughter to be proud of a father who left both her and a racist, consumer-driven society. In short, I propose reading Rom's madness as a symptom of neoliberalism.

The film opens with a small crowd of people watching the spectacle of Rom's daily rumination. Acutely aware of their spectatorship, he bellows, "Do you think you're going to crawl into my brain and see a show?" A diminutive man at the forefront of the crowd responds that he is from social services. To which Rom replies, "You're all Stuyvesant." Film reviewers seem to miss the metaphor implied through Stuyvesant and his fabulous abode and instead understand him as the characters in the film do, as a figment of Rom's schizophrenic imagination—as an imaginary figure that Rom believes lives in the penthouse of the Jazz Age Art Deco Chrysler Building. The building's spire is lit up and always seems to be visible from any location in Manhattan; it is seemingly omnipresent.

I do not think it is a coincidence that Stuyvesant controls people's minds through rays emitted from the Chrysler Building. Both Stuyvesant and Chrysler are historical figures in the development of industry and capitalism in New York and around the world. Peter Stuyvesant was a Dutch colonist who was appointed by the West India Company to govern New Amsterdam in 1647. The colony was plagued by chaos and corruption, prompting Stuyvesant to impose strict rules, some needed and others resented. Stuyvesant was religiously intolerant and sought to expel or refuse residency to Quakers, Jews, and Catholics. Ultimately, he is the white patriarch of what is now known as New York City, and the Bedford-Stuyvesant neighborhood in Brooklyn is named after him. It is fitting, then, that the original patriarch resides in the Chrysler Building. Stuyvesant is linked to imperialism, and Walter P. Chrysler, the auto-industry mogul who built the Chrysler Building, is the embodiment of capitalism. Chrysler amassed his fortune during the Progressive Era by participating in the pursuit of the American dream that was facilitated through white male homosocial relationships. The representation of Stuyvesant in *Cavemen* is, therefore, not random. Stuyvesant and the Chrysler Building serve as constant reminders to both Rom and his estranged wife of the fear of failure and inadequacy that led Rom to leave Juilliard and eventually take up residence in a cave.

It is no wonder, then, that many of Rom's rants about Stuyvesant are racialized. For example, Bob, a blond-haired, blue-eyed, wealthy bankruptcy attorney first meets Rom outside his condo building and is curious when he sees Rom writing music; Bob does not believe Rom when he says that he attended Juilliard. When he asks Rom why he is homeless if he attended Juilliard, Rom invites him to follow him down the street to a location with a good view of the Chrysler Building. Once there, Rom points toward the building and exclaims: "I'm here because that bastard wants me here. He sits in his tower and he watches. What he sees, he doesn't like . . . what he sees is a free man. Good ole Stuyvesant, you know what he says to that? He says we're gonna crush that nigger. Oh yeah, send some y-rays that nigga's way." At the mention of the word "nigger," Bob begins inching away, compelling Rom to turn and holler: "Don't back off Pin-Stripes, you fuckin' coward! Stuyvesant's gone and laced your mind with y-rays. You're living like a jackrabbit." According to Rom, Stuyvesant represents a particular epistemology that is damaging not just to black men like himself, but also to all humankind who succumb to a capitalist market that constantly drives competition and production.

There are two additional scenes where he expounds on the damage perpetrated by Stuyvesant and his mind-controlling, omnipresent y-rays. After being kicked out of Leppenraub's party for accusing him of abusing and killing Scotty, and subsequently being roughed up by two thugs as he walks aimlessly down the country road, Rom returns to Leppenraub's country house and goes to Moira's (Ann Magnuson), Leppenraub's sister's, quarters. As she tends to his scrapes, he explains his conspiracy theory to her: "Stuyvesant uses y-rays to terrify and destroy. Y-rays are crude. Y-rays are tax collectors, and police brutality, and drug wars and backed up toilets. But this new weapon . . . z-rays, z-rays are green and soft like moonlight and seductive. Much more vicious. Z-rays smell like a rich man's bank account. They smell like success." Y-rays, then, are the tools of a neoliberal state—the neoliberal state that crushes social movements and cuts social welfare in order to redistribute goods upward to benefit men and corporations like Chrysler. Social activists during the 1960s and 1970s rallied against the evils of y-rays, but by the 1980s and 1990s many of those activists had been bought or co-opted by neoconservative politics and embraced neoliberal agendas that do not champion the rights of racial minorities. Z-rays differ from y-rays in the sense that once y-rays have already beaten down and desensitized people, all that is needed is the calming effect of z-rays, as they brainwash society into compliant constituencies.

Rom specifically expresses the precarious state in which racial minorities exist when he crashes Bob and his wife Betty's party. As he enters their condo and sees a room full of wealthy, almost exclusively white women and men, he announces:

This is a "Bob and Betty" festival.
(*Laughter*)
Rom: May I propose a toast?
Bob: Sure.
Rom: To the eternal and everlasting cycle of failure and resuscitation. To the fact that the cycle seems to be stuck and the Bobs and Bettys are always on top.
(*Laughter*)
Rom: Let's drink to those on top, stay on top. (*He walks toward their balcony that has a magnificent view of the Chrysler tower, with its lit spire and radiating rays of light.*) And let's drink to those poor slobs down below, cuz they'll always be shit(sloggers?) down there, am I right? They'll believe all the lies we tell them.

After this final statement, Sheila appears as an apparition, as she does throughout the film, and cautions him, "You're losin' it, baby," prompting him to come in from the balcony. He informs his host: "Don't bother yourself, Betty. There's no need to call the cops. You're safe up here. Nothing can touch you."

Yes, Rom registers that the neoliberal state is designed to keep Bob and Betty on top, but he also points out the racial dimension of the hierarchy. The increased inequalities and racial injustices are linked to the hierarchy that Bob and Betty are positioned atop and the safety they experience there. During a strained meeting with his daughter, Lulu, in a cathedral, Rom boisterously declares: "You tell your boss he can't snake this one over on me. Tell him he can't kill me, cuz I'm reachin' for my wallet. He can't talk to me with his anal broomsticks. You tell Stuyvesant I'm gonna tear his house down"; and the volume of his voice reaches a crescendo with the final sentence. While Lulu cannot tolerate what she believes to be nonsense produced by his mental illness, Rom's reference to racialized police brutality alludes to the nineteen bullets that killed Amadou Diallo in New York City in 1999 when he was approached by plainclothes police officers who claimed he fit the description of a serial rapist. Diallo was unarmed and when showing his wallet, was shot nineteen times by the officers, who were acquitted by an Albany jury. The anal broomstick reference is to Abner Louima, a Haitian immigrant, who was brutally assaulted on his way to jail and sexually assaulted with the handle of a toilet plunger while in NYC police custody in 1997.

Perhaps, then, Rom's fear is not a fear of recitals, which the film suggests is his reason for quitting Juilliard; it is a fear of something far more damaging and seemingly irreversible—social structures that are penetratingly undemocratic and racist. Rather than participate in that system, Rom chooses to retreat to a world beneath. He literally creates a dialectical relationship between those who live outside the cave and cannot see what is going on because they believe what they are told about democracy and equality and himself, a man who lives in the dark of both the cave and presumably his brain, but sees the mechanisms that thwart a racial democracy. Rom becomes the philosopher who can see the true form of the shadows in the cave, and thus is freed from them.

His freedom comes at a price, however. Just as the self-definition that Stan strives to negotiate through the subtleties of sitting and working in his kitchen with his friends and daughter does not come to fruition in *Killer of Sheep*, it does not in *Caveman* either. Perhaps, at the conclusion of the film, Lulu has become reconciled to the fact that her father's choices are his own to make, and the public might see him as a helpful crazy-man, but the self that he imagines is one that is not haunted. Rom found the world of Chryslers and Stuyvesants and Bettys and Bobs to have an imprisoning effect, to literally be something he could not avoid, whether at Juilliard or in a cave in Central Park. Like Stan, then, Rom can imagine grace. He can imagine a self that is not defined by others based upon his race, gender, sexuality, or class. But just as critics and scholars have been unable to see the grace Stan imagined for himself, Rom, too, is unsuccessful in getting society to see him as more than a crazy black man living in a cave and shouting nonsense.

Aurochs, Deltas, and Southern Gothic, Oh My!

The black male protagonist in Benh Zeitlin's *Beasts of the Southern Wild* is perhaps more successful than Stan and Rom in escaping the haunting of a past that is so intricately bound to the present. Zeitlin's first feature-length film is and is not about Hurricane Katrina, the massive Category Four hurricane that crashed into New Orleans and the surrounding Gulf Coast area on August 29, 2005. There is no hurricane in the film; nonetheless, the film is both didactic and dialogic, offering a lesson on what happens when people disregard the well-being of the environment, as well as that of other human beings. It, therefore, exists in dialogue with the angry critiques of the government in the aftermath of Katrina. The film addresses "a vision of American apartheid in the new millennium," as legal scholar Lolita Buckner Inniss describes what mainstream Americans saw during and after the storm.[57] Like Watts, New Orleans was a geographical space that was of little importance to the government, outside of tourism in the case of New Orleans. Black people who, like Rom, were viewed as problems, or in the case of Katrina, as "refugees," rather than as disenfranchised citizens or victims of racial and class discrimination, populated both spaces.

Beasts of the Southern Wild presents an imaginative alternative to the spectacle of black victimhood. The film is set on Isle de Charles Doucet, a fictional island just off the coast of New Orleans. The island is inhabited by a motley crew of black, white, and creole men, women, and children who survive off the land with little modern technology. They live this way by choice. Hushpuppy (Quvenzhané Wallis, an Academy Award nominee for her inaugural performance in this film) lives in two ramshackle abodes, one her "house" and the other her father Wink's (Dwight Henry) house. They raise chickens, catch fish and crawfish, and the adults drink lots of beer. Though lacking what mainstream US society would deem basic necessities, the people who live in "The Bathtub," as the community has named itself, appear to be happy to be removed from a consumer culture manipulated and controlled by neoliberal economic agendas. In fact, residents of The Bathtub seem to be much happier and content with their lives than their counterparts on the mainland.

The film chronicles mundane daily life in The Bathtub—catching food, preparing food, going to Ms. Makeba's "school," visiting with friends, and so on—until a storm and floods strike their community. Many of the residents leave before the storm, but Wink and Hushpuppy remain with a handful of other residents who ride out the storm. Juxtaposed to the mundane are Hushpuppy's lessons about apocalypse and aurochs, ancient cattle-like horned creatures who inhabited Europe, Asia, and North Africa but became extinct during the seventeenth century.[58] Ms. Makeba teaches a bedraggled, multiracial group of children about apocalypse and survival with an environmental consciousness, as she attributes the inevitable apocalypse to global warming and compassionately instructs the children, "You got to learn how to take care of the people [by which she means all living things] smaller and sweeter than you are." There are consequences for failing to follow that seemingly simple creed. The film suggests that the aurochs became extinct during a previous apocalyptic event, the Ice Age. Thus, the aurochs serve as harbingers of the future of a world that does not respect the earth, something emphasized by the looming drilling rigs and oil refineries.

Hushpuppy learns lessons at school, but the crux of her learning happens with her father. His unidentified terminal illness offers a logical explanation for why he is invested in teaching her basic survival skills. What he is teaching her, however, is not simply fueled by an awareness of his impending death. The Bathtub is more than a community; it is a family, so Hushpuppy will not be homeless or abandoned at Wink's death. Wink is teaching Hushpuppy what Stan seems to hope to convey to Angie through his silence and what Rom hopes his rants will one day make clear to Lulu—black people and poor people are expendable. For Wink, this means that as a father, he must teach his daughter how to depend on no one other than herself.

Analyzing the father-daughter relationship in *Beasts* is not easy, because it surely is not what the government's "responsible fathering" campaign has in mind. At one point, when Wink has presumably gone to a medical clinic on the mainland and left Hushpuppy in The Bathtub, she searches for him. She appears to want to know where he is, but does not seem to be alarmed by his disappearance. Instead, she matter-of-factly mutters, "If daddy don't get back soon, it's gonna be time for me to start eating my pets." Her response, simply put, registers the cycle of life, something her father and Ms. Makeba have taught her is natural and necessary. When Wink does return, he appears to be in state of delirium, and he chastises Hushpuppy when she inquires about his absence. In response, she runs off to her house (an old trailer) and deliberately ignores the can of food she began to cook on the gas stove. When the fire starts, Hushpuppy crawls into a large cardboard box with hieroglyphic drawings on the interior. Wink eventually rescues Hushpuppy, but she does not answer when he is calling her name and trying to find her. Once he gets her to safety, she runs away, saying she is running away like her mother, who abandoned her and Wink when she was just an infant. Wink chases her, and when he catches her, he slaps her. He hollers at Hushpuppy: "I gotta worry about you all the damn time. You're killing me. You're killing me." Hushpuppy replies with equal frustration, "I hope you die and after you die, I'll go to your grave and eat birthday cake all by myself." She then punches him in the chest, and he falls down on the ground, trembling.

This is neither *Leave it to Beaver* nor *The Cosby Show*. Murray's black middle-class family in which the father affectionately dotes on his wife and children and wisely instructs them on social issues is not in this script. What is in this script, however, is a father who probably never experienced a loving family and leisurely life like the Cleavers' or Huxtables', yet he knows he loves his daughter—a daughter that he knows few people outside The Bathtub will love. One of the implicit and sometimes explicit critiques of black fathers is that their failure to be "responsible" fathers is due to innate sociological and psychological predispositions that allow them to either abandon their children or remain present without caring for their children's well-being. Many sociological studies have found that critique to be untrue, however. A study of psychosocial outcomes and family processes of 634 African American adolescents found that many nonresidential fathers were still present in their children's lives, and their nonresidence did not necessarily produce negative psychosocial outcomes.[59] A study on race and ethnicity differences in father involvement in two-parent households found that numerous variants determined residential fathers' involvement with their children, producing differing results across races depending upon the variable (e.g., economic differences, residential neighborhood, cultural differences, and family structure).[60] The root of the issue, then, goes back to policy. What are the political policies that have produced communities of people who have been disenfranchised, marginalized, and told they do not matter? It is policies implemented through the President's Fatherhood Initiative, "responsible fathering" programs, and PRWORA that ignore the social factors producing the inequalities that limit the ability of black men to parent in ways that assure the physical, emotional, and social safety of black children.

Acutely aware of how racial discrimination shapes policy, Wink warns Hushpuppy: "Someday when I'm gone you're gonna be the last man in The Bathtub. You have to learn how to feed yourself. Now, stick your hand in this water!" Wink makes this command when he is trying to teach Hushpuppy how to noodle.[61] Conservative politicians and policymakers have used similar rhetoric—"You have to learn how to feed yourself"—to support welfare reform, arguing that surely people will have greater respect for themselves through independence from the government and its social-welfare programs; yet, black men were still as underemployed in 2010 as they were in 1975. In a neoliberal hegemony, employment is critical to surviving independently of the government, and it would seem Wink is not only aware of this reality, but very consciously rejects that option. Instead, he sharply admonishes Hushpuppy that they "can't cry like a bunch of pussies!"

Wink has imagined grace. The grace he has imagined is subsistence living in a community that has rejected the capitalist, consumer-driven culture that has perpetually kept black men like Wink at the bottom.

Stan and Rom imagine grace similarly to Wink, but only Wink has completely divorced himself from the sociocultural practices and political economy that deny black men subjectivities that are not polarizing or in crisis. The counterculture, commune-style living he has chosen for his daughter and himself seemingly exists free of "isms," as there appear to be no race, gender, or class hierarchies, or separations based upon sexuality, nation, or religion. As "the last man in the bathtub," Hushpuppy, too, is afforded some grace, as Wink seems to envision "man" as a gender-neutral subjectivity. His ultimate hope seems to be that she will be free to simply be a human being who respects the earth and lives off its bounty. He surely imagines a dystopian space, but as Baby Suggs instructs in *Beloved*, the only grace black people can have is the grace they can imagine. Imagination is the first and necessary step.

It is ironic that a scholar lauded in my introduction for being critical of the limited ways of imagining black masculinity in the twenty-first century, and lamenting the failure of her own work and that of other advocates of feminist politics to influence "the more mainstream writing about black masculinity that continues to push the notion that all black men need to do to survive is to become better patriarchs," seems to have made a 180-degree turn in her critique of race, gender, and class in *Beasts*. Again, in *We Real Cool*, bell hooks criticizes both conservatives and radicals for being more invested in "talking about the plight of the black male than they are at naming strategies of resistance that would offer hope and meaningful alternatives."[62] Yet, these sentiments are the opposite of those in hooks's review of *Beasts* on Mark Anthony Neal's blog site *New Black Man*. hooks insists that *Beasts* participates in perpetuating race and gender stereotypes, stereotypes of alcoholic, violent black men and gender-neutral black girls who attract pornographic gazes. These are hefty claims—claims that fail to see the possibility that Wink has identified a "strategy of resistance" that he believes offers him and his daughter "hope and meaningful alternatives" to the neoliberal state he has abandoned.

Describing the film as a "crude pornography of violence," hooks's review is troubling because it seems invested in black victims at the same time that it lambastes the film for victimizing and violating black children. hooks claims the film's

spectacle is the continuous physical and emotional violation of the body and being of a small six year old black girl. . . . While she is portrayed as continuously resisting and refusing to be a victim, she is victimized. Subject to both romanticization as a modern primitive and eroticization, her plight is presented as comically farcical.[63]

I viewed the film in a theater only once, but, based upon the lack of laughter I observed, the primarily white middle-aged to older audience viewing the film with me did not seem to find much in the film comical.

Having cloaked Hushpuppy in victimhood, hooks, then, reverses gears and claims she has a resilient spirit and is a survivor, "a miniature version of the 'strong black female matriarch,' racist and sexist representations have depicted from slavery on into the present day."[64] Her commentary is interesting given that it comes from someone who has written about how black people should raise their children but has not raised any herself. hooks imposes a normalized ideation of childhood onto Hushpuppy, an ideation in the same vein as that of those who read the children in *Killer* as despairing. hooks and other dissenting viewers are entitled to read the film as they chose, but inherent in the dissent in hooks's case is an uncritical acceptance of the film's title—an acceptance that disallows imagining the realities and self-realized subsistence of coastal existence in that region. The notion that Hushpuppy is reared in the "wild," then, becomes ironic in my reading, because I propose that is the only space in which Hushpuppy and her father can live outside of civilization's strictures and policies and imagine themselves otherwise. It is also ironic because of the "community" and, to a certain extent, the "enlightened" but different civilizations that exist there.

The critique of Wink that hooks offers is just as narrow as her reading of Hushpuppy. Hushpuppy's father, hooks proclaims, "is the most vocal advocate of a lawless reckless independence. Wink is the representative hard badass black man. His character is a composite of all the racist/sexist hateful stereotypes that mass media projects about black masculinity."[65] She reads him as the alpha male of The Bathtub, yet I did not register anyone as the alpha male or alpha female. The very point of The Bathtub seemed to be an escape from authoritarian and imperialist rule. The disdain hooks holds toward Wink emits from the page like a dagger. Thus, where I see a man trying to see himself differently from the racist/sexist stereotypes, hooks sees a man who embodies them. Wink is no saint, and there are clear problems with him slapping his child, but I did not see a "badass black man," just as I did not see a victimized child whom the camera encourages us to view through a pornographic lens of wanton sexual desire and eroticization. I similarly did not read Wink as preferring Hushpuppy to be male, as hooks asserts. Instead, I saw a man who knew how to be one thing—a self-assured black man; as a result, he bestowed the only knowledge he had upon the only child he had, a child who just so happened to be a girl. In Wink's mind, his daughter could, indeed, be the "last man in the bathtub."

I believe hooks treads on dangerous ground in her gender critique. So much of her previous work has been grounded in the fact that gender is socially constructed. If she believes that to be true, then why must we understand Wink to be teaching Hushpuppy to mimic "the behavior of a raging patriarchal male" in the "Beast It" scene, where Wink commands Hushpuppy to demonstrate the proper way to eat a crawfish, or beast it? And, why would hooks suggest, "In the absence of the body and being of the mother to establish object constancy, to teach her 'female roles' showing her own [sic] to live as a female in the wild, Hushpuppy projects that she hears the voice of the mother guiding her."[66] Compartmentalizing gender and assigning certain behaviors to women and girls and others to men and boys is what patriarchy is all about. Such a conclusion does not strike me as feminist, not at all. Thus, I am left to wonder the same thing about hooks that she wonders about those who instructed her to see what they insisted was a remarkable film: how did she see what she saw?

Perhaps the challenge for black men, and by extension, black families, is not simply going to be the need for *them* to imagine grace, but also for society—society including black women like bell hooks—to imagine grace for black men. Wink was an imperfect father who loved his daughter. hooks pathologizes him no differently than Moynihan, in spite of her insistence that he is a dangerous, prevalent stereotype of black masculinity. Hushpuppy is a six-year-old black girl who seems perfectly content with where she lives and how she is being raised. That does not mean we cannot critique whether The Bathtub is an ideal space for rearing children, but to make the child a victim and the object of an erotic gaze suggests a very limited imagination of black resistance.

I critique hooks because she has positioned herself as a black public intellectual and cultural critic whose work in critical race and gender studies is received by many students and scholars as if it were an academic bible. Thus, I think it is important to identify the contradictory rhetoric; the *Black Looks* hooks seems to have been absent at the viewing of *Beasts*, and in her place was the hooks whose numerous books in the last decade have been self-help-oriented texts that are marketed and sold in the popular press. Ultimately, neoliberalism needs black and poor victims to rally against. If those victims see themselves as perennial victims, then it is much easier to manage them. Black men bear a particularly problematic burden in this game. *Beasts* certainly does not liberate black men from the burden—no film could—but it does shed light on how gender intersects with race and class in the neoliberal project.

Killer, Caveman, and *Beasts* seemingly have little in common with the Cosby family Hwesu Murray insists was his creation. The families in the films are not the Cosbys, first and foremost, because the films are dramatic representations of black life; *The Cosby Show* was a sitcom. What does connect the sitcom and films, however, are black (and white in the case of Zeitlin) cultural producers who say here's a story you don't know. It's not *Amos and Andy* or *Step 'n' Fetchit,* or *Gone with the Wind.* Therefore, while the filmic families do not represent Murray's black middle class, they are just as novel in the twenty-first century as his proposal was in 1980. Society has such a narrow way of imagining black life that there is still a high demand for creative, diverse representations. Furthermore, the inherent link between neoliberalism and nationalism creates precarious public and private spaces for black men. The black male protagonists in *Killer, Caveman,* and *Beasts* demonstrate how challenging that link can be when one is defining a sense of self and the law and society have said that in order to be a man, you must be a certain type of man. Moreover, you must embrace patriarchy, and you must participate in and valorize a neoliberal state; otherwise, you have nothing to offer the state or your family. These films demonstrate just how shortsighted such logic is, and propose that black families might be most free if the script for black fathers is rewritten, bestowing grace upon both their families and the men themselves.

FIVE

Twisted Criminalities: Contradictory Black Heroism

It was with reservation that I got up, dressed, and argued with my oldest two children about getting dressed for church on a Sunday morning. Up until that point, our attendance at church had been random and infrequent, although, as a rule, I never go on Christmas, New Year's Eve, Easter, or Mother's Day. I admittedly questioned and resisted much of what came out of the pulpit at the church I sometimes would attend, and at churches in general, because of what feels like a limited variety of churches in the large midwestern city in which I reside. The message on the particular Sunday I am referencing was framed around healing and wholeness, two concepts that, for a long time, I have found to be so philosophically and psychologically complex that the words never fail to make me bristle.

The pastor made (what I am certain he perceived to be clever) allusions to Bill Sandusky and Bishop Eddie Long in a sermon that made homosexuality synonymous with pedophilia. He covered all of the "unnatural," "abnormal," and "abomination" rhetoric that is expected from evangelical ministers, but he also offered his own corollary on tolerance: "First you're asked to tolerate, then you're asked to accommodate, and then, before you know it, you'll be asked to celebrate." He then proudly boasted that he would be receiving some phone calls and e-mails about his statements, and offered the disclaimer that he was not preaching hate. Although he never used the word *hate* outside of his disclaimer, regardless of whether one embraces or rejects evangelical philosophies on sexuality and biblical interpretations, his rhetoric surely fosters hate. Homosexuals, according to his sermon, are a threat to God's nation, and their "lifestyle" cannot be tolerated; they are diseased, and they need God to turn their "softness" into a manly firmness, he proselytized in his sermon.

This sermon was given in early 2012, and I have not attended that church since then. The sermon itself was probably not an unusual one across many denominations of Christianity. In fact, this pastor's rhetoric was mimicking a national rhetoric espoused by many evangelical churches, across racial demographics, throughout the United States. California's Proposition 8 is a prime example of how rhetoric in a different region of the country was being employed in black churches in order to vocalize intolerance. On November 4, 2008, by a 52 percent vote, California voters approved Proposition 8, legislation that terminated same-sex marriage. African Americans supported Proposition 8 by a higher percentage than voters as a whole.[1] In a report released by the National Gay and Lesbian Task Force, scholars Patrick J. Egan and Kenneth Sherrill provide a variety of quantitative data linking African American support for Proposition 8 to higher-than-average levels of religiosity. Although this chapter is not about the role of religion in shaping the political viewpoints of African Americans, I open with this anecdote because it offers a context for the social construct I do introduce—twisted criminalities.

The designation *criminal* in US society is quickly and frequently read as "black and male." Images of black men as criminal or threatening fill the media. As a consequence, countless social science studies insist black men are in a state of crisis or endangered. In addition to associating crime with black men, the popular media depicts black men as hypersexual, tough, and often scary. It is not surprising to me, then, that when I teach courses on black masculinities and ask students to provide me with adjectives that describe black men or black masculinity, they produce a list of adjectives that describe black men as deviant, criminal, pathological, possessing athletic prowess, and having a seemingly innate ability to entertain. Such narrow prescriptions for black men produce a dialectical tension I call "twisted criminalities."

Twisted criminalities are framed by a dialectical logic that is produced from instances in which socially and politically marginalized groups respond collectively to a social phenomenon that they perceive to be intricately connected to their relationship to the nation.

In the context of this chapter, a twisted criminality is when African Americans excuse criminal behavior perpetrated by African Americans—especially African American men—because of the contemporary economic and social realities that black communities experience as a result of a historical legacy of disenfranchisement and inequalities. Every type of criminality—murder, rape, drugs, domestic violence, and so on—can be accepted as normative and morally excusable, except for homosexuality. This ideology is contradicted when, in response to social and political exclusion, African Americans develop an essentialist notion of blackness in order to construct a sense of belonging and, in doing so, identify certain characteristics—in this case homosexuality—as criminal, as a crime against the community (the black nation). The complex irony here is that because homosexual sex was once actually a criminal act under the law, black gay men, then, are always already criminals because they are nonnormative; their sexuality itself is criminal, and, in the minds of those who criminalize gay men, their sexuality impedes the effort of the black community to be incorporated into the nation through assimilation.

The proposition and contradiction in the model I present—black thug versus black gay man—is reconciled through the "homothug." The homothug exists in a tension between the proposition and contradiction; all of his behavior—law abiding or not—is criminalized by his inherent sexual "deviance." This criminalization means that even if he is committing a crime that responds to racial oppression, it is always read as a crime against the black community. For the state, this means the homothug becomes the site where nonnormative behavior *and* crimes against racial oppression are prosecutable. By developing and employing the concept of twisted criminalities, I hope to intervene in the current discourse on black men and "crisis" by offering a nuanced analysis of one way in which black male subjectivity is not controlled and shaped solely by the dominant culture.

My argument proceeds from the premise that African Americans create their own culturally specific structures that manifest prominently through religion and various other social values, as well as through a distinctive epistemology of oppression and exclusion. In other words, time, space, and the law have comingled to produce ideas of social justice and respectability among a critical mass of African Americans—an idea of social justice that can logically accept particular criminalities as just and, simultaneously, make criminal certain identities that threaten efforts to be granted full incorporation into the nation. I intend for my analysis to demonstrate the complex and often invisible structures that inform intergroup dynamics; further, I intend to think critically about how acts of exclusion contribute to the reinforcement of the very structures that so often oppress African Americans socially and politically. In order to examine how this phenomenon works, I perform close readings of Ridley Scott's film *American Gangster* and Cornelius Eady's poetry cycle "The Running Man Poems," along with a critical analysis of Antoine Dodson's news media spectacle and a query about why Tyron Garner is never a Black History Month hero. Read together, these texts and bodies exemplify how imagining grace requires introspective analysis of what role black men, and the black nation generally, might play in perpetuating crisis.

When Thugz Cry

While the thug performs actions that are against the law in popular culture, the thug is often not viewed as a criminal in popular culture representations; instead, he is simply a black man trying to get by in a system that is designed to keep him down. Many criminal activities can, thus, become forgivable, if not worthy of admiration. Ridley Scott's *American Gangster* portrays the quintessential beloved thug. The film casts Denzel Washington as the real-life drug lord Frank Lucas, a North Carolina-born New York hustler who seized control of the heroin industry in New York City during the 1970s. The story of Frank Lucas's illustrious criminal career spurred a pseudodocumentary BET series, with the same title as the Ridley Scott film, which spotlighted notorious black gangsters in large US cities.[2] Public response to both the film and the series has in general been admiration, for the man who created a business that no one imagined a black man could run, rather than condemnation, for all of the black people who died as a result of his business enterprises.

Although *American Gangster* is based on Lucas's real life, countless fictive representations of glorified thug life exist in popular culture and predate Scott's film. Gangster rap has appropriated the lives and even the names of notorious Italian mobsters such as Al Capone, and the idolized body of writing by Iceberg Slim and Donald Goines continues to be popular among black urban populations. Until *American Gangster*, however, aside from the legendary Iceberg Slim,[3] rappers and everyday men and boys had no real-life black underworld icons that had been immortalized in the pages of history or on the silver screen, as well as on posters and the covers of cassette tapes and CDs. Frank

Lucas was black, and he was "the real deal," constructing a drug and money-laundering industry that did not just rival the Mafia, but outdid it through intellect. Frank Lucas was legend come to life.

African Americans may not have had a historical Frank Lucas to revere or condemn, but African American folk culture is full of tales of black men who are African American folk heroes. African American folk culture is, therefore, an important resource for understanding the genealogy of twisted criminalities as a phenomenon produced by cultural ideologies. In his classic text on African American folk heroes, *From Trickster to Badman: The Black Folk Hero in Slavery and Freedom*, John W. Roberts begins by defining the concept of a hero within the context of African American folk culture through a critical lens. Roberts observes that "figures (both real and mythic) and actions dubbed heroic in one context or by one group of people may be viewed as ordinary or even criminal in another context or by other groups, or even by the same ones at different times."[4] It is significant that Roberts's definition acknowledges that heroes are not static figures. Roberts demonstrates his point by examining two classic hero archetypes in African American folklore, the trickster and the badman. The trickster figure is a West African retention in the Americas. Modeled after Anansi, the Ghanaian spider trickster, trickster figures were both real and mythical during slavery. West African trickster figures were mediums of resistance during slavery. After slavery, the feats of the trickster no longer had an applicable context, and thus, the badman emerged. Roberts explains how the badman served as a model of adaptive behavior to deal with postreconstruction racial oppression; this figure was largely the product of the relationship between African Americans and the law in the thirty-year period after slavery ended. The badman was created as an outlaw folk hero whose actions were situated primarily in the black community, in contrast to the trickster figure of the slave period. The black community felt ambivalence toward badmen because, unlike the trickster of slavery, the badman's bad acts could be directed toward the black community rather than the white oppressor. There was also a clear recognition that the badman's violence could bring "the law" into the black community.[5]

One contemporary cultural space in which the badman often emerges is film. The evolution of the badman in black film almost certainly begins with Melvin Van Peebles's classic, *Sweet, Sweetback's Baadasssss Song* (1971), which is now identified as the inaugural film of the 1970s blaxploitation cinema era. *Sweetback* was a very low-budget independent film that brought in $10 million in box-office receipts, helping save a sluggish US film industry. The film is noted for breaking from the binary mode of black representation in film as either servile (Hattie McDaniel) or honorable and accommodating (Sidney Poitier) by employing the stylistic technique of black American realism in which the poverty, violence, hypersexuality, and other aspects of urban life were on display. In the film, Sweetback, a black male prostitute, intervenes in a police assault on a Black Panther in South Central Los Angeles—an action that results in Sweetback's flight toward the US-Mexico border. Sweetback and his most popular blaxploitation contemporary, Shaft, became black cultural icons because they were characters who reacted against the oppressor to protect the black community, blurring the line between the trickster and the badman.

By the 1990s, however, the line was no longer blurred, and characters like the infamous Nino Brown (Wesley Snipes) of *New Jack City* (1991)—a film directed by Melvin Van Peebles's son, Mario Van Peebles—were emerging as clearly defined badmen.[6] Brown is traitorous to his blood, his extended "family," and his community—almost as a warning and emblem of the remorseless, individualistic, capitalist monstrosity created when Reagan-era ideologies brainwash any man, but particularly a black one. Mario Van Peebles, arguably, directed a film showing what the "beloved badman" became when he lost the conscience that Sweetback, Shaft, Dolemite, and Petey Wheatstraw had and began to use his charisma and ingenuity for evil. Brown is both loved and loathed by many because he responds to victimization with agency, but it is agentic greed, remorselessness, and ruthlessness, which mirror so many aspects of normalized capitalist white masculinity that, in doing so, he illustrates precisely how damaging assumption of this space is for black males and the black community as a whole. In the end, he assumes this identity so fully that he will do little time because he smugly displaces blame onto a fall guy (his loyal "friend"); he lies, cheats, steals, has others do his violence and dirty work for him, punishes those who cross/steal from him (including family), and lives in excess. He is no hero, largely because he has no true affinity to the community or family whence he came, and he exploits them without regard for any consequence. His final monologue, then, is telling:

I'm not guilty. *You're* the one that's guilty. The lawmakers, the politicians, the Colombian drug lords . . . all you who lobby against making drugs legal, just like you did with alcohol during the prohibition. *You're* the one who's guilty. I mean, c'mon, let's kick the ballistics here: ain't no Uzis made in Harlem. Not one of us here *owns* a poppy field. This thing is bigger than Nino Brown. This is big business. This is the American Way.

Brown's indictment of a purported racial democracy explains why and how Nino Browns are born and why the government is disingenuous when it orders reports on the social status of black families while simultaneously reinforcing a system designed to marginalize and exploit those same families. It becomes difficult, then, to register Brown as the villain.

This abridged folk hero and film genealogy is intended to provide historical background and insight with regard to why the representation of Frank Lucas's life and crimes in *American Gangster* was not widely condemned. Precedents had already been established that allowed badmen to be heroes.[7] In addition to these precedents, there are specific elements of *American Gangster* that diminish the severity of the violence and crime perpetrated by Lucas. The casting, soundtrack, and selective biographical focus help viewers to understand this film as strictly entertainment, and thus allow them to ignore the social implications of Lucas's activities for the "black community."[8]

Denzel Washington definitely creates a character when he plays the role of Frank Lucas. In real life, Lucas fled rural North Carolina when he was a teenager because he had assaulted his boss, stolen $400 from him, and burned his property down. In interviews with Lucas, his region of birth and limited education are easily detectable; his North Carolina accent is garbled by poor enunciation and grammar, making him sound as if he has marbles in his mouth. In fact, a 2007 interview in *New York* magazine with Frank Lucas and Nicky Barnes, one of Lucas's real-life rivals in the drug world, reveals that Barnes was known to mock Lucas's "'country boy' lack of education."[9] Washington, however, depicts Lucas as suave and sophisticated—a performance that underscores and makes believable Lucas's ability to mastermind an international drug trade. Furthermore, as an Academy Award winner who holds a permanent spot on Hollywood's "acceptable blacks" list, Washington is beloved by Americans across racial lines. Although he broke many hearts in the role of Detective Alonzo Harris in *Training Day*, and although there was nothing redemptive about Lucas's criminal activity, it was difficult for viewers and critics to truly feel the contempt that the character played by Washington deserved. Even given the uncertain and tumultuous state of the United States after the terrorist attacks of September 2001, film critic Roger Ebert was clearly dazzled by the character Washington created and his performance. As for Harris's violence, Ebert offered an example of when he prevented a rape and instead of arresting the men, "thoroughly and competently beats them." Ebert's admiration of Washington's performance is palpable in his review.[10]

The soundtrack further accentuates the allure of Washington starring as Lucas. It is a mix of classic R&B, the blues, neo soul and rap, featuring Bobby Womack, John Lee Hooker, Sam & Dave, the Staple Singers, Lowell Fulson, Anthony Hamilton, Public Enemy, and Hank Shocklee. The music evokes a nostalgia that minimizes Lucas's moral depravity. A recent study by a team of psychologists found "the source of music-evoked nostalgic experience to be idiosyncratic associations that people have formed between particular songs and events in their past."[11] I would hope this study explains why every viewer did not feel contempt for Lucas during the scene in which a baby is crying on the bed next to his dead mother who overdosed on heroin—a scene that has no musical soundtrack but that functions as an ironic flashback to an earlier montage of Lucas's drug world in which a different mother was purchasing Lucas's Blue Magic "trademarked" heroin while Sam & Dave's "Hold On, I'm Coming" played. Indeed it may, for as film scholar David Shumway notes, film soundtracks did not exist until the late 1960s, and while they initially served the purpose of providing emotional cues for audiences, they have since become a marketing tool. When tracing this trend in *The Graduate* and *Easy Rider,* Shumway explains that the intent of soundtracks is consumer oriented, intending to establish "a bond between the consumer and product while also arousing a feeling of generational belonging in the audience."[12] The song genres on the *American Gangster* soundtrack, then, evoke memories of a past that make both those who experienced it and those who did not feel a connection through the sounds of soul, which is often understood as the essence of blackness and the black experience.

Shortly after the premier of *American Gangster,* the film, hip-hop mogul Jay-Z released his own soundtrack titled *American Gangster.* The soundtrack is not the official movie soundtrack, but the tracks directly engage the film, and the music videos incorporate clips from the film. Jay-Z's soundtrack is not nostalgic; it is very contemporary, but it undoubtedly produces an emotional response from viewers who listen to his music. In an interview with Charlie Rose, Jay-Z explains his fascination with the film.[13] As a Brooklyn native, who grew up in the Marcy Projects, Jay-Z says he can connect to the film, not just through familiarity with the setting, but also through the stories and lore his father and uncles shared of the period in which the film is set. He notes that the film is complex. The life of Frank Lucas outside of his business dealings is "normal"—he has a family, he buys his mother a house, and he entertains family and friends (and business associates, as family and friends often fit dual categories). The normalcy of Lucas's life is contrasted to the corrupt cops and to the dysfunctional personal life of the lone good cop, Richie Roberts (who later becomes Lucas's lawyer in real life). The complexities Jay-Z describes, combined with the nostalgia and racial confraternity that the official soundtrack produces, make it much easier to focus on Frank Lucas as the family man and philanthropist who gives away a truck full of turkeys, than the cold-blooded killer who shoots a man in the head on the street or sells heroin to mothers who overdose and leave their children unprotected; the soundtrack does not play music that captures the tragedy of the scene.

Where No Black Man Has Gone Before

When Lucas meets with his new recruits—primarily his relatives from North Carolina— over breakfast in a Harlem diner, he tells them integrity, hard work, and family frame his business, emphasizing that never forgetting where they came from is critical. He schools his underlings in entrepreneurism: "The man I worked for had one of the biggest companies in New York City, but he didn't own his own company. White man owned it, so he owned him. Nobody owns me though." Owning one's self, and the challenges inherent in that feat for African Americans, stretch back to slavery, when blackness was equated with slavery and property, but it extends to the present. What historian and cultural studies scholar George Lipsitz refers to as a "possessive investment in whiteness" has shaped the ways in which black subjectivity and social advancement occurred postemancipation. Lipsitz insists that whiteness has a cash value in the United States; whiteness is "a social fact, an identity created and continued with all-too-real consequences for the distribution of wealth, prestige, and opportunity."[14] Lipsitz identifies discrimination in the housing market that restricted post–World War II Federal Housing Authority loans, difficulty accessing use of the GI Bill, and living in environments that were home to a variety of health hazards as just a few of the many social and economic disadvantages that African Americans have experienced and continue to encounter. Frank Lucas, and Jay-Z protraying Lucas in his music videos and CD tracks, identify a niche in which black men can own themselves, be their own bosses, and have access to the material goods that institutionalized and structural racism has kept from them. Accomplishing such a feat, whether through legitimate means or illegitimate, is heroic in the eyes of many African Americans, particularly those who would not be inclined to register Nat Love or my grandfather as successful because the neoliberal state measures success by material excess.

Lucas declares, "You are who you are in this world, and this is one of two things: either you're somebody or you ain't nobody." Black men who are not "anybody" can look to Lucas as an exemplar. He has made himself somebody in spite of the odds. He has branded a product. Lucas claims trademark rights to Blue Magic, his nearly 100 percent–pure heroin that black people overdosed on. He proudly asserts, "Blue Magic. That's a brand name. Like Pepsi, that's a brand name. I stand behind it. I guarantee it. They know that even if they don't know me any more than they know the chairman of General Mills." Lucas delivers this lecture to Nicky Barnes after discovering Barnes has been diluting Blue Magic and reselling it, which according to Lucas is trademark infringement. Branding, then, is important for understanding the contradiction of Lucas as simultaneously badman and hero. The attempts by black people in the United States to own businesses, copyrights, and patents have been vexed. Many early twentieth-century race riots were motivated by whites' desire to usurp black businesses. Elvis Presley is perhaps the best-known white performer accused of "stealing" from black music artists whose work was not copyrighted. This history of usurpation and exploitation helps to inform the perception of Lucas as not being a *real* criminal.

Lucas creates an opportunity for black people in general, and black men in particular, to see themselves as American first and foremost—not as black Americans or African Americans, as Du Bois famously laments in "In Our Spiritual Strivings," the first chapter of *Souls of Black Folk*. Owning one's own business and crafting one's own brand through integrity and hard work is the American dream, and finally, Lucas stands as exemplar that the dream includes more than just the European immigrants who assimilated and became "white"; it also includes the very people whose uncompensated labor built this nation. Lucas registers this reality when he claims Harlem as "my home" and the United States as "my country." It is ironic that Lucas becomes The Man only a few years after the Memphis sanitation workers' strike, where black men wore protest signs with the simple yet poignant statement "I Am a Man." The significance of the black manhood Lucas embodies is apparent when Richie Roberts seeks the assistance of the FBI, and they ask who Frank Lucas is. They want to know which family of the Italian Mafia he works for. When Roberts explains that Lucas is black and works for no one, the FBI agents exclaim, "No black man has accomplished what the American mafia hasn't in a hundred years!"

When I teach this film and read blogs about the film and Frank Lucas, one constant in people's responses to why it is difficult to condemn Lucas is that he ran a business enterprise that not only outsmarted the white man, but also put Lucas at the top. This film was released in 2007, prior to the election of the first black president, so there have been very few instances, particularly in the public sphere, in which a black man was at the top of anything other than athletics and the entertainment industry. A black man at the top as a businessman, which is both how Lucas constructs himself and how many viewers read him, represents the transformation of a self once defined as property into a self that possesses agency—that is, a subject rather than an object.

Not only is Lucas a businessman, but he is also ingenious in the way in which he smuggles his product into the United States directly from Southeast Asia, eliminating the middleman and securing a pure product. That is the popular understanding of his genius, but a more symbolic understanding of his genius is the relationship between his drug-trafficking business and the Vietnam War. Protests against the Vietnam War were often intertwined with civil rights protests fueled by the disenfranchisement and discrimination directed toward racialized US citizens. The Vietnam War was the first fully integrated war; and for African Americans the opportunity to prove their patriotism and receive educational and vocational benefits resulted in their being represented disproportionately on the front lines of battle, making the Vietnam War what some have called "a white man's war but a black man's fight."[15] Thus, while there is something morbidly unpatriotic about Lucas smuggling heroin in the coffins of fallen soldiers in the film, there is also a twisted poetic justice in what he does—a senseless war that, in spite of full integration, has not truly incorporated African American soldiers is increasing the capital of an African American drug lord. Ultimately, through criminality, Lucas is able to do what men do—take care of his family, buy his mama a house, and care for his community (to some extent). Therefore, a slippery space is created wherein it is easy to register Lucas as an American man who does what American men do—patent a product, build a business, accumulate wealth, and so on. It is important to note, however, that his portrayal of hypermasculine, capitalist manhood in the film falls within the confines of a heterosexual male space.

The Running Man

The inherent contradictions in US democratic ideals are what makes it possible for black people to defy the commonsense logic that crime is bad and, instead, to understand certain crimes committed by black people, and black men in particular, as forgivable or justifiable. This twisted criminality is the way in which gay black masculinity is understood, by many, as a threat to both the black community and black progress toward full incorporation into the nation; yet, it defies the commonsense logic of both racial unity and solidarity. I will examine this contradiction through Cornelius Eady's cycle of poems titled "The Running Man Poems."

Eady's "Running Man" is the second cycle of poems in a collection titled *Brutal Imagination*, which is also the title of the first cycle of poems. "The Running Man" cycle was originally written as a score for a jazz opera. It is set in a small town somewhere on the Virginia coast between the 1930s and the 1950s. Running Man, or Tommy, as he was known as a child, is smart and gay, both of which are read as white by his family and small black community. A childhood of ridicule, condemnation, and verbal, sexual, and physical abuse culminate in the boy who could have had a promising future becoming a calculating, cold criminal who is killed as a result of his thug lifestyle. In a small southern town that still has architecture that retains the residue of slavery—shackles and various other remnants of slavery in slave quarters—and during an era still resplendent with racial uplift ideologies, one would think that both family and community would idolize Tommy. With his high grades and masterful vocabulary, Tommy hardly seemed a threat, especially compared to Frank Lucas; yet, the clever criminal is revered and the smart gay black boy is despised.

"When He Left," the first poem in the cycle, is in the voice of Miss Look, Tommy's youngest sister, who describes Tommy as a child:

He was good with words.
He had a way of looking
Into the heart of an object.
He was on a first-name basis
With a bloom or a motor.
He'd unlock books
And tame the jargon,
Take the white man's

Arithmetic
And make it spit
Silver dollars.
When he left,
The birds and trees lost
Their Latin names,
Our world shrank back
To just a world.[16]

Miss Look describes Tommy as "good with words," an attribute black boys are not often described as possessing. Being "on a first-name basis/ With a bloom or a motor" suggests a child who has a variety of interests and who is curious. It also reveals he is adept at things deemed masculine (motors), while also appreciating things deemed feminine (a bloom); it is only one segment of his "self" that is criminal. Furthermore, his vocabulary is well developed, as he cannot only read proficiently, but also turn "jargon" into something comprehensible. He has a penchant for math, and he knows the Latin names for birds and trees. Tommy is a quintessential Renaissance man, but a small black town in Virginia during the World War II era could not imagine such a black boy.

At the end of the cycle, and presumably the end of Running Man's life, he signifies on the New Negro Movement poet Countee Cullen's "Yet Do I Marvel!" when he describes the cruel joke he feels his life has been: "God made me pretty/God made me smart/God made me black/Which only proves/God's infinite sense of humor."[17] In this stanza, Running Man describes his physical and intellectual gifts as cruel jokes because of his race. Cullen, too, saw cruelty in being given talents when one is black. In "Yet Do I Marvel!" the speaker laments, "Yet do I marvel at this curious thing:/To make a poet black, and bid him sing!" In the next stanza, Running Man uses a simile to describe his misfortune: "Where I come from/A smart black boy/Is like being a cat/With a duck's bill."[18] He is unnatural. He is a freak. While Running Man has his love affair with books, the neighbors observe: "*He's so bright*/But mean/*He's so white*." They call him a "useless miracle."[19] Through books, Running Man sees and dreams a world that is different from Old Nancock, Virginia, on the Chesapeake that has only four or five buildings and a dirt road, and is haunted by the ghosts of slaves who lived in the old slave shacks. He describes the world to his baby sister as a great adventure: "I bring to her attention olives and Roman columns/I bring her Charlemagne/And Louis Armstrong."[20]

The perceived unnaturalness of Running Man's intellect and choice of activity during leisure time is compounded by his sexuality. In the poem "Sex," Running Man describes how he dreams about a boy, "but I know I'm not supposed to do this." In a retrospective voice, he acknowledges, "I am still too young to know what to make of this," and he reveals he is punished for describing his dreams out loud. He is more than punished—his father sodomizes him with a toothbrush. In his childish innocence, Running Man says: "Every time I say this out loud I must feel pain/This, they say, will make me stop." The pain is justified through religion: "My father takes me/To the bathroom, he removes my pants/He takes a toothbrush and this pain he gives/Is approved of by Jesus."[21] The repeated correlation between justifiable pain and punishment with religious approval resonates with the sermon I described at the beginning of this chapter about the dangers of tolerance. As I noted, the pastor never explicitly said gay men should be hated or even physically "punished," but the correlation he drew between gay sexuality and pedophilia encourages behavior like that of Running Man's father.

Early in his youth Running Man accepts his punishment, but he later seeks revenge. In the poem titled "Revenge," Running Man describes his evolution from Tommy to Running Man. A girl at his church shows an interest in him, causing his parents to be relieved and the parishioners to nod in agreement, but Running Man admits, "When she looked at me, I knew I would take/Her goodwill, her lust, and abuse her heart."[22] From this point, he turns into a monster, brutally beating people, murdering women, stealing from people, and being everyone's worst nightmare.

The perceived criminality of being black and gay by Running Man's community is tragic. The inability of his black community to claim him as one of their own produces a violent and loathsome black assailant who is foregrounded in the first cycle of poems, which chronicle the Susan Smith child murders in Union, South Carolina, in 1994. The "Brutal Imagination" cycle is written in the voice of the unidentified black man Susan Smith creates as a cover when she straps her two young sons into the back seat of her car and rolls it into a lake. Smith claims she was carjacked by a black man. The title of the cycle is a commentary on the type of imagination—a brutal one—that would permit not just the Union, South Carolina, Sheriff's Department and townspeople to believe Smith's vague story, but also an entire nation to easily and readily believe her story. The front matter of the collection functions as Eady's personal message for white America, a *brutal nation*, that needs to *cry* and seek penance for yet *again* criminalizing an innocent black man—a brutal nation whose mentality understands the intersection of black and male to mean prone to criminal behavior.[23] But it is not just the white nation that needs to cry and seek penance for its brutality. The black nation, too, is culpable. The black nation cannot imagine a black man being defined as anything other than heterosexual. To be a "real" black man, then, is to be straight. Far too often, gay black men are understood as always already criminals, as obstacles to black incorporation into the nation.

Antoine Dodson as Queer Synthesis

To synthesize the queer contradiction that emerges when examining the intersections of race, gender, sexuality, and nation, it would be simple, and perhaps logical, to analyze the "homothug" as an identity that synthesizes the dialectic. Omar Little from the hit HBO series *The Wire* is an exemplary embodiment of homothug—a gay black man who embraces and performs acts of violence and "badness" that permit the black public sphere to overlook his sexual orientation. Omar is a provocative synthesis because he lives by a moral code that restricts his violent acts to those involved in his criminal underworld. He walks the streets with large caliber guns and a trench coat, and his face marked by a scar. Like Lucas, Omar's cunning and intelligence compel the audience to revere him in spite of his crimes.[24] The homothug that Omar represents, however, exudes a heterosexual masculinity in both appearance and performance in spite of his being openly gay. For this reason, I want to propose a riskier synthesis.

Antoine Dodson became an Internet celebrity in November 2008 when his interview on WAFF-48, an NBC affiliate in Huntsville, Alabama, went viral. Dodson was interviewed because someone had broken into the apartment he shared with his sister, Kelly, and her daughter in the Lincoln Park projects, and attempted to rape Kelly. Dodson scared off Kelly's attacker, and during the interview, Dodson sent a warning to the Lincoln Park community, as well as to the intruder. He warned the community "to hide your kids, hide your wife, and hide your husband cuz they rapin' everybody out here," and to the intruder, he said: "You don't have to come and confess that you did it, we're lookin for you, we gonna find you. I'm lettin' you know now, so you can run and tell that, homeboy!" Dodson's interview probably would not have gone viral if it had not been for his unabashed flamboyancy.

During the interview, he was wearing a black "wifebeater" undershirt and had a red scarf tied kerchief style around blown-out but unpressed shoulder-length hair. His body gestures and voice intonations invited viewers to read him as gay. In his discussion of legible and illegible black masculinities in *The Wire*, Neal references Guy Trebay's classic *Village Voice* essay, "Homo Thugz Blow Up the Spot," in which Craig Henderson makes a distinction between "gay" and "faggot," explaining that the projects are a (safe) space for gay black men; however, he warns, "You can't walk through the projects and be a faggot."[25] While Dodson's slight build and blown-out shoulder-length hair could be read as Henderson's definition of "faggot"—soft and feminine—his "wifebeater" and blown-out hair, which is not untypical of black "thugs" who wear cornrows, trouble his legibility in spite of the body language of a snap queen.

In addition to his sartorial style, Dodson's bravado in his warning to the community disallows an easily read legibility. His warning echoes the prelude to "Bucktown" by hip-hop duo Smif-n-Wessun. The track opens with "Lock your doors, nobody's safe." The duo then rhymes about how one survives on the streets of Brooklyn (Bucktown): "I walk around Town with my pound strapped down to my side/No frontin' just in case I gotta smoke some" (Da Shinin'). The implications of Smif-n-Wessun's "Lock your doors, nobody's safe" echo Dodson's insistence that you need to literally hide your entire family "cuz they rapin' everybody out here." Dodson's hip-hop stylized warning invokes a bravado that is at odds with his flamboyance; yet, Dodson's statement simultaneously reminds us of just how vulnerable black people are—including black men—in a nation that places little value on their lives and safety. When was the last time there was a media frenzy over a missing or abducted black child? How many unarmed white men are shot by police officers and civilians? In spite of the violent and virile performances of masculinity, black men remain vulnerable as citizens of a nation that refuses to grant them full citizenship.

Dodson's warning identifies the emptiness of performances of hypermasculinity. How tough are you really when your toughness cannot protect your own community? Yet, the second warning Dodson issues has linguistic significance because of his use of "we." Rather than using the first person singular, "I," to threaten the intruder, Dodson uses the first person plural, "we." *We* are looking for you and *we* will find you—a collective effort by a community that can only count upon itself. In this regard, Dodson adds a queer synthesis that is more compelling than Omar Little, who incited such fear in the community that his violence could never serve the community usefully. The threat of violence that Dodson issues is about communal retribution, a threat that is more in-line with Sweetback's and Shaft's acts of violence than Lucas's or Nino Brown's. Thus, Dodson inserts himself into a liberating tradition that has resisted incorporating queer bodies and identities.

Although Dodson paradoxically queers the homothug by troubling legibility when he blurs the line between homothug and "faggot," his insistence upon being a legitimate protector of his family and community becomes fodder for social media and the black entertainment industry. He is neither a thug nor a homothug. Unlike Running Man, Dodson is not deemed a pariah, or a diseased black body that contaminates the black community and undoes efforts of incorporation; instead, he is turned into a commodity. Although it was Antoine's sister, Kelly, who was the victim, Antoine became famous. He recorded "Bed Intruder Song" with the Gregory Brothers, performed at the BET Awards, and has his own app, which locates sexual predators. His acceptance, however, is difficult to call acceptance because his flamboyancy functions as spectacle. People can laugh *at* him as they laugh *with* him. Neither the local news interview nor his song would have gone viral if he had been read as a heterosexual black man, protecting his sister from a rapist—there is nothing particularly spectacular about that scenario. Thus, Dodson as protector of his family becomes no more than fodder for visual pleasure.

The reduction to fodder makes it difficult to register Dodson's need for grace, and by extension, the difficulty gay black men experience in imagining grace in both the larger nation and the microcosmic black nation where their bodies are often criminalized. This reality is perhaps most evident in Dodson's recent resurfacing in the public sphere as a "reformed" homosexual and an initiate of the Hebrew Israelites, who "is no longer into homosexuality."[26] His Internet sensationalism was rekindled in May 2013 when he renounced his homosexuality on his Facebook page and Twitter account. In a Huffpost Live interview with Alicia Menendez, Dodson nonchalantly explained he is "trying to move away from that and become a better person." When Menendez challenged his previous identification as openly gay and his new proclamations of renunciation, Dodson offered another explanation for Menendez to again reject: "I like the art of a woman. I've always liked that, and I guess it got to the point so much that I tried to, like, be that instead of being with that." Dodson consistently returns to religious doctrine that opposes homosexuality as the ultimate determining factor in his renunciation, but he is quick to emphasize his disinterest in condemning or demonizing nonnormative sexuality. Although the media is clearly dubious about Dodson's heterosexuality, his purported girlfriend, and the supposed recent birth of his and his girlfriend's child, whether these details are true or fabricated, Dodson continues to be fodder for visual pleasure, and there is no sincere clamor to incorporate him into the black nation.

Nobody (Still) Knows My Name

The gay black hero continues to be an oxymoron in the twenty-first century, not only for African Americans but also for the nation as a whole. In conclusion, then, I want to consider the heuristic possibilities of *Lawrence v. Texas* (2003) for understanding the emancipatory limits of twisted criminalities. Tyron Garner was John Geddes Lawrence's co-petitioner in *Lawrence*. Garner's name is not as recognizable, because the legal case is named after Lawrence. On September 17, 1998, four deputies from the Harris County Sheriff's Office (just outside the jurisdiction of the Houston Police Department) responded to a dispatcher's alert about "a black male going crazy" in Lawrence's apartment. The recent in-depth examination of *Lawrence* by legal scholar Dale Carpenter helps to piece together a story, especially regarding events on the evening of September 17, 1998, that previously was often presented piecemeal. Through interviews with virtually every person involved with the case, Carpenter reveals that Tyron Garner, a young gay black man, and his older gay white boyfriend, Robert Eubanks, were visiting Lawrence at his apartment. Lawrence and Eubanks were friends. Eubanks and Garner would clean Lawrence's apartment once a month, and on the evening of the incident, Eubanks and Garner were visiting in order to prepare to move furniture that Lawrence was donating to them. Speculation has consistently been that Eubanks, a well-known alcoholic, had been drinking and became belligerent, resulting in Lawrence telling him to leave and allowing Garner to stay. Eubanks did not comply initially, but eventually searched for change and left the apartment. Upon his departure, he went to a nearby pay phone, called the police, and reported "a black male going crazy." Carpenter reports uncertainty about whether Eubanks said "black male" or "nigger," a term Eubanks frequently used to describe black people, including his boyfriend, Garner.[27] When the police arrived, an accurate story of events does not exist, as everyone's story differs, and the nuanced details of the course of events that evening are not the concern of my narrative. The concern of this narrative is with the fact that, as a result of being arrested and charged with sodomy, Garner joined Lawrence as a petitioner in this landmark gay civil rights case, yet no one knows his (Garner's) name.

Prior to their arrest, Garner and Lawrence were not active in the gay rights movement. Garner was from a poor, working-class background, and he was not educated beyond high school. At the time of his arrest, he was unemployed and spent his adult life as a transient, working low-wage jobs. His grammar and locution in oral interviews confirm his lack of formal education. Thus, it is not likely that Garner himself would have questioned the legal precedent for his arrest. Rather, some serendipitous events and the interest of gay civil rights groups that had been waiting for just such a case—charges against gays or lesbians[28] for same-sex intercourse in their own home[29]—resulted in Garner becoming a civil rights hero. On June 26, 2003, the US Supreme Court ruled antisodomy laws were unconstitutional, making *Lawrence* the leading gay rights decision[30] until the Supreme Court struck down the federal Defense of Marriage Act (DOMA) as unconstitutional on the tenth anniversary of *Lawrence*. Given the significance of this civil rights victory for the entire nation, why is it that Tyron Garner faded into oblivion even before his premature death in 2006? The Supreme Court indirectly marked the ten-year anniversary of *Lawrence* with a second landmark decision advancing LGBT civil rights. Various (white) LGBT organizations and media also celebrated the tenth anniversary of the ruling. I have been unable, however, to locate any commemoration of the *Lawrence* case by African American civil rights groups. This silence is compounded by the fact that, beginning in 2013, there have been numerous decennial anniversary commemorations for race-specific civil rights legal decisions and major events, but none for the history Garner made.[31]

Tyron Garner is never on the agenda when Black History Month rolls around each year. How is it that entertainers like Chris Brown and R. Kelly, individuals who have committed heinous crimes against black women, can be awarded and nominated for NAACP Image Awards, but Garner is seemingly not even known in the first place, let alone remembered? Instead, Antoine Dodson, a faux homothug, serves as synthesis to a troubling dialectic. The race-specific civil rights commemorations and Black History Month are part of a global tradition of celebrating important historical events, and they are also examples of how each subsequent generation of African Americans creates usable pasts. In that process, however, someone like Garner cannot become a usable black hero. His sexuality is certainly a prime reason. It took decades to begin giving due recognition to Bayard Rustin, and even now, most African Americans still do not know his name. The multidimensionality of Garner's identity, however, makes his erasure about far more than sexuality. Unlike Nat Love, who had complete control over his representation and how we remember him now, Garner's poverty and lack of education extended him little agency. These factors influenced his physical appearance. In photographs, Garner wears his hair in an Afro shag cut, using what looks like hair grease to create a light Jheri-curl appearance, a style that, by the early twenty-first century, was terribly dated and associated with "countriness" or being a "bama." Coupled with his "countrified" speech, his physical appearance did not invoke the race pride attributed to the images of a race leader like Malcolm X, whose photographic images exude strength, determination, and heterosexual manliness, and whose prose and enunciation were forceful and precise.[32] The fact that Garner's boyfriend was white, as well as the man he was accused of having either anal or oral sex with—the story differed among "witnesses"—also diminishes the possibility of Garner becoming a black hero.

Garner did not desire fame or recognition as a hero, however. Yet, in spite of his publicly shy and passive demeanor, he did believe his rights had been violated, and he agreed to move forward with the legal suit led by Lambda Legal Defense Fund. When Carpenter interviewed Garner after the ruling, he contrasted Garner's response to the politicized response from Lawrence. On the day of the ruling, Garner revealed, "I felt like a celebrity." When Carpenter brought up heroism, however, Garner quickly resisted such identification: "I'm not a hero. But I feel like we've done something good for a lot of people. I feel kind of proud of that."[33] It is unfortunate that Garner's pride in *his* accomplishment was never reiterated in the public sphere—not in the mainstream, LGBT, or African American community.[34] He truly has been erased. Silence is a criminalizing act, too.[35]

Race has also frequently been erased from analysis of the events leading to the case, the ruling itself, and the political aftermath of the ruling. Whether describing Garner as a "black male" or "nigger," Eubanks raced Garner and conjured the popular perception of black men as violent. The pathology Eubanks relies upon to take his drunken vengeance upon Garner speaks to the illogic of how black masculinities are policed. Patricia Hill Collins emphasizes this illogic when she insists that understanding "racism and heterosexism [as] constitut[ing] two separate systems of oppression masks how each relies upon the other for meaning."[36] As a gun-wielding black man, or as a black man engaged in same-sex intercourse, Garner is depicted as a deviant whose body is in need of policing by both white and black America. White racism is not simply reliant upon socially constructed ideologies around "race"; social constructions of race, gender, and sexuality all collide, one feeding upon the other in order to give meaning to "gun-wielding black man," which, Athena Mutua registers as a "gendered racism."[37]

In order to maintain racial oppression, the white nation's regulation of black rights relies upon the role the black nation plays in producing the twisted logic that disallows Garner's heroism. In this scenario, the structural forms of racism that Lucas encounters in North Carolina can be overcome through a life of crime. The social structures that put him at a disadvantage because he is black disappear in the crime underworld. Being able to sympathize with and often empathize with black men who break the law, the black community often excuses crime committed by black men, especially when the crime is not understood to directly affect the black community; hence, Lucas's stealing of the drug business of white mobsters is not understood as criminal. Tommy, however, casts shame on the black community. His sexual orientation is a metaphorical crime, and, thus, the book lover is condemned. The black community, then, develops a structural practice of exclusion that produces inequitable outcomes for the black LGBT community with regard to being incorporated into the black community, quietly and literally leaving them homeless, since racism often excludes them from the white LGBT community. These often-invisible structures that inform intragroup dynamics contribute significantly to reinforcing the very structures that so often oppress African Americans socially and politically.

SIX

"I'm Not a Businessman, I'm a Business, Man": A Hip-Hop Genealogy of Black Entrepreneurship

We have started an agitation all over the world. It is the agitation of self-reliance wherein the Negro must do for himself.

MARCUS GARVEY, ADDRESS TO UNIA SUPPORTERS IN PHILADELPHIA, 1919

The promise of free enterprise has been and continues to be a pursuit of black men. The premise of the American dream has been driven by the idea that one can become whoever one wants to be and attain whatever material goods and social standing one desires through hard work and dedication. Even today, while there are surely success stories, the ideals that shape the American dream have not been extended equally to African Americans as a minoritized group. The unfettered access to free enterprise is impeded by various structural systems—education, immobile geographies, lack of social and cultural capital, and so on—that perpetuate systems in which African Americans do not have the same opportunity to build capital as white (or Asian) Americans. This chapter focuses on three black men who are iconic, which does make them exceptional, but their exceptionalism is instructive for thinking about how black men have imagined grace through acts of self-determination and subject making.

Marcus Garvey, Berry Gordy, and Jay-Z (aka Shawn Carter) are a seemingly unlikely trinity for comparison, but they share a distinctive characteristic. All three men are successful entrepreneurs who intertwined nationalism with entrepreneurship to produce a brand. I am working with three iconic figures whose lives and careers have been well studied by scholars and journalists, so my contribution is not to rehearse their biographies. Instead, my goal is to map a specific genealogy that emerges when examining their lives and political choices through the lenses of nationalism and entrepreneurship. The title of this chapter borrows from Jay-Z's feature on Kanye West's "Diamonds from Sierra Leone."[1] When Jay-Z raps, "I do this in my sleep/I sold kilos of coke, I'm guessing I can sell CDs/I'm not a businessman/ I'm a business, man!" he does much more than demonstrate the ingenuity of his flow. Black men have routinely been excluded from entering the market as entrepreneurs, as well as from entering the corporate world. Thus, the distinction between being a businessman and you yourself being a business is profound. The men studied here registered the bleak opportunities offered to them to become businessmen and, instead, made themselves into businesses. They branded themselves as businesses that were raced and gendered—businesses that had a nationalist component, though varying with each individual, and blended it with a propaganda that, over the course of time, manifests as the "swagger" of contemporary hip-hop—what I call a hip-hop genealogy.

This chapter analyzes the nuances of how a hip-hop genealogy infuses how Garvey, Gordy, and Jay-Z imagine black entrepreneurship as a nationalist site of redemption that literally positions them at the helm of empires. Each man negotiates empire building differently, but central to each man's plight is the determined force of white supremacy to squelch black subjectivity formation and prevent African American access to wealth building. And although only central to the life experiences of Garvey and Jay-Z, each man finds certain aspects of the law play a role in thwarting his free enterprise efforts. For Garvey, it was mail fraud and a coalition of black leaders willing to sell him out. For Gordy, it was Jim Crow laws that indirectly controlled black music production and influenced the imposition of European values and conceptions. For Jay-Z, it was initially illegal commerce, and more recently, trouble with intellectual property.

Marcus Garvey intertwined liberation theology with entrepreneurship as a means of imagining grace when full citizenship fails, as was made clear after World War I. His contemporaries in the cultural realm founded the New Negro Movement (popularly known as the Harlem Renaissance) to serve a similar purpose, but unlike the culture producers,

Garvey denied white Americans the opportunity to judge his work or him, as they had as benefactors of the New Negro Movement. Garvey's brand was by black people and, most definitely, only for black people. His empire failed, but his relentless political nationalism memorialized him as the godfather of black empire building. Gordy emerges during the civil rights era at a time of renewed hope and belief that legislation could effectively incorporate black Americans into the nation, creating widespread images of black redemption that were framed by integration, rather than Garvey's segregated vision. Gordy capitalized on the period and created a new enterprise and sound—black pop, a crossover genre that would build a music empire. Jay-Z came of age during Reaganomics and the devastating realities of racial and social inequality that drove urban blight and white flight. A demoralized black economy birthed hip-hop. As Jay-Z notes in "Diamonds," he is the heir to a Dynasty—"The Dynasty like my money last three lifetimes"—and his Dynasty, or black empire, was a hip-hop nation that he built through a New Jack entrepreneurship that offered black men, in particular, the opportunity for economic success in a sophisticated network of often unlawful activity. Before analyzing each man's empire building, it is important to consider the historical significance of property ownership, entrepreneurship, and self-help.

This Land Is Your Land, This Land Is My Land

The abolishment of slavery in the United States meant far more to the emancipated slave than the simple right to own his own body and labor; inherent in freedom was the right to participate in free enterprise and the accumulation of capital. In the throes of the culmination of the Civil War, the federal government seemed to register the inherent nature of freedom in a democratic nation when, even before the passage of the Fourteenth Amendment to the Constitution, Union general William T. Sherman issued his Special Field Order No. 15 on January 16, 1865. Sherman's order confiscated 400,000 acres of land owned by Confederate planters that stretched along the Atlantic coastline from Charleston, South Carolina, to the St. Johns River in Florida, including the coastal sea islands and stretching thirty miles inland.[2] The confiscated land was to be redistributed in forty-acre segments to newly freed black families. The redistribution project is popularly referred to as "forty acres and a mule."[3] The act of reparation was short-lived, however. When Andrew Johnson succeeded Abraham Lincoln as president, Johnson overturned Sherman's directive and returned the confiscated land to the planters who "originally" owned it, or, to put it differently, those who had declared war on the United States.

Land redistribution was neither Sherman's nor Lincoln's idea. On the one hand, land redistribution served the pragmatic purpose of providing a means to support the freed slaves. On the other hand, land redistribution was a response to direct inquiries posed to black people about what they wanted, and it was this response that spurred Sherman's order.[4] On January 12, 1865, four days before Sherman issued his order, both he and the secretary of war, Edwin M. Stanton, met with twenty black ministers at Charles Green's mansion on Macon Street in Savannah, Georgia. Literary historian Henry Louis Gates Jr. notes Stanton's recognition of the historical significance of that meeting, as evidenced by the verbatim transcription of the meeting that he presented to Henry Ward Beecher, the famous pastor and brother of Harriet Beecher Stowe. Beecher read the transcript to his congregation at New York's Plymouth Church, and the transcript was printed in full in the February 13, 1865, edition of the *New-York Daily Tribune*.[5] According to Gates, Stanton told Beecher, "For the first time in the history of this nation, the representatives of the government had gone to these poor debased people to ask them what they wanted for themselves." Stanton had proposed asking something that, according to Gates, no one else had thought to ask: what did they want? What they wanted was self-reliance, and the route they envisioned producing self-reliance was land ownership. A Baptist minister, Rev. Garrison Frazier, who bore the responsibility of answering the twelve questions posed by Sherman and Stanton, explained: "The way we can best take care of ourselves is to have land, and turn it and till it by our own labor . . . and we can soon maintain ourselves and have something to spare. . . . We want to be placed on land until we are able to buy it and make it our own."[6]

Thus, even before the Fourteenth Amendment had granted black people citizenship, these men registered the most fundamental principle of citizenship in a democratic nation—the opportunity to accumulate wealth, and in the agrarian South, wealth accumulation was rooted in land ownership. These insightful ministers had thought beyond the ideals of freedom being rooted in free enterprise and also considered the means by which they could best accomplish the production of capital. For this reason, when asked whether they preferred integrated or segregated living quarters, Frazier quickly retorted, "I would prefer to live by ourselves, for there is a prejudice against us in the South that will take years to get over."[7] Ironically, just over thirty years later, Justice Brown in *Plessy v. Ferguson* echoes a similar sentiment about the inability of the law to change what is in people's hearts. The dissolution of the Freedmen's Bureau, President Johnson's shocking veto of the Freedmen's Bureau Bill, and Congress's installation of the 1866 Civil Rights Act, after Johnson vetoed that as well, made it clear that Reconstruction was not going to incorporate African Americans into the nation. Rather, blacks would be nominally free and "equal," yet decidedly positioned at the social, political, and economic margins of society.

In order to emphasize the significance of the legislative history regarding black free enterprise postemancipation, I want to provide a brief overview of that historical moment, especially 1866, and the political ideologies that shaped it. The Thirteenth Amendment freed the slaves, and land redistribution was an on-the-ground effort to begin offering former slaves a chance of survival postemancipation. Aside from plain old racism, the biggest challenge to incorporating African Americans into the nation was the debate over state rights versus the power of Congress and federal action. Most of the rights that would assure that African Americans were equal to their white compatriots had, theretofore, been state concerns. Both radical and moderate Republicans shared some degree of understanding that secession actions by Southern states meant those states, while remaining members of the Union, had nonetheless forfeited, at least temporarily, voting and governing rights until "essential rights of the freedmen had been guaranteed."[8] Registering this need, Congress, through the leadership of Lyman Trumbull, chairman of the Judiciary Committee, presented two bills to Johnson: the Freedmen's Bureau Bill and the Civil Rights Bill of 1866. The former bill basically functioned to extend the life of the Freedmen's Bureau, assuring funding, as well as doling out punishment for noncompliant state officials who failed to extend freedmen "civil rights belonging to white persons."[9] As the logical move after the abolition of slavery, and as a harbinger of the Fourteenth Amendment's granting of citizenship and equal protection to African Americans, Congress also presented a civil rights bill. Section 1 of the bill strove to grant African Americans citizenship, protect that citizenship, and punish any who violated the civil rights of African Americans:

Be it enacted by the Senate and House of Representatives of the United States of America in Congress assembled, That all persons born in the United States and not subject to any foreign power, excluding Indians not taxed, are hereby declared to be citizens of the United States; and such citizens, of every race and color, without regard to any previous condition of slavery or involuntary servitude, except as a punishment for crime whereof the party shall have been duly convicted, shall have the same right, in every State and Territory in the United States, to make and enforce contracts, to sue, be parties, and give evidence, to inherit, purchase, lease, sell, hold, and convey real and personal property, and to full and equal benefit of all laws and proceedings for the security of person and property, as is enjoyed by white citizens, and shall be subject to like punishment, pains, and penalties, and to none other, any law, statute, ordinance, regulation, or custom, to the contrary notwithstanding.

This bill was the first legislative act by Congress for civil rights, and it followed a rather basic logic that one must be a citizen of the nation in order to be protected by the laws of the nation, and if one is a citizen, then one must be able to participate in the same activities and possess the same rights as one's fellow citizens. The ability to participate in the legal system through contracts and the court, as well as the right to be the possessors of real and personal property—what Congress called "fundamental rights"—was critical for African Americans to participate in free enterprise and the rise of capitalist commerce in the nation. Historian Eric Foner points out that although the bill was "a profound change in federal-state relations and reflected how ideas once considered Radical had been adopted by the party's mainstream,"[10] the ability of federal courts to police discrimination at the state level would prove difficult and most often impossible. There remained an issue, then, of political rights, as Trumbull would point out. Until the passage of the Fifteenth Amendment, however, suffrage was not allotted to black men.[11] The issue more preeminent for Congress than suffrage was Johnson's unexpected veto of both bills.

Regarding the Freedmen's Bill, Johnson "derided it as an 'immense patronage' unwarranted by the Constitution and unaffordable given 'the condition of our fiscal affairs.'"[12] Johnson employed divisive pronouns, charging that Congress "had never felt called upon to provide economic relief, establish schools, or purchase land for 'our own people'; such aid, moreover, would injure the 'character' and 'prospects' of the freedmen by implying that they did not have to work for a living."[13] Johnson obviously failed to register that freedmen had spent their entire lives working and receiving no wages. He also did not register how critical a mistake he made when voicing his conviction that "clothing blacks with the privileges of citizenship discriminated against whites" and suggested (European) immigrants knew more about "the nature and character of *our* institutions" than did native-born freedmen.[14] His actions resulted in the Radical and moderate Republicans declaring war on Johnson, as Congress, for the first time in history, overrode a presidential veto, and eventually, impeached Johnson. This course necessitated pursuit of a constitutional amendment to avoid future skirmishes with the president. The Fourteenth Amendment was understood to function as a constitutional basis for the 1866 Civil Rights Act, "guarant[eeing] blacks the same rights as whites with regard to property, contracts, court access, and legal protection."[15] An important distinction should be made between civil, political, and social rights, as issues pertaining to each type of rights entered into debates around legislation and constitutional amendments. Civil rights are exactly what the 1866 Civil Rights Act enumerated—"freedom of contract, property ownership, and court access"; political rights involved such rights as voting and jury participation, and social rights involved activities such as interracial marriage and school integration.[16]

This social and political backdrop drove emerging race leaders to advocate self-reliance and self-determination, and often, separatism for African Americans. Economic fortitude that embraced civil rights was consistently at the heart of plans of action and is expressed pragmatically in the November 18, 1882, issue of the *Richmond Virginia Star*:

We would like to see more [black businesses] started on a larger scale. If single individuals are not able to conduct such, let several unite their means. Must we sit and pray and hope for better times when the white man will see our need and give us better wages? Certainly not. Let us put our shoulders to the wheel; imitate our white brother instead of abjectly depending upon him: establish and carry on every species of industrial enterprise for ourselves, employing and paying fair wages to our people.[17]

Black economic endeavors and entrepreneurship have existed since Africans arrived in this nation, and, even during slavery, there were some free and enslaved blacks who managed to participate in business enterprises. There were, of course, limitations on black economic endeavors during the antebellum period, and those limitations did not dissipate after the Civil War. An acute awareness of how industrialization would produce serious economic impediments for those who could not or did not participate in the free enterprise of the developing capitalist economy compelled race leaders during the late nineteenth and early twentieth centuries to advocate property and business ownership. The means of accomplishing capitalist participation differed from one leader to the next, but business and property ownership was consistently pushed, and doing so within segregated black communities was a prevailing logic espoused by many race leaders and orators.

For Us, by Us

Former slave and president of the Tuskegee Institute, Booker T. Washington, sociologist W. E. B. Du Bois, and Pan-Africanist Marcus Garvey were the leading voices of social uplift ideology during the early twentieth century. All of these men advocated black economic empowerment, and while the differing approaches to their individual ideologies often positioned these men in conflict with one another, Garvey stands out with distinction from Washington and Du Bois for his social uplift philosophies framed by separatist rhetoric. Like Du Bois and Washington, Garvey preached self-help strategies, but his attention to a self-reliance that had no interest in charity or governance by white benefactors is distinctive from the approaches of his contemporaries, whose livelihood and work for the racial cause were wedded to white organizations and individual benefactors.[18] Historian Juliet E. K. Walker notes another critical distinction between Garvey and Washington and Du Bois: only Garvey actually established a business conglomerate that included the masses, even though Washington and Du Bois also advocated for cooperative black business development.[19] Ultimately, Garvey instilled in his worldwide black disciples the notion that the grace they see for themselves must be produced for them and by them, not by nonblack others whose own personal benefit from bestowing grace would undoubtedly infringe upon black self-reliance and economic, political, and social mobility. The self-help business model that Garvey designed and employed through the Universal Negro Improvement Association (UNIA), therefore, serves as a compelling lens for thinking about how black entrepreneurship could become a nationalist site of redemption for two of the greatest music moguls of the late twentieth and twenty-first centuries. Through the business ventures of the UNIA and his political philosophies, Garvey positioned himself and black people in a marketplace that often excluded them as both workers and proprietors.

Marcus Mosiah Garvey Jr. was born in St. Ann's Bay, Jamaica, in 1887. He apprenticed with a printer during his teens, and, after traveling in Central and South America, as well as living in London from 1910 to 1912, Garvey returned to Jamaica and established the UNIA in 1914. He moved to the United States in 1916 and established a thriving base for the UNIA in Harlem. The philosophy of the UNIA encouraged black people globally to embrace and be proud of their blackness. Under the auspices of the UNIA, Garvey also advanced anticolonial philosophies and insisted upon "Africa for Africans," a proclamation that called for all Europeans to leave Africa and for diasporic Africans to return to Africa and help develop "civilized" modern nations. In order to facilitate his "back to Africa" movement, Garvey founded the Black Star Steamship Line in 1919. That same year, he also founded the Negro Factories Corporation, a venture that encouraged black economic independence.

In order to map the hip-hop genealogy that I argue will influence how Gordy and Jay-Z register black entrepreneurship as a nationalist site of redemption, this section on Garvey will examine the basic tenets of his liberation or redemption theology, the intertwining of that theology with his economic independence instructions, and the government's swift and damning end to Garvey's organizing efforts in the United States. I will then analyze how gender and sexuality intersect with race, class, and nation to construct a black Self-Made Man that provides a foundation for the black music industry in the second half of the twentieth century.

Before his arrival in the United States, Garvey's intercontinental travel revealed to him that black people were subordinated and disenfranchised throughout the world. Once he had arrived in the United States, his visits to thirty-eight states led him to conclude that black leadership was ineffectual and opportunistic.[20] Garvey arrived in the United States during the New Negro Movement, a period of prolific black cultural production that emphasized racial pride, progressivism, and economic independence. Culminating after World War I and during a period of heavy black migration from the rural South to the urban North, the movement understood the New Negro to be distinctive from the "Old Negro," or ex-slaves, who embodied racial stereotypes and represented an inferior class of human beings. In contrast, the New Negro embodied modernity, demonstrating a fitness to be fully incorporated into the nation. The New Negro ideology, then, also marked a transitory period of moving away from the "accommodationism" of Booker T. Washington, who had passed away in 1916, and embracing the more militant demands for inclusion espoused by Du Bois. Garvey entered this scene and adapted the New Negro ideologies to fit his own political agenda.

It was important to Garvey that black people come together globally as a unified, collective front, and Garvey wanted them to be understood as modern when doing so. The New Negro, according to Wilson Jeremiah Moses, "would be crisp, efficient, and decisive," while "the 'Old Negro' was putatively lethargic, dreamy, and sensual."[21] In the

global context of building a Pan-African nation, Garvey acutely understood industrialization and modernization to be a necessary component of empire building. He, in fact, castigated Ethiopian emperor
Haile Selassie because of a belief that Ethiopia failed to subdue Italian
attacks because Ethiopia had failed to become modern. Literary theo-
rist Mark Christian Thompson explains Garvey's antagonism toward
Selassie as rooted in Garvey's "appropriation of a reactionary modern-
ist stance" that informed his "high appraisal of industrialization and
modernization, and his incorporation of technology in his nationalis-
tic scheme," because Garvey understood "the rigors of modern life and
modernity" to be essential for African nations to be prepared for and to
ward off colonial aggression.[22]

A sign, for Garvey, that the New Negro was indeed modern was a
commitment to separatism. Garvey was a strong opponent of integration. He felt that each race should have its own nation and that races
should work to maintain racial purity. The sixth point in Garvey's
"Lesson 3: Aims and Objects of the U.N.I.A." from *Lessons from the
School of African Philosophy: The New Way to Education* outlines his plan
and logic:

6. To assist in the development of independent Negro nati[ons] and Communities.

The Negro should not have but one nation, but work with the hope that these
independent nations will become parts of [the] great racial empire. It is necessary,
therefore, to strengthen the hand of every free and independent Negro state so
that they may be able to continue their independence.

Every community where the Negro lives should be devel[oped] by him in his
own section, so that he may control that section or part of the community.

He should segregate himself residentially in that community so as to have political power, economic power, and social power in that community.

If he should scatter himself about the community, if other people live in that
community, he will be scattering his power and dividing it up with other people.
If there are 10,000 Negroes in a town, they should live close to each other, and so
if there are 1,000, 500, or a million, they will have the power of their numbers to
do business, to appeal to the governor and to voice their rights as citizens—in this
respect segregation is good, to do [o]therwise is bad.[23]

Garvey could not imagine, or was not interested in imagining, black
people possessing political power, economic power, and social power
outside of an independent black nation, or "great racial empire," as he
called it. And, in the minds of Garvey's followers, there was a clear
logic supporting his ideologies. The failure of the 1866 Civil Rights

Act to guarantee the civil rights of black Americans was made clear in
nearly every facet of black life, but particularly through the 1918 Anti-
Lynching Bill, sponsored by the National Association for the Advancement of Colored People (NAACP), and the 1921 Tulsa race riot. If black
people did not have the most basic protection—that of their corporeal being—under the law, then they would never achieve any type of
power. Unlike Washington, who believed that with time and through
industrial labor, black people could prove they were no different than
whites and then be incorporated into the nation, and unlike Du Bois,
who believed agitation through interracial cooperation would compel
black incorporation, Garvey suggested that both positions diminished
black power and self-respect. Thus, he advocated self-segregation, or
separatism, and believed "the most appropriate strategy for social advancement required that economic development supersede demands
for political and civil rights."[24]

Garvey identified "Three Stages of the Negro in Contact with the
White Man." The first was slavery, the second emancipation, and the
third stage was the post–World War I era, when he declared that "after
two hundred and fifty years of slavery and fifty eight of partial freedom under your leadership we are going to try but fifty years under our
own direction."[25] The third stage, he insisted, "calls for all the manhood within the race and means that we must throw off all the conditions that affected us in the first and second stages, and go out and
do—acquit ourselves like men in the economic, industrial and political
arena."[26] In this statement Garvey not only makes clear his position on
racial uplift; he also makes clear it is a gendered position that defines
black manhood through a lens of self-reliance and modernity.

Garvey readily conceded that the way to convince people to follow
his directions through the "third stage" was through propaganda. Racial pride propaganda, then, went hand-in-hand with separatist rhetoric. Lesson 16 in his *Lessons from the School of African Philosophy*, therefore, implored black people to

tear down from your wall all pictures, that [do not] glorify your race. Tear up and
burn every bit of propaganda that does not carry your ideas of things. . . . You
should always match propaganda with propaganda. Have your own newspapers,
have your own artists, have your sculptors, have your pulpits, have your own plat-
forms, print your own books and show your own motion pictures, paint your own
pictures and sculpture your own subjects. . . . Keep your homes free and clear of
alien objects, of other races on glorification, otherwise your children will grow up
to adore and glorify other people. Put in the places of others the heroes and noble

characters of your own race. . . . Customs, therefore, are based upon acceptance of propaganda skillfully engineered. Have your own propaganda and hand it down the ages. . . . Never allow false statements or allegations against your race to become current and pass into history, as if it were a fact.[27]

Merging civil and social rights, Garvey advocates freedom of contract and property ownership, while offering his own version of social rights.

His plan for achieving equality extended beyond simply building a great racial empire and independent Negro state; capitalism was a critical element. Garvey was virulently anti-Communist. Thompson notes, "His antipathy toward Communism and Marxism well known, Garvey excoriated black and white Communists and Marxists in his writing and speeches, accusing them of attempting to disenfranchise blacks of the very thing that would gain for them political power: private property."[28] In "Capitalism and the State," Garvey extols capitalism as "necessary to the progress of the world, and those who unreasonably and wantonly oppose or fight against it are enemies to human advancement: but there should be a limit to the individual or corporate use or control of it."[29] A capitalist system was critical for the development of a modern black nation that would be industrially competitive and have the fortitude to defend itself against colonial aggression. The UNIA and the Negro Factories Corporation served as the means of achieving a black capitalist system that had certain limits in order to ensure the survival of the entire community.

"Lesson 10: Economy" in Garvey's *Lessons from the School of African Philosophy* outlined basic, commonsense rules for financial economy, such as the importance of savings, the importance of a profit for businesses, purchasing with cash rather than credit, and only purchasing goods that are necessary. Practicing good financial economy is moot if one has no means to produce capital. Supporting the UNIA solved the problem of access to capital production, as Garvey used a self-reliance logic to explain why depending on white employment was unwise: "By supporting the U.N.I.A. to the point of success, opportunities of employment will be created in the establishment of factories, mills, commercial enterprises, farming enterprises, shipping enterprises, etc."[30] The "Application" section of *Lessons from the School of African Philosophy*, then, specifically outlines how the UNIA will function as an economic trust:

All the funds of the U.N.I.A. are supposed to be directed in these channels. The funds of the U.N.I.A. must be [us]ed for the race, and the race only, and belongs to no one individual or group of individuals, but is held in trust for the race, and all the profit it makes out of its investments through different companies which it controls must be ultimately used for the good and welfare of the Negro race at large.

Its property will be held in trust for the Negro race. Its wealth will be held in trust for the Negro race for serving generations yet unborn.

It shall go on eternally, one generation handing down to the next. No one person or persons can claim such wealth because it is for the race in perpetual existence. Stress this everywhere you go, so that people may know that what they contribute to the U.N.I.A. is not lost to them, in that their generations may benefit from the gift they give today.[31]

The propaganda Garvey espoused was very effective apparently, as the UNIA raised large amounts of capital, but, in spite of Garvey's lessons on economics, squandered the capital, often inexplicably, through poor business management and treachery.[32] Although the poor business management, coupled with government's and black political leaders' antagonism, would result in the demise of the Black Star Line and Garvey's community power, the funds raised through the UNIA did successfully support the Negro Factories Corporation, which "was comprised of firms in the service-industry (one laundry, one printing plant, and three restaurants), retail (three groceries stores), and manufacturing (two uniform assembly factories). The industrial and transportation sector was represented by the Black Star Line, which was to carry African Americans to and from Africa and transport UNIA goods worldwide."[33]

There was legitimate cause, urgency even, for Garvey's propaganda. Although the period 1900–1930 is what Walker refers to as "the Golden Age of Black Business," the first of three waves of critical black presence in corporate America, blacks continued to have limited participation in free enterprise. While Walker notes the significance of blacks entering the banking and insurance industries, as well as the success of the hair-care industry, she also reports, "In 1900 the total wealth of black America, $700 million, amounted to less than that of the nation's first billion-dollar corporation, United Steel, organized in 1901."[34] The problem of black wealth was inextricably linked to labor. Very few blacks, in the North or South, had accumulated wealth after emancipation. As a result, the accumulation of black wealth was reliant upon blacks being able to enter the labor force either as laborers or as proprietors. The Harlem Jobs-For-Negroes Boycott of 1934, urban history scholar William Muraskin contends, was a climactic event resulting from an intolerable labor situation in Harlem prior to 1934.[35] Even in their own neighborhoods, blacks had limited access to employment, and those who were employed were excluded from white-collar positions and restricted to menial positions as janitors and floor sweepers; one store proprietor even boasted, "In fact one Negro college graduate worked the elevator."[36] This environment made Garveyism appealing to the black masses. Garvey's commitment to black economic power attracted black people more than his pageantry. Moses contends, "For the black working people who bought five-dollar shares in the Black Star Line, the enterprise represented, not a desire to escape from America, but the basis of a financial and industrial empire, which would command universal respect."[37]

A lack of respect for black workers was not unique to Harlem—it was a national and global phenomenon. The college-educated black elevator operator was not an anomaly, but more the norm for educated blacks. It is no wonder, then, that in the mid-1920s "there were more than 700 branches of the UNIA in 38 states, along with 200 international branches, most of them in the West Indies and in Central and South America."[38] The stockholders in the Black Star Line, Moses explains, "were seemingly attracted by the opportunity to become involved in an enterprise that represented, not only black capitalism, but an attitude of assertiveness and militancy in defiance of white power."[39] In spite of Reconstruction-era legislation, which was passed with the intent of protection and equality for black citizens, both ambiguity of language, as in the Fourteenth Amendment, for example, and the challenge of compelling local enforcement of laws and punishment for infractions made protection and equality an all-too-often failed reality. This reality fueled Garvey's insistence upon a separate black nation that was self-reliant.

More importantly, perhaps, for Garvey, capitalism was critical, but so was common sense. One of the many seemingly commonsense lessons Garvey passed on to his following was this: "In acquiring property for commercial, ind[u]strial or personal purposes or use, always see that you get value for your money."[40] Garvey, unfortunately, did not have strong business acumen, and his commonsense financial lesson proved to be his demise. The Black Star Steamship Line was composed of three steamships, and all three proved to be unseaworthy in spite of the issuance of seaworthiness certificates at their purchase. The *Yarmouth*, the first steamship purchased, was commissioned to deliver whiskey to Cuba and also made stops in Jamaica, Panama, and Costa Rica. The details of the commissioning and subsequent contract, however, suggest incompetent management and the likely dishonesty of high-ranking officials, in addition to a vessel that needed numerous repairs, many of which were the result of white engineers' tampering.[41] The second ship, the *Shadyside*, took passengers up and down the Hudson River, but never made it out to sea before encountering repair problems. The third steamship, the *Kanawha*, made it to Havana, with numerous repair problems and sabotages along the way. The purchase of the fourth ship, which was to be named the *Phyllis Wheatley*, was never completed, encountering problems with financial deceit and general incompetency as in the case of the first three ships.[42]

When Garvey was indicted for mail fraud in 1922, Edmund David Cronon explains, "postal authorities charged that Garvey and the Black Star Line had knowingly used 'fraudulent representations' and 'deceptive artifices' in the sale of stock through the mails and had advertised and sold space on a mythical vessel."[43] Basically, Garvey was charged with using the mail to sell stock in a company that was nearly bankrupt; the stock, therefore, held no value. In addition to the bad business deals and treacherous associates that led to the failure of the Black Star Line, a number of black leaders led campaigns that also contributed to the demise of both the Black Star Line and Garvey's empire building. Cyril V. Briggs, Robert S. Abbott, editor of the *Chicago Defender*, and W. E. B. Du Bois published public allegations of mismanagement, dishonesty, and fraud against Garvey. In response to these allegations, Garvey did exactly what he preached—he fought propaganda with propaganda. I will discuss that battle in more detail below, but first I want to address a secondary approach to battle that Garvey seemingly also took—a gangster-mafia-style approach that, once again, positions him as laying a foundation for a hip-hop genealogy of black nationalist entrepreneurship that has to resort to creative, and sometimes unethical or illegal, means for full participation in free enterprise.

Garvey is quoted in the August 18, 1924, issue of *Daily Worker* proclaiming, "Only crooks and thieves and cowards fear to go to prison. Men with principles don't care about jails."[44] Apparently, in addition to not fearing prison, Garvey did not fear those who betrayed him and spoke ill of him. Du Bois was able to publish UNIA financial statements in his magazine, *Crisis*, when Rev. J. W. H. Eason was expelled from the UNIA and delivered the documents to Du Bois.[45] Eason was shot in the back and killed on January 1, 1923, in New Orleans. It was widely speculated that Garveyites committed the crime, but it was never proven in a court of law,[46] and the UNIA insisted upon its innocence.[47] Yet, previous gangster-mafia-style activity makes it seem likely that either Garvey or Garveyites were complicit in Eason's murder. Asa Philip Randolph, the Socialist labor organizer and onetime friend of Garvey, initiated a campaign to have Garvey deported after Garvey gave a speech in New Orleans in which "he was quoted as saying, in terms reminiscent of Booker T. Washington, that America was a white man's country and the black man could not insist on riding the white man's jim crow streetcar, since he had not built any streetcar of his own."[48] Randolph launched his anti-Garvey speech campaign in Harlem and published hostile editorials in the magazine he cofounded with Chandler Owen, the *Messenger*. His position was clearly articulated when he declared in the July 1922 *Messenger*: "*Here's notice that the* MESSENGER *is firing the opening gun in a campaign to drive Garvey and Garveyism in all its sinister viciousness from the American soil.*"[49] Less than two months after the editorial, Randolph received a package through the mail containing the severed hand of a white man, the race presumably based upon red hairs on the hand.[50] A note was included warning Randolph that the same would happen to him if he did not become a dues-paying member of the UNIA.[51] While there was no proof Garvey or Garveyites had anything to do with the delivery of the hand, "increasing thuggery" attributed to the UNIA in numerous cities made logical associations understandable.[52]

Shortly after the Eason murder, Robert W. Bagnall, contributing editor to Randolph's *Messenger* and director of branches of the NAACP, and William Pickens, NAACP field secretary, joined ranks with Randolph and others to launch a relentless anti-Garvey crusade that culminated in a letter to Attorney General Harry M. Daugherty dated January 15, 1923, declaring "Marcus Garvey Must Go" and enumerating reasons such as his anti-integration position; his fraternization with the KKK; his "foreignness"; the composition of the UNIA being primarily "the most primitive and ignorant element of West Indian and American Negroes"; and the pending Eason and mail fraud cases.[53] The ultimate goal of the crusaders and letter was to have Garvey deported. The fact that those who had been identified by the government as black radicals would enlist the government to eliminate a political foe has often been noted by scholars.[54] Scholars also consistently note that the legal charges against Garvey were brought after a period of desperately searching for some crime to charge him with, since he was an "alien," and agitation was perceived as a serious threat to the US government. Garvey scholars such as Wilson Jeremiah Moses, Tony Martin, and Judith Stein all acknowledge that the charges against Garvey did not match his offense. The disproportionate charges compared to Garvey's purported offenses will also later animate some of the engagement with politics through rap and hip-hop culture. The incongruity between Garvey's charges and offenses also resonates with the late twentieth-century criminalization of crack cocaine in disproportion to powder cocaine, the racialization of drug sentencing and punishment, and also the troubling punishment for marijuana possession in some states where possession is a felony.[55]

Gender Matters

To this point, my exposition and analysis have focused on a self-reliant black nationalism and entrepreneurship as a means of empire building, with attention to race and class, but without a consideration of how gender and sexuality intersect with race, class, and nation. The construction, performance, and perception of masculinity, actually of heteromasculinity, are paramount in the production and dissemination of hip-hop, and these elements also influenced the philosophies, positions, and actions of Garvey and his political foes. Bravado, braggadocio, and a militant disregard for law and order are understood by some scholars to be survival mechanisms for disenfranchised black men who have no access to white social and economic institutions. Richard Majors and Janet Mancini Billson refer to such performances as "cool poses," black men's efforts to gain self-respect and control through expressive performance.[56] As Garvey's enemies grew from a hostile government to include other black men of prominence in the black community, he adopted an attitude by which he determined to control his political and economic ventures, as well as his own destiny, through actions and activities—the violent criminal acts could not be proven—that were deeply concerned with not just sovereignty and citizenship, but also with manliness.[57]

Both individual and the nation's manliness were preoccupations during the early twentieth century, and the discourse was intricately linked to race and class. This anxiety affected both men and women, and historian Martin Summers contends, "The overarching question of what constituted manhood . . . dominated the ways in which most men and women in the United States conceptualized, among other things, economic prosperity, national belonging, and, for many, their position within racial, ethnic, and class hierarchies."[58] As sociologist Michael Kimmel notes, proving one's manhood became a cultural practice in the early nineteenth century, and it continues to frame society's most fundamental understanding of what it means to be a man.[59] The focus of black race leaders on economics and capital production during the early twentieth century was about survival, but it was also driven by the reality that the Industrial Revolution meant that men's collective economic, political, and social identity was no longer fixed, as it had been in the previous social order of the genteel patriarch landowner, artisans, and laborers—all of whom occupied fixed positions in society. The Industrial Revolution created what Kimmel refers to as the Self-Made Man, "a model of manhood that derives identity entirely from a man's activities in the public sphere, measured by accumulated wealth and status, by geographic and social mobility."[60] Garvey understood this newly constructed manhood. He also understood what people like Du Bois did not seem to register—it was a "white only" manhood, and no matter how efficiently or spectacularly black men performed this manhood, they would never become "men," with no appended racial signifiers—a status available to white men and European immigrants, who would eventually be granted admission to "manhood." This realization is the crux of Garvey's separatist politics. Choosing separatism—as opposed to having segregation imposed upon him—or voluntary ex-patriotism was not simply about sovereignty; it was also about manhood.

When Garvey entered into a public debate with Du Bois through the press, he did exactly what he encouraged his UNIA followers to do: "You should always match propaganda with propaganda."[61] In 1921, Du Bois ended his private quips with Garvey and indirect attacks in the magazine *Crisis*, beginning direct attacks in the December 1920 and January 1921 issues of *Crisis*.[62] Garvey responded to the attacks publicly at Liberty Hall and in *Negro World*. My intent is not to rehash a debate that was ideologically rooted in class differences and colorisms, but I do want to consider Du Bois's critique of Liberty Hall in Harlem, the headquarters of the Harlem UNIA chapter. Du Bois describes the building distastefully: "There was a long, low, unfinished church basement roofed over. It was designed as the beginning of a church long ago, but abandoned. Marcus Garvey roofed it over, and out of this squat and dirty old Liberty Hall he screams his propaganda. As compared with the homes, the business and church, Garvey's basement represents nothing in accomplishment and only waste in attempt."[63] Garvey responds by referring to Du Bois as a "lazy dependent mulatto" and proceeds to explain how significant Liberty Hall is in the grand scheme of Garveyist self-reliance. He emphasizes that Liberty Hall is "the only independent Negro structure" in Harlem, and, as far as Garvey is concerned, the fact that Du Bois compares it to white-owned property that blacks occupy, but do not own, is evidence of Du Bois's problematic allegiances to white people whose philanthropy supports both the NAACP and Du Bois himself as an officer of the organization. From there, Du Bois deals a low blow and defames Garvey's father, claiming he died in an almshouse.

Garvey's retorts are as much about class and colorisms as they are about gender. While Garvey does not disparage Du Bois's father, he does attack the dignity and manhood of Du Bois himself. He paints a picture of Du Bois being in love with white people as a child in Great Barrington, Massachusetts, and proposes that his disdain for poor blacks and love for whites has produced a fifty-five-year-old man "still living on the patronage of good white people."[64] In contrast, "with the thirty-six years of Marcus Garvey (Who was born poor and whose father, according to DuBois, died in a poor house) he is able to at least pass over the charity of white people and develop an independent program originally financed by himself to the extent of thousands of dollars, taken up by the Negro people themselves."[65] Garvey then asks: "Now which of the two is poorer in character and in manhood? The older who had all these opportunities and still elects to be a parasite living off the good will of another race, or the younger man who had sufficient self-respect to make an effort to do for himself, even though in his effort he constructs a 'dirty brick building' from which he can send out his propaganda on self-reliance and self-respect."[66] Garvey defines Du Bois as less than a man because Du Bois has opted for white charity over ownership of himself. Interpreting the NAACP as white hegemonic power over black political thought and social uplift, Garvey ascribes to the black men involved in the organization an effeminate nature and subordinate position in a male-dominated society; yet another reason for Garvey to shirk interracial cooperation. While critiquing Du Bois's assimilationist and reliant tendencies, however, Garvey fails to register that his own ideologies are rooted in Emersonian values and thus in elements of white manhood.

Nonetheless, in Garvey's mind, his critique of Du Bois's agentic deficiencies positions him as modern, or as the New Negro, who is invested in entering the marketplace as a Self-Made Man, while Du Bois becomes the Old Negro, invested in a genteel patriarchy bestowed upon him by white philanthropists. Garvey easily concludes of Du Bois, "DuBois cares not for an Empire for Negroes, but contents himself with being a secondary part of white civilization."[67] Garvey's conclusion actually stands in stark contrast to Du Bois's often-cited appeal in the first chapter of *Souls of Black Folk* to recognize "the Negro" as a first-class citizen, as American without hyphenation. For Garvey, first-class citizenship is not something bestowed upon you. Rather, it is something you gain when you create your own nation and control your own enterprise and capital production; it, consequently, is also the same means by which you become a bona fide man—a man both self-reliant and modern—by Garvey's standards.

I'm Coming Out

The post–civil rights business enterprises of Berry Gordy and Jay-Z demonstrate an investment in black independent enterprise, as well as an investment in capitalism—both of which have become markers of modern manliness. Both men have acted as their own agents, defining themselves against white mainstream definitions of black manhood. In some ways, Gordy is a complicated figure to include in this threesome, but in other ways, it is impossible to exclude him. My attention to Gordy, then, functions more as a brief interlude between Garvey and Jay-Z that helps to map a hip-hop genealogy that several major figures in hip-hop—namely, Jay-Z, Dr. Dre, and Sean "P. Diddy" Combs—have followed: branding themselves as a consumable product for the masses.

Berry Gordy is a controversial figure in black music history. Many scholars and journalists have addressed the controversy of Gordy's pointed development of his record production company, Motown Records Corporation, as one that would cross racial lines and appeal to mainstream audiences in a period in which both the radio and performance venues were either white or black. I do not intend to revisit that controversy or to critique Gordy's business ventures in that context. I am, instead, interested in how, despite his undeniable desire to produce a black pop rather than soul sound, Gordy worked within a black nationalist paradigm that links to Garvey's philosophies regarding nation, entrepreneurship, and self-reliance. Gordy is the post–civil rights godfather of crossover black branding that lays the integrated era's blueprint for black empire building, one followed by Jay-Z and his hip-hop industry compatriots, but also by black entrepreneurs like Oprah and Tyler Perry.

The founding of Motown was the outcome of risk taking and vision. Prior to Motown, Gordy tried a short-lived career in boxing. He also borrowed money for a record shop that failed. The idea of working for himself was familiar to Gordy because his father owned a grocery store and a contracting business, and his mother started an insurance agency. Borrowing $800 from his family's Ber-Berry Co-operative,

Gordy set out to establish his first record label, Tamla, named after Debbie Reynolds's hit song "Tammy." His success as a cowriter of some of Jackie Wilson's hits proved to be more than sheer luck; Motown Records produced more than one hundred top-ten hits between 1960 and 1979.[68] Over the course of his career at Motown, Gordy produced legendary stars, including the Supremes, Marvin Gaye, Diana Ross, (Little) Stevie Wonder, the Jackson 5, Michael Jackson, Mary Wilson, the Temptations, Smokey Robinson, Gladys Knight and the Pips, Eddie Kendricks, and Lionel Richie. Motown hit its low point, however, when Michael Jackson left the label in 1975. The corporation continued to produce notable artists, but with its heyday clearly over, Gordy sold Motown to MCA for $61 million in 1988, retaining publishing rights to the original hits.[69]

Gordy was a savvy businessman, who, seeming to depart from Garvey's Pan-Africanist philosophies for entrepreneurial success, actually practiced them with a different spin. During Garvey's heyday in Harlem, it would have been difficult to imagine blacks and whites coexisting in the United States since both social customs and the law failed to grant blacks equality and protection. Thus, the grace Garvey imagined was ideally repatriation in Africa, but, at best, a separatist nation within a nation. The civil rights movement had hardly waned in 1959—its grandest victories would not come until the mid-1960s—but the political climate certainly would have suggested Gordy was warranted in expecting "a change is gonna come."[70] The federal legislation resulting from the movement redressed social, political, and civil equality. *Brown v. Board of Education* spearheaded the movement in 1954, attending to social equality in public education, and *Loving v. Virginia* (1967) addressed interracial marriage. The 1965 Voting Rights Act addressed political rights. And a variety of legal action worked to make explicit what the Fourteenth Amendment failed to do when, as legal scholar Michael J. Klarman points out, it "[did] not specifically forbid racial classifications, and 'equal protection of the laws' [did] not plainly bar 'equal but separate' facilities."[71] The 1964 and 1968 Civil Rights Acts made explicit the ambiguities of the Fourteenth Amendment, which enabled states to disregard black rights to property, contract, court access, and legal protection. Anticipating the freedom of free enterprise, in the sense of market expansion and capital gains, Gordy set out to create an African American sound—"The Sound of Young America"— that would appeal to a mainstream (read white) audience. His capitalist venture proved highly successful, and following in Garvey's footprints, Gordy did not limit his business pursuits to one product market; he produced *Lady Sings the Blues, Mahogany,* and the film adaptation of the Broadway musical *The Wiz.*

Business and nation were intricately linked, if not inseparable, in Gordy's venture, as "Motown's success depended on the extraordinary web of family and friendship ties which brought its musicians together in the first place and kept them all involved with each other thereafter."[72] Marvin Gaye, for example, was married to Gordy's sister Anna. And Harvey Fuqua, who eventually became head of Motown's Artists and Repertoire office, was married to another one of Gordy's sisters, Gwen. Gordy surrounded himself with almost only black employees, many of whom were family members, and he only produced black artists. Although Gordy was trying to acquire the dollars of young white America, he was wholly invested in a certain brand of black nationalism. Mary Wilson of the Supremes, for example, remembers in her autobiography: "The building on West Grand Boulevard was a home away from home for many young singers and musicians then. The company was still serving hot family-style meals for everyone who happened to be around."[73] On 2648 West Grand Boulevard at Hitsville USA, Gordy created a microlevel black nation based on black entrepreneurship that was in direct response to white supremacy—a logic not much different from Garvey's when he founded the Negro Factories Corporation as a "for us, by us" capital-building business venture.

Although some music critics and scholars during Motown's heyday, and even now, have characterized Gordy's business practices as invested in commercialization (read assimilation) rather than black nationalism, the point made by Mary Wilson is no small matter. Creating a "home space" for black music artists during a period in which they were socially and economically marginalized required a race-based ideology about nation and community. In 1963, Motown reproduced Martin Luther King Jr.'s "Great March to Freedom" speech given in Detroit the day before the now-famous March on Washington.[74] The Black Forum label, albeit short-lived, featured spoken word performances and speeches by Amiri Baraka, Langston Hughes, and Black Panther leader Elaine Brown, as well as Stokely Carmichael's "Free Huey" speech.[75] As Gordy reveals in his autobiography, the Black Forum was intricately linked to his financial contributions to the Southern Christian Leadership Conference (SCLC). When Jesse Jackson solicited funds on behalf of Dr. King and the SCLC, after an extended inquisition, Gordy reports, he told Jackson, "Not only am I goin' to give you the money . . . but I'd like to do more."[76] The "more" was to memorialize Dr. King's speeches on albums. In his autobiography, Gordy juxtaposes that story of financial and cultural uplift to a later meeting with Jackson when Jackson was running for president of the United States and Gordy was attending a fund-raiser for Jackson and Jackson's Rainbow Coalition.[77] This public, and often behind-the-scenes, investment in civil rights and black incorporation into the nation positioned Motown in what Mark Anthony Neal insists was a "historical role in providing the music and the cultural cover for Black American demands for social justice and equality."[78]

The black nation Gordy built at Hitsville USA was a nationalist operation, even though he was undeniably packaging black music for a white audience. Free enterprise changes with time. For Gordy, it meant an integrated market, and, like millions of other black Americans, Gordy wanted what the lyrics to the first hit song he penned for the Tamla label on Anna Records emphatically state: "Now give me money/that's what I want."[79] Yet, if black people want to exponentially increase their capital through business ventures at any time in the United States, they cannot depend solely upon a market composed only of African Americans, as that racial group makes up less than one-fifth of the nation's market. Recognizing Gordy's black nationalism, as well as the logic of his business strategy, Tom Brokaw points out that Gordy "didn't sport a big Afro, or wear a dashiki, or hold up a clenched fist"; yet, the absence of those signifying gestures does not change the fact that "he had a real and meaningful financial and cultural black power that came from building a recording empire based on a marketing strategy that relied on emotions and sexual fantasies crossing racial lines instead of polarizing them."[80] Like Garvey, Gordy located black power in capitalist-driven empire building, but unlike Garvey, Gordy found a way to build his empire without racially polarizing the nation. Gordy, according to Neal, was, therefore, able to assist "blacks [in] integrat[ing] American society in general and corporate boardrooms in particular."[81]

Gordy's success in integrating both black sound and the boardroom was a nationalist project and also a hustle. In spite of his best efforts and even threats of libel suits, Gordy still cannot shake the rumors he had mob ties. Both Gerald Early and Gerald Posner report rumors that Gordy "was just a figurehead," and organized crime had taken over Motown for any variety of reasons—"silly stories of mysterious shootings, runaway gambling debts, loan-shark beatings, and even a rumor that a close friend of his had supposedly gone to jail in his place on a tax rap."[82] Gordy and "virtually everyone connected with Motown past and present" deny the validity of such claims.[83] Considering Detroit was a union town, and the popularity of payola during Gordy's start-up period, the rumors are not without logical rationale. Yet, framing empire building around a nationalist paradigm in the music and entertainment industry sets the stage for urban youth of Gordy's grandchildren's generation to take branding to a new level, and literally make *themselves* the business.

Tryin' to Catch Me Ridin' Dirty

The image of black men holding white signs with the simple statement "I Am a Man" above their heads or in front of their chests as they walk single file down a street, passing National Guard troops with rifles pointed at them, is now an iconic visual representation of a disenfranchised black masculinity that epitomizes black men's social, political, and economic history in this nation. The Memphis sanitation workers' strike in 1968 was spurred by the refusal of the mayor of Memphis, Henry Loeb, to recognize the workers' union, unsafe working conditions, and poor wages. During his visit, Martin Luther King Jr. encouraged the workers, assuring them that they would get to the "Promised Land" and must "give [themselves] to this struggle until the end."[84] King was assassinated that very evening, and riots and looting broke out across the nation. King's murder in 1968 marked a definitive end to nonviolent resistance and the civil rights era, but the violence that erupted during his first visit to Memphis to help organize the workers and the violence following his death were indicative of a growing impatience with passive resistance before his death.

The civil rights legislation passed by Congress during President Johnson's administration marked progress, but it had serious limitations. African Americans continued to encounter major obstacles in obtaining employment, housing, and education, and a critical mass of young people who had supported King's nonviolent movement were losing faith in his approach by the mid-1960s. This loss of faith is perhaps best memorialized in Stokely Carmichael's speech on October 29, 1966, at the University of California, Berkeley, in which he coined the term "Black Power." By the mid-1960s, nonviolent marches in southern states shifted to violent conflict between black activists and federal, state, and local government agencies and police. As in the civil rights movement, a primary concern of Black Power activists were the economic disadvantages that affected black people's social and political lives. The transition from "We Shall Overcome" in the civil rights era to Public Enemy's "Fight the Power" laid the groundwork for Jay-Z and "Dynasty" building through hip-hop.

When Marcus Garvey responded to Du Bois's public attack, his response positioned manhood at the center of the debate. Garvey developed his movement and intellectual philosophy around the interconnected goals of self-reliance and modernity. These two goals would, in his view, deliver black people globally from disenfranchisement and subordination. Left unstated, but absolutely imperative, was the fact that self-reliance and modernity were inherently linked to manliness—hence Garvey's berating of Du Bois for being a grown man still reliant on the good graces of white people to provide for himself. Although Garvey's status in the black national imaginary dwindled by the late 1960s,[85] when Black Power was on the rise and hip-hop was being birthed by African American and Latino youths in the Bronx, his ideology of black business ownership as both a property asset and an employer of black people resurfaced in Black Power rhetoric—rhetoric that was deeply invested in recouping the manhood stripped from the Memphis sanitation workers and declared lost in the Moynihan Report.

The black economic empowerment that the 1960s civil rights legislation was expected to accomplish, but universally fell short of accomplishing, became the rallying cry as King's movement lost its grounding, and political agendas began aligning with Malcolm X and leaders with more radical approaches. This political transition was felt in black popular culture. Before Black Power, any political messages in black music were coded. Media scholar S. Craig Watkins notes that white retaliation, censure, and commercial failure prevented black musicians from being explicitly political, and he identifies three specific barriers that were eventually removed: white music executives began to see the financial gains available to them; it became fashionable for artists to incorporate politics in their work; and the support of black performers was sought when white financial support of the civil rights movement waned.[86] Thus, artists like James Brown and Marvin Gaye began to incorporate a level of political protest and social consciousness into their performances. The melding of political commentary and artistic performance with an economic and political climate that was volatile and demoralizing for many black youths, who logically should have been benefactors of the civil rights movement, created a fruitful climate for both the birth of hip-hop and an unprecedented increase in illegal black enterprises.

It is true that informal economies have always existed in the black community. Number running, payolas, and other illegal enterprises employed a large number of blacks who otherwise would have been jobless. The heroin epidemic during the 1970s and the crack cocaine epidemic of the 1980s created the opportunity for an additional informal economy in the black community. Both dealing and using drugs have a direct connection to the lack of employment opportunities for African Americans. Whether it was starting a business or being gainfully employed in the workforce, black men, in particular, found that they could not escape discrimination—even when laws were put in place to remedy the problems. Title VI of the 1964 Civil Rights Act stipulates, "Every Federal agency which provides financial assistance through grants, loans or contracts is required to eliminate discrimination on the grounds of race, color, or national origin in these programs."[87] It would seem, then, that black entrepreneurs would have better access to loans to create small businesses, but that was not the case. The Economic Opportunity Loan program, which was funded through the Office of Economic Opportunity, is an example of how so many civil rights programs have failed black people. Walker explains that "individuals with high personal income or savings and those with technical expertise in business management who could or had demonstrated a capacity to succeed in business" were denied the EOL loans.[88] Furthermore, Johnson's War on Poverty failed to increase black employment. Failure after failure to achieve justice and equality created the socially and economically disadvantaged environment of the Marcy Projects in Brooklyn, where Shawn Corey Carter, aka Jay-Z, was born and raised.

For many black youths growing up in impoverished urban spaces, as Jay-Z did during the 1970s and 1980s, the manhood that was diminished by lack of employment and political power could be reclaimed through violence and a hardness that recouped their masculinity. The Self-Made Man that Garvey embodied and berated Du Bois for failing to become continues to be valued in US society. But, for black men who did not have either the wherewithal or the social capital to pull themselves up by the bootstraps and achieve the American dream, the illegal drug industry offered an opportunity to redefine the Self-Made Man in terms that they could achieve. By the time Jay-Z entered the hip-hop scene, the music genre and culture more generally had transitioned from good-time party music to gangster-themed, and the culture made black men always already criminal suspects.

There are two connections that create a genealogical link between Garvey, Gordy, and Jay-Z. The first is a nationalist framework that critiques racial inequalities and supports a subculture within which resistance can take place; Jay-Z does this through his lyrical aptitude. The second is Jay-Z's capitalist enterprises; Garvey heralded such ventures, and Gordy followed suit, according to scholars like Neal, making Motown, and by extension, himself, an internationally recognized brand. The nationalist-oriented art coupled with the capitalist pursuits situate Jay-Z as uniquely modern because he takes an indigenously black art and culture and uses it, literally, to turn himself into a product that can be marketed and consumed. Like Garvey and Gordy, then, Jay-Z amasses a global black empire, but unlike his forefathers, Jay-Z is successful at rooting his empire in both ideology and commerce—something he is able to accomplish, in large part, because of the crossover appeal of hip-hop (Garveyism was adamantly opposed to such pursuits) and the buying power of African Americans in the late twentieth and twenty-first centuries.

Ideologically, Jay-Z's early work, in particular, capitalized on the fact that, for all the black boys growing up in places like the Marcy Projects that he touts, hustling was what made you a man—what made you able to bring home food for your mother and siblings, clothe yourself, and enjoy material goods. Hustling offered black men a place in a patriarchal, capitalist society. Hustling as a form of grace is a far cry from the other examples I have examined thus far of black men who seek to imagine selves that society refuses to see, yet in the context of how Jay-Z presents the hustle lyrically, it is bound up in imagining grace. His lyrics demonstrate a clear consciousness about what social circumstances create his precarious position in society.

It is well noted that Jay-Z is a drug dealer turned rapper. His track "99 Problems," on *The Black Album*, became famous initially for its controversial hook, "99 problems but a bitch ain't one," and, subsequently, for its many reuses, most recently in the final hours before President Barack Obama's reelection, when Jay-Z performed "99 Problems but Mitt Ain't One" at an Ohio campaign rally. In his monograph, *Decoded* (2010), Jay-Z offers a mix of his own intellectual genealogy with explication of his discography that does not hide his belief that many critics and listeners, alike, do not understand his lyrics. He describes the hook as "a joke, bait for lazy critics." In spite of an immediate "here we go again" critique of sexism in rap lyrics, Jay-Z insists: "At no point in the song am I talking about a girl. The chorus really makes that clear if you bother listening: the obvious point of the chorus is that I wasn't talking about women."[89] Now, he does not claim that he never refers to women as "bitches," which surely contributes to the confusion among many critics; however, it is true that the lyrics clearly are not about a woman. They are about being young, black, male, and, therefore, automatically fitting a guilty profile. The real events he says he reimagines through the song, however, do, indeed, describe the experience of "riding dirty" and the anxiety and risk inherent in such activity. Verse 2 opens with "The year is '94 and in my trunk is raw." He includes a footnote, as he does for all slang in his lyrics, that insinuates "raw" references the "stash" location in his car. A few lines later, once he is stopped by the police and asked if he knows why he was stopped, he spits back, "Cause I'm young and I'm black and my hat's real low?"

Setting the song in 1994, Jay-Z is telling a tale that is a real story— his own personal story, but also a much larger national narrative that plagued black men's lives during the 1990s in very particular ways. He ran drugs up and down the I-95 corridor, and during the 1990s, police stops of black men without probable cause on that highway were exponential. A US Supreme Court case decided in 1996, just two years after "99 Problems" is set, exemplifies the dilemma both those innocent and guilty of riding dirty experienced.[90] In *Whren v. United States*, the court unanimously decided against the petitioners, holding that Michael A. Whren's and James L. Brown's contention that they were stopped and their truck searched without reasonable suspicion or probable cause was unsupported by the evidence. The court held that the petitioners were stopped on a traffic violation for speeding away from a stop sign and not using a turn signal, and since an actual traffic violation occurred, the personal intent of the officers does not affect the legality of the search and seizure. Whren and Brown were, in fact, in possession of crack cocaine, and they were sitting in an SUV in a "high drug area" of Washington, DC. "Driving while black" stops and Terry stops create daily problems for black men, who, to so many people, look "suspicious." And the officers stopping Whren and Brown on a legitimate traffic violation, just as the police officer in "99 Problems" stops Jay-Z/ the lyricist for a legitimate traffic violation—"Well you was doing fifty-five in a fifty-four"—raises concerns. My husband, who is a police officer, concedes that there are so many traffic codes that an officer does not have to watch or follow someone long before he or she violates one of the codes. Jay-Z, Whren, and Brown were wrong for breaking both traffic and criminal laws, but at the same time, there has never been a national phenomenon of white men being stopped, because, as white men, they do not "look" guilty. Thus, there is something wrong with a system that ascribes guilt to specific bodies. And as Jay-Z notes, he chose hustling because simply existing in East New York during the mid-1980s was such a precarious endeavor that, at thirteen years old, he "started to think that since I was risking my life anyway, I might as well get paid for it. It was that simple."[91]

Jay-Z emphasizes that rhyming is an art form and that he has always been conscious of the type of picture he wants to paint. He says he was not interested in painting pictures of violence and thug life, as was so common in hip-hop. Instead, he "was interested in something a little different: the interior space of a young kid's head, his psychology."[92] *Decoded*, ultimately, is not the autobiography of a superstar; simply telling his life story is not what the book is about. Just as he insists critics either do not bother to listen to his lyrics or simply do not possess the cultural competency to interpret the lyrics, he analyzes his life experiences and choices for readers who also might not know how to read him as a black boy living in the projects, former drug dealer, and entertainer. The first page of his book prepares a careful reader for what is to come when describing the Marcy Houses as being "like tunnels we kids burrowed through" and explaining that "housing projects can seem like labyrinths to outsiders, as complicated and intimidating as a Moroccan bazaar."[93] The five-sentence paragraph that begins the book is a prelude to the intellectual genealogy in the pages that follow. Jay-Z's vocabulary—"burrow," "labyrinth," "intimidating," and "bazaar"—is well developed and creative; he uses figurative language, and his prose is lyrical and registers knowledge of geography. In the first few pages that follow, he describes his fascination with rhyming and reveals that, in his preparation for rhyming battles, he spent his free time reading the dictionary to build his vocabulary.[94]

In the end, this book is propaganda, and that is fitting, for Garvey said the best way to fight propaganda is with propaganda. Although there was a time when even black radio stations would not play hip-hop, the genre is now global, but that does not mean the artistry of hip-hop is regularly acknowledged. One of Jay-Z's three goals in writing *Decoded* was to make the case that the hip-hop lyrics of every great MC are poetic. He makes his case by explicating the lyrics for readers. As he explicates lyrics and tells tales, readers are introduced to a black boy who imagined a self that was not what black or white society might think he was supposed to be. This boy gets caught in a world that can imagine no grace for poor black people, and, as a teenager and young man, he has to use his intellect to decide which world he wants to be in—the only one society can imagine a black boy from the projects inhabiting or the one he imagines. He imagines a world of contradictions, which is fitting given how messy and complicated the grace that

Baby Suggs tells folk they must imagine actually is; nothing is simple or comes easily in Morrison's philosophical stances. I think that people readily register Marcus Garvey as a revolutionary with a Pan-African nationalist agenda, and while Berry Gordy is not understood to be a revolutionary, his business enterprises were indeed revolutionary. Garvey wrote treatises that were rigidly prescribed and true to his investment in modernity; Gordy adhered to similar prescriptions through his investment in black middle-class respectability.

I do not think that people as readily view Jay-Z as a revolutionary, and I believe that is because he, too, is complicated. Jay-Z understands himself, and by extension, hip-hop, as full of contradictions, or as academics would say—postmodern. As an example, he describes the response from a journalist to his wearing a Che Guevara T-shirt and rapper Biggie Smalls's "Jesus piece" chain around his neck. The journalist asked: "You don't feel funny? You're wearing that Che T-shirt and you have—" She stopped speaking and motioned with her hands toward the chain around his neck, and then concluded, "I couldn't even concentrate on the music. . . . All I could think of is that big chain bouncing off of Che's forehead."[95] Jay-Z acknowledges being caught off guard and not having an answer for her because he had not thought about her perceived contradiction before. As food for thought, the journalist gave him a copy of an essay she had written about him. He actually read it and saw that she critiques him for calling himself "the soul of Mumia" on a track titled "Dope Man." She says he's almost convincing when rapping about representing for Rosa Parks, Malcolm X, and Martin Luther, but then she cites an MTV *Unplugged* show in which "he rocks his Guevara shirt and a do-rag, squint and you see a revolutionary. But open your eyes to the platinum chain around his neck: Jay-Z is a hustler."[96] He admits he could have been a "hater" and simply dismissed her critique, but, instead, he was fascinated by it and thought about it. He thought about Rosa, Malcolm, and Martin's "struggle" and concluded that the race leaders have disappeared, and the struggle is no longer organized or coherent—"There wasn't even a list of demands." His track "Public Service Announcement" provides him the opportunity to identify what connects the two struggles and to respond to the journalist. The second verse opens with the line "I'm like Che Guevara with bling on, I'm complex." His self-analysis resonates with the way Rebecca Walker and other third-wave feminists of color discuss fluid, malleable feminism. He explains that both he and Che share contradictions, and such contradictions are human. Although his rap is not explicitly revolutionary, he offers his own theory of semiotics in postmodern culture: "For any image or symbol or creative act to mean something, it has to touch something deeper, connect to something true."[97]

Jay-Z asserts: "Rap was the ideal way for me to make sense of a life that was doubled, split into contradictory halves. . . . Rap is built to handle contradictions."[98] The notion of contradictions is what makes Jay-Z function as a more compelling contemporary representative of how the hip-hop genealogy is pieced together. Among the other high-rolling hip-hop millionaires, Jay-Z stands out, because the significance of the relationship between black nationalism and black entrepreneurial prowess is reflected in his empire building—perhaps with contradictions, but it is there. Russell Simmons, Sean Combs, and Andre Young, aka Dr. Dre, all have philanthropic foundations and are brands—especially Dr. Dre—but there is something about Jay-Z that puts him, and not the others, on the president's speed dial.

Bow Down

That something of distinction, I would argue, is "Mrs. Carter." The odds of a drug dealer turned rapper turned entrepreneur being on the president's speed dial would seem highly improbable. In addition to performing at the eleventh-hour campaign rally for President Obama's reelection campaign, Jay-Z and his wife, Beyoncé Knowles, hosted a campaign fund-raising dinner at Jay-Z's New York City 40/40 Club in September 2012. This couple is an unlikely, but interesting, power duo. Barack and Michelle reign over the political realm, and Jay-Z and Beyoncé reign over the public sphere. Both of these relationships are essentially a partnership between two entrepreneurs who are exceptionally business savvy.

As the king of hip-hop and the queen of pop, Jay-Z and Beyoncé make a powerful couple. As entrepreneurs, they both reflect Jay-Z's rap about not being a businessman, but rather a business. As a couple, they have a net worth of over $1 billion; in Beyoncé's world, girls apparently do really run the world, because on *Forbes* magazine's most powerful celebrities list, she beats both her man and recent billionaire Dr. Dre when she comes in first place for 2014.[99] Her "Mrs. Carter Show World Tour 2014," according to *Forbes*, brought in an average $2.4 million at each of her ninety-five stops on the tour, which catapulted her to number one on the list. While successful, none of Jay-Z's fellow hip-hop businessmen have made their brand a family affair.

I am certain the everyday public takes pleasure in registering the duo's marriage as romantic, and their child makes them the hip-hop couple to love. Perhaps the marriage is romance and love, but it is also a brilliant business move, one that both Garvey and Gordy modeled, too. Garvey was married twice, both times to women named Amy. The first marriage to Amy Ashwood Garvey was short-lived and involved a messy divorce. The second marriage to Amy Jacques Garvey endured. What both wives have in common was their close work with Garvey in the movement. According to her biographer, Ula Taylor, in Jacques's own recorded descriptions of Garvey's impression of her, Jacques insists Garvey fell in love with her intellect, not her "feminine charms."[100] Jacques might have wanted to emphasize this point for more reasons than privileging her brain over her body: she lived in Garvey's home and traveled with him while he was still married to, but estranged from, his first wife; emphasizing that he was pleased with her efficiency and intelligence preserved a respectable womanhood. In fact, Taylor reveals that Jacques was invested in presenting a public image, at least, of her marriage as purely a business relationship. Jacques never suggests she was attracted to Garvey and proposes their marriage was strictly for the sake of the movement.[101] As reported by Jacques, Garvey chose her over his other "secretary," because Henrietta Vinton Davis was older than he was, and he wanted a son. Jacques ultimately positions herself as savvy, acknowledging, "Other eligible women among the membership . . . lacked the sum total qualities of what he wanted for a wife now—a stand-in, in an emergency."[102]

Perhaps Garvey was clairvoyant because he did soon need Jacques to repeatedly stand in during his emergency—being indicted for mail fraud and incarcerated. In addition to having, quite literally, to raise money for his legal fees and bail—because much to her surprise, they were broke—Garvey called upon Jacques to handle his business outside while he was incarcerated. At one point, this involved her bringing a gun to the office because a male UNIA employee had threatened to throw her down the stairs for reporting Black Star Line certificates he had lost.[103] Later, she also had to develop slick maneuvers to raise Garvey's defense funds and prevent them from being confiscated by the district attorney's office: she used banks in nearby states, a small bank in New York, and diverse routes for getting to the banks, to ensure she was not followed.[104] She even began giving propaganda speeches, much to the pleasure of Garveyites. Her intellect, determination, and rhetorical skills when subsuming his role garnered her praise from Garvey, "Now I have a rival, but I am glad she is my wife."[105]

Jay-Z's wife is Mrs. Carter, even if she is, sometimes, his "babymama," as in "Part II (On the Run)," and he is her "babydaddy" in her "Drunk in Love" video. They regularly express desire for one another through their song lyrics, music videos, and even Jay-Z's surprise appearance on stage with her during some of her Mrs. Carter Tour stops, which is different from Garvey's and Amy Jacques's account of the purpose of their marriage. On the business side, however, the Carters are a power partnership just like the Garveys, both working to build an empire, and neither seeming to resent the ascension of the other. Both Garvey and Jay-Z have an "Outlaw Chick" who will "hold your heart and your gun." In "Part II (On the Run)," an overture to the couple's first musical collaboration, "Bonnie & Clyde," Jay-Z raps that with "matching tatts," his "babymama harder than a lot of you niggas." The freedom to enter into contract granted by the 1866 Civil Rights Act becomes a double entendre for the Carters, as their marriage seems to be a play on and blurring of both business and marriage contracts.

Gordy also relied upon wives who were intricately involved in his business endeavors, but his sisters, especially Esther and Anna, seem to have been the more formidable businesswomen in his life. Moreover, Gordy lived his life and ran his business under strict rules of decorum and respectability—a team trained the artists in these performances—so there are no tantalizing accounts of mayhem and betrayal to recount in his case. There is, however, a class factor that links Gordy to Jay-Z in his "second life," the life of respectable husband and father, as opposed to drug hustler. Phillip Brian Harper makes the point that it was not as simple as Gordy offering whitewashed soul music to the world. The crossover appeal, according to Harper, is better "understood in terms of the manipulation of various class markers than in terms of the manipulation of the 'racial' identity of the musical products."[106] And that is where Gordy fits into the hip-hop genealogy; his crossover ventures and the tool he employs—a respectable black nationalism—open the doors for rap and, specifically, for Jay-Z to be in the boardroom.

Jay-Z swapped Pan-Africanist separatism for a new brand of nationalism, and even his crossover appeal differs from Gordy's prescriptive respectability in grooming his artists. Jay-Z ultimately links *swag* to grace. As a scared and careful child, to a stressed and cautious teen, the world of language was his safe retreat. In that space, amid dictionaries and hard tabletops, he manipulated language and rhythm to define a subjectivity far more complex and nuanced than that allotted to black boys and men in the Marcy Projects. It is a subjectivity full of contradictions. He stands in for the genteel patriarch in a white linen suit or through his clothing line at Barney's. He is the Self-Made Man, yet he is without doubt "Jigga that Nigga." Granted, he received a lot of breaks that enabled him to imagine the possibility that he could become the business maverick he is today, but Jay-Z recognized the relationship between nationalism, entrepreneurship, and redemption.

Black Boys Making Sense of Race

I would not say that my parents pretended race did not exist when I was growing up, but they certainly were not vocal about racial politics. What this means is that when I was maybe six years old and asked about the headline and accompanying image on the front page of our local newspaper addressing a Ku Klux Klan rally in my hometown, my mother matter-of-factly explained they were a racist organization who terrorized black people, and returned to whatever she was doing. It meant that, at probably too young an age, I would watch *Lady Sings the Blues* with my father and listen to his pointed answers to my inquiries about disturbing events in the film. It also meant that when my father was serving on our inner-city neighborhood commission, he would express frustration to my mother that only had meaning for me much later in life; he had been out asking neighbors to place paper-bag candles at the foot of their yards for Martin Luther King Day, and one of the few older white women left in the neighborhood spitefully retorted when asked, "Why can't you do anything for the Kennedy boys?" So, I heard my parents occasionally discuss race, but they did not politicize it; they just left it hanging there, I guess, for me to figure out on my own terms. In contrast, my oldest son often comments that everything I do at my job seems to be about African Americans. Something about his tone always makes me ask (similar to when he recently began commenting on my "big hair" when I don't flatiron it), "Is there anything wrong with that?" He always responds no, but seems deep in thought, too, so I never quite discern what he is really thinking—how he is piecing it all together in his head.

I could conclude this study by rehearsing the vicissitudes of black men's efforts to navigate spaces between the poles of pathology and celebrity, but I believe that would not be nearly as interesting as a brief glimpse into the minds of black boys, my boys, who never cease to fascinate me with their astute observations and the conclusions they draw. I am grateful that they have not yet begun to draw correlations between blackness and maleness, because that means my husband and I have had some success as we work vigilantly behind the scenes to protect them from some of the realities of *black maleness* that many of their black male peers have already experienced. I feel confident that attending what I refer to as their "racial uplift" school, Mansion Day School—a preschool–fifth grade preparatory school whose student body is almost exclusively black—has aided us in protecting them. Not yet being cognizant of the multidimensionality of *black maleness*, however, has not prevented them from trying to make sense of race.

Vignette 1: The War

July 24, 2013

Note: Seth and Isaac, my oldest boys, were seven and nine years old during the summer of 2013, which is when this story took place. Solon was two, so his race stories have not yet emerged, but, rest assured, Solon, your stories will one day be part of Mommy's work, too.

The kids were talking about their outdoor adventure camp during dinner, and Isaac pointed out that Seth was the only black kid in his group. Seth bluntly replied, "I know that," which was interesting because, at this time, Seth was a bit ambivalent about being black when he knows he is partly white (he has more European genomes than African). Isaac went on to point out that few black kids attended that camp, and asked why. I just said that's the way that camp is and pointed out that their basketball camp was nearly all black, which received the emphatic response from Seth, "That's because it's in the 'HOOD!'" I, then, asked if they notice when there aren't many black people at places, and they both quickly said yes. At that point, I thought Isaac said he wished he was white, but I guess he was actually saying a kid at school—a little chocolate one—wished he was white and has a white girlfriend. I asked why the kid wanted to be white. Isaac responded that white people are aliens, evil aliens, which produced lots of laughter from him and Seth.

In response, I asked Isaac if he ever wished he was white. He quickly said no and that black is better. I asked why black is better. He said because we won the war. I asked what war. He said the white-black people war. I said there was no such war. He said, yes, there was—the war when black people got their freedom. In case I did not understand, he explained that it is better to be black because we won. Isaac has always been very disturbed by the African American experience and not being able to understand why or how many white people could do the things they have done to black people. I had once thought that his rather blunt identification of and bewilderment around white people being in our family was because he was not sure about being black, but I now think it is because he perceives them to be evil aliens and black people to be superior because, well, black people won the war.

Vignette 2: White History Month

March 18, 2013

Isaac: Why isn't George Washington part of Black History Month?

Me: Because he wasn't black.

Isaac: Well, why don't we have White History Month (*sincerely*)?

Me: Every month is White History Month (*bluntly*).

Vignette 3: The Tan Americans

Spring 2009

Me: This is one of my favorite books (*opening Joy Harjo's* The Good Luck Cat). (*I stop reading when we get to the part about going to a powwow.*)

Me: Have you learned about Native Americans/American Indians at school (*Montessori*) yet?

Seth: No, we have only learned about Black-African Americans (*said with no sense of connection*).

Me: Well, you are a Black-African American.

Seth: (*Holding out his arm*) I am a Tan American.

Me: Well, have you learned about the Tan Americans yet?

Seth: No (*thoughtfully*).

For some time after this conversation, my husband and I would amuse ourselves by asking Seth if he had learned about Tan Americans yet in school. His answer remained the same—no.

Vignette 4: "I Don't Want to Be the Only One!"

There are two elite, coeducational private preparatory schools in central Ohio. In March 2013, when Seth was in third grade, he told his father he wanted to attend Wellington for middle school. I asked him why, and he said most of his friends were going there for middle school (we later concluded it was more about a specific girl who was going to go there). A week or so later, he told me he did not want to go to Columbus Academy, the other private prep school. When asked why, he said there are no black kids. I told him there were, and he insisted I was wrong; kids in his class visited the school. I assured him I knew of some black kids who went there, and one of my previous graduate students worked there and said there are black students (you can find them, if you look really hard). Out of curiosity, I asked why he would not want to go there if there were no black kids. "I don't want to be the only one!" he exclaimed.

Vignette 5: Bastions of Whiteness—Costco and Powell, Ohio

The entire family loves Costco. One day, during spring 2014, when Isaac and I were walking down the dairy aisle, Isaac asked why he hardly ever saw African Americans shopping at Costco. I explained that there are not a lot of African Americans who live in the part of town where that Costco is located. Fast forward to summer 2014, and out of the blue, he asks me if there will be other black kids at the neighborhood school he will switch to for the upcoming school year. I tell him there will not be many. He looks me in the eyes and asks, "Other than the lady across the street, why doesn't Powell have black people?" All I can say is that a lot of black people cannot afford to live in Powell. Isaac says, more than asking, "Because black people do not have as much money as white people." I confirm his conclusion, explaining that white people, generally, are wealthier than black people. He says, "So, we are really lucky."

Vignette 6: The Multiracial Dilemma

Race, like slavery, produced a truly peculiar institution. Trying to explain race to my children always requires that I ask them to suspend logical thinking in order to understand the illogical.

Every year, the boys' private school requires us to fill out reenrollment forms. For the 2013–14 school year, I decided to ask them how they wanted me to fill out the racial demographics section, ignoring my husband's directive to mark "African American." I was curious about how they were processing the idea of race, particularly in relationship to their own identity formations. Isaac immediately answered, "African American," which caused Seth to frown. After hearing all of the categories, Seth pointed to "Caucasian" and asked what it was. I said, "White." He frowned again, so I pointed to "multiracial" and I said because he is two races, he could chose that category if he preferred. His frown persisted, as he declared the list confusing and reluctantly settled on "multiracial."

Vignette 7: We Almost Had a Black President

Summer 2014
(*Driving in the car on a summer evening.*)
Isaac: I know who the first black president is.
Me: Who is it, Isaac?
Isaac: Barack Obama.
Seth: We almost had a black president before Barack Obama; it was Jesse Jackson.
Me: Jesse Jackson would have never been elected president.
Seth: Why not?
Me: Because he spoke in rhymes, but more seriously, because he was black, as well as saying bad things about Jewish people.

Vignette 8: Seth and Law Class

During the summer of 2014, I cotaught a law and culture seminar. Just before I left home for one of the final evenings of class, Seth and his father simply were not having a good day, so I told Seth to come to class with me. He attended class with me four or five years ago and found it incredibly boring, so I wondered if taking an almost eleven year old to a three-and-a-half-hour class was a good idea, but he had an epic Percy Jackson book he was reading. He did fine in class. He sat in the front row and seemed engrossed in his book, stopping now and then to look up or around the classroom. When we were driving to Chipotle—his favorite food choice and reward for behaving—he noted that the class was focused on "African American struggles." When I revisited his comment days later, he expounded by saying that he thought it was supposed to be a class about the law, but instead it focused on "African American struggles." I explained that the law and struggle are linked for African Americans, offering slavery and Jim Crow laws as examples. Isaac interrupted, "Yeah, yeah, we already know that—it's why African Americans don't have money."

The Last Word: Beautiful Black Boys and Grace

In these vignettes, I talk about black boys because it only seems logical when all black men were once black boys. The boyhood experiences of black men surely inform their adulthood efforts at subject making. That cute little boy my grandfather was so proud of in the portrait sitting on his piano had not yet been made aware of his blackness. He was black. He was poor. Yet, his confident smile reflects a self-assuredness that makes his extraordinary accomplishments defeating the odds not so surprising. My boys, thankfully, do not live in poverty as my grandfather did as the child of Georgia sharecroppers. They also do not live under Jim Crow laws. They will nonetheless experience racism, no doubt, and they will inevitably learn what it means in US society to be black and male. Given this demoralizing reality in a nation that touts democracy and is condescending toward nondemocratic nations, I can only hope that my husband and I, and all of the family and friends who love my children, can provide them with the tools to imagine grace. I have been blessed with three very strong-willed children—payback, my father tells me. I am confident that it is not their social class that will allow them to develop agentic senses of self—since many middle-class black boys and men are victims of various structural inequalities—it is their recognition that black is beautiful and worth loving. Blackness, as Baby Suggs insists, is something you yourself must love. Loving one's self is not going to fix a broken system, but self-love surely is critical to believing one is worthy of grace.

Notes

1. The Ohio State University, 2014–2015 Enrollment Report, http://enrollmentservices.osu.edu/report.pdf.
2. OSU provides enrollment statistics for "underrepresented" minorities as groups, but does not offer separate statistics that divide the racial groups along gender lines. However, a WOSU online news article from October 23, 2007, addresses the low African American enrollment and notes 2.5 percent are male and 4 percent female. I would imagine those numbers have changed as a result of the creation of the Bell National Resource Center to address low African American male enrollment among other issues affecting that group of students.
3. In every incident my husband has discussed with me, the assailants have never been students enrolled at OSU; they are instead members of the local black community that surrounds OSU, a low-income, working poor community that is steadily being displaced by OSU gentrification projects.
4. *Williams v. Alioto* (1977), 549 F.2d 136, http://openjurist.org/549/f2d/136. In this case, after seventeen white people were seemingly murdered at random by black assailants, the San Francisco Police Department declared a "stop and frisk" policy that relied on very generic suspect descriptions. A civil liberties suit was filed, but it was dismissed as moot because the killers were apprehended and "less objectionable" instructions were issued prior to apprehension. See Derrick Bell, *Race, Racism, and American Law,* 6th ed. (New York: Aspen, 2008).

5. In *Lankford v. Gelston* (1966), 364 F.2d 197, http://openjurist.org/364/f2d/ 197/samuel-james-lankford-v-gelston, the Baltimore Police Department conducted warrantless searches of over three hundred mostly private dwellings after one police officer was shot and another seriously injured; nearly every search was based upon unverified, anonymous tips.

6. Bell, *Race, Racism, and American Law*, 258.

7. "About Us," *Scholars Network on Black Masculinity*, 2009, http:// thescholarsnetwork.org/.

8. Ed Guerrero, "The Black Man on Our Screens and the Empty Space in Representation," *Callaloo* 18, no. 2 (Spring 1995): 395–400.

9. Amy Abugo Ongiri, "We Are Family: Miscegenation, Black Nationalism, Black Masculinity, and the Black Gay Cultural Imagination," in *Race-ing Representation: Voice, History, and Sexuality*, ed. Kostas Myrsiades and Linda Myrsiades (New York: Rowman and Littlefield, 1998), 231–46, 242.

10. Avery Gordon, *Ghostly Matters: Haunting and the Sociological Imagination* (Minneapolis: University of Minnesota Press, 1997), 139.

11. Toni Morrison, *Beloved* (1987; New York: Vintage Books, 2004), 102.

12. Ibid.

13. Phillip Brian Harper, *Are We Not Men? Masculine Anxiety and the Problem of African American Identity* (New York: Oxford University Press, 1996), x.

INTRODUCTION

1. Hazel V. Carby, *Race Men* (Cambridge, MA: Harvard University Press, 1998), 5.

2. https://www.whitehouse.gov/my-brothers-keeper.

3. The title of this section references an often-quoted line from Anna Julia Cooper's *A Voice from the South* (1892; New York: Oxford University Press, 1988), 31. Cooper, a renowned author, educator, and activist famously declared: "Only the BLACK WOMAN can say 'when and where I enter, in the quiet undisputed dignity of my womanhood, without violence and without suing or special patronage, then and there the whole Negro race enters with me.'" Paula J. Giddings borrows from this now often-cited passage when she titles her seminal work on African American women's history *When and Where I Enter: The Impact of Black Women on Race and Sex in America* (1984; New York: Morrow, 1996).

4. Beverly Guy-Sheftall and Evelyn M. Hammonds, "Whither Black Women's Studies: An Interview," *Differences* 9, no. 3 (1997): 31–45, 43.

5. Devon Carbado, ed., *Black Men on Race, Gender, and Sexuality: A Critical Reader* (New York: New York University Press, 1999).

6. Kimberlé Williams Crenshaw coined the term "intersectional" in her essay "Mapping the Margins: Intersectionality, Identity Politics, and Violence against Women of Color," *Stanford Law Review* 43, no. 6 (July 1991): 1241–99.

7. Athena Mutua, ed., *Progressive Black Masculinities* (New York: Routledge, 2006), xii (emphasis mine).

8. This absence is also glaring in the increasingly popular realm of the public intellectual. Aside from that of Melissa Harris-Perry, commentary by academics on any public issues relating to black people is relegated to black male scholars, and primarily black male scholars at Ivy League and elite East Coast institutions, such as Cornel West, Michael Eric Dyson, Henry Louis Gates Jr., and others.

    Joy James offers a very candid discussion of the patriarchal dominance she sees at play when black men enter black feminist discourse in "Antiracist (Pro)Feminisms and Coalition Politics: 'No Justice, No Peace,'" in *Men Doing Feminism*, ed. Tom Digby (New York: Routledge, 1998), as does Michele Wallace in her critique of Henry Louis Gates Jr.'s opportunistic role in the heyday of black feminist literary criticism in "Negative Images: Towards a Black Feminist Cultural Criticism" (master's thesis, City College of New York, 1990). James and Wallace raise important points that continue to be relevant.

9. Michael Awkward, "Black Feminism and the Challenge of Black Heterosexual Male Desire," *Souls* 2, no. 4 (2000): 32–37, 32.

10. Ibid., 33.

11. bell hooks, *We Real Cool: Black Men and Masculinity* (New York: Routledge, 2004), xiv. Prior to *We Real Cool*, hooks had interrogated the relationship between black men and feminism in *Feminist Theory: From Margin to Center* (Boston: South End Press, 1984).

12. hooks, *We Real Cool*, xv.

13. The success of Ntozake Shange's choreopoem, *for colored girls who have considered suicide when the rainbow is enuf* (1976), and Michele Wallace's *Black Macho and the Myth of the Superwoman* (1978) catalyzed a rather ugly debate regarding the themes and intent of black women's writing. Black male critics accused black women writers of castration, emasculation, being sexually repressed, battering the black man in return for popular media attention, and being brainwashed by white feminism. Black male scholars and critics like Robert Staples, Mel Watkins, David Bradley, Addison Gayle, Darryl Pinckney, and Ishmael Reed accused black women writers of being unduly influenced by white feminism and, thus, being rewarded by the white media, which explained black women's "unprecedented" literary popularity from the 1970s onward. Staples, for example, published a virulent response to Wallace's and Shange's work in his essay "The Myth of Black Macho: A Response to Angry Black Feminists," published in *The Black Scholar* 10, no. 6/7 (March/April 1979): 24–33.

    In "Reading Family Matters," in *Changing Our Own Words: Essays on Criticism, Theory, and Writing by Black Women*, ed. Cheryl A. Wall (New Brunswick, NJ: Rutgers University Press, 1989), Deborah E. McDowell argues that these responses are grounded in a "family romance" that black women writers are determined to deromanticize. Black male opposition to black women's writing consistently reiterated family unity. According to these black male critics, when black women writers depicted the hetero-sexual fissures and negative images of the black family, especially negative acts performed by black men, they betrayed the black "community." They were not only airing black America's dirty laundry, so to speak, but they were also contesting sexual hierarchies that the responding male critics apparently did not view as problematic. The bottom line for the male critics was that race allegiance ought to trump awareness along sexual lines. McDowell argues that the black male readers of the debate possess gazes that are fixed on themselves—they mourn the black male writers' loss of status as a result of black women writers' being "midwifed" by white feminists.

14. Hazel V. Carby, *Reconstructing Womanhood: The Emergence of the Afro-American Woman Novelist* (New York: Oxford University Press, 1987).

15. Michele Wallace, *Black Macho and the Myth of the Superwoman* (1979; New York: Verso, 2015).

16. Mark Anthony Neal, "Critical Noir: Taking One for the Team—Michele Wallace," *AOL BLACK VOICES*, Time Warner, March 2, 2005.

17. Rudolph Byrd and Beverly Guy-Sheftall, eds., *Traps: African American Men on Gender and Sexuality* (Bloomington: Indiana University Press, 2001)

18. Aaronette M. White, *Ain't I a Feminist? African American Men Speak Out on Fatherhood, Friendship, Forgiveness, and Freedom* (Albany: State University of New York Press, 2008).

19. Candice Marie Jenkins, *Private Lives, Proper Relations: Regulating Black Intimacy* (Minneapolis: University of Minnesota Press, 2007).

20. Nicole R. Fleetwood, *Troubling Vision: Performance, Visuality, and Blackness* (Chicago: University of Chicago Press, 2011).

21. Ann DuCille, "The Occult of True Black Womanhood," in *Skin Trade* (Cambridge, MA: Harvard University Press, 1996), 95.

22. See Gail Bederman, *Manliness and Civilization: A Cultural History of Gender and Race in the United States, 1880–1917* (Chicago: University of Chicago Press, 1996); E. Anthony Rotundo, *American Manhood: Transformations in Masculinity from the Revolution to the Modern Era* (New York: Basic Books, 1993); and Michael Kimmel, *Manhood in America: A Cultural History* (New York: Free Press, 1996).

23. Greg Tate, *Flyboy in the Buttermilk* (New York: Fireside, 1992).

24. In the past two decades, a growing cadre of scholars working on black masculinity studies have identified black feminist criticism and theory as integral to their work. These scholars include Marlon B. Ross, *Manning the Race: Reforming Black Men in the Jim Crow Era* (New York: New York University Press, 2004); David Ikard, *Breaking the Silence: Toward a Black Male Feminist Criticism* (Baton Rouge: Louisiana State University Press, 2007); Rolland Murray, *Our Living Manhood: Literature, Black Power, and Mascu-*

line Ideology (Philadelphia: University of Pennsylvania Press, 2007); and Maurice O. Wallace, *Constructing the Black Masculine: Identity and Ideality in African American Men's Literature and Culture, 1775–1995* (Durham, NC: Duke University Press, 2002).

25. The history I invoke has been percolating for nearly forty years in both the media and academia. The public black male backlash toward black feminists and black women writers during the 1970s has been repeated numerous times since then and is exemplified in uncivil debates between Henry Louis Gates Jr. and Houston Baker, as they tag-teamed Joyce Ann Joyce in a debate on the black literary canon and criticism; Molefi Asante, former chair of Temple University's Black Studies Department, his brainchild, and his successor, Joyce Ann Joyce; and most recently, Cornel West and Melissa Harris-Perry, as West threw noncollegial, sexist rhetorical jabs.

26. Two studies presented at the 2015 American Educational Research Association propose that universities' public responses to racial crises are more invested in public relations and image than actually addressing racism. See "Colleges Respond to Racist Incidents as If Their Chief Worry Is Bad PR, Study Finds," *Chronicle of Higher Education*, http://chronicle.com/article/Colleges-Respond-to-Racist/229517.

27. Butler identifies four other metatexts: claims that fault African American women for African American men's social, political, and economic subordination; the claim that it is more important to remedy African American men's problems than those of African American women; the suggestion that African American men have been more adversely affected by white supremacy than have African American women; and the claim that recuperation of a black heteromasculine power structure ought to be a matter of public policy. Paul D. Butler, "Black Exceptionalism? The Problems and Potential of Black Male-Focused Interventions," *Du Bois Review* 10, no. 2 (2013): 485–511. 488, 492.

28. My grandfather's surname was actually Booth without the letter *e* on the end, but the story my mother tells is that when he enlisted in the military, his penmanship was so sloppy that the army interpreted his script as Booth*e*, which officially made him Gilbert A. Boothe.

29. Jeanes Supervisors are named after Anna T. Jeanes, a wealthy Quaker who donated $1 million in 1907 to create a program to improve education for blacks in rural southern schools.

CHAPTER ONE

1. Susan Neal Mayberry's *Can't I Love What I Criticize? The Masculine and Morrison* (Athens, GA: University of Georgia Press, 2007) takes up this issue.

2. Bederman, *Manliness and Civilization*, 180, 187.

3. Kimmel, *Manhood in America*.
4. Morrison, *Beloved*, 322.
5. Ibid., 133.
6. Ibid., 8–9.
7. Ibid., 81.
8. Ibid., 21.
9. Ibid., 321.
10. Ibid., 322.
11. Mark Anthony Neal, *New Black Man* (New York: Routledge, 2005).
12. http://www.huffingtonpost.com/2012/08/10/owens-gay-marriage-civil -rights_n_1764570.html.
13. The Lilly Ledbetter Fair Pay Act of 2009 is named after Lilly Ledbetter, who worked at a Goodyear Tire plant in Alabama and sued her employer when she found out that her male coworkers were paid more than she was.
14. Mariel Concepcion, "Eric Benet Says Lil Wayne Shout Was 'Huge Compliment,'" *Billboard.com*, October 6, 2010, http://www.billboard.com/columns/ the-juice/955032/eric-benet-says-lil-wayne-shout-was-huge-compliment.
15. *Rainbow* was the term used to describe the pickaxes used by chain gang workers because the reflection of the sun on the pickax's metal would create a rainbow effect on the metal.
16. Although "Rainbow" would often have a ethnically mixed ensemble of performers—mostly Asian and black men—the politics driving the performance were always entangled in a paradigm of resistance for marginalized men.
17. It is interesting that Richard Pryor stars in Paul Schrader's *Blue Collar* (1978), which in many ways offers a more developed scenario of the "everyblackman" Willy represents.
18. "Industrial Metamorphosis," *Economist*, September 29, 2005, http://www .economist.com/node/4462685.
19. Thomas LeClair, *New Republic*, http://www.newrepublic.com/article/books -and-arts/magazine/95923/the-language-must-not-sweat.
20. *My Brother's Keeper Task Force Report to the President*, https://www.white house.gov/sites/default/files/docs/053014_mbk_report.pdf.
21. Council on Women and Girls, https://www.whitehouse.gov/adminis tration/eop/cwg/data-on-women.
22. US Department of Commerce, *Women in America: Indicators of Social and Economic Well-being*, https://www.whitehouse.gov/sites/default/files/rss_viewer/ Women_in_America.pdf.
23. Ibid., 29.
24. Ibid., 31.
25. Ibid., 32.
26. *My Brother's Keeper Task Force Report to the President*, 5.

27. Ibid., 8.
28. Teaming up with "celebrities, athletes, CEOs and current and former government officials, including singer John Legend, former Pittsburgh Steeler Jerome Bettis, NBA legend Shaquille O'Neal, former Attorney General Eric Holder, former Secretary of State General Colin Powell, and Democratic Sen. Cory Booker of New Jersey" the foundation mirrors MBK. http://www.cnn.com/2015/05/04/politics/president-barack-obama-brothers-keeper/.
29. See, for example, Monique W. Morris's *Pushout: The Criminalization of Black Girls in Schools* (New York: New Press, 2016), in which she identifies how black girls also experience discipline and educational achievement disparities, but for different reasons than boys. Threats of violence, for example, are a critical factor in the overdiscipline of black boys, whereas black girls are disproportionately punished for failing to conform to white gender standards of female respectability. http://aapf.org/wp-content/uploads/2012/08/Morris-Race-Gender-and-the-School-to-Prison-Pipeline.pdf.
30. Lincoln's essay was published in the September 1966 issue of *Negro Digest*.
31. https://www.whitehouse.gov/the-press-office/2013/07/19/remarks-president-trayvon-martin.
32. Connie H. Choi and Eugene Tsai, eds., *Kehinde Wiley: A New Republic* (New York: Brooklyn Museum and Delmonico Press, 2015), 123.
33. Mark Anthony Neal, *Looking for Leroy: Illegible Black Masculinities* (New York: NYU Press, 2013), 5, 8.
34. This portrait appropriates Jacques-Louis David's *Napoleon Bonaparte Crossing the Alps at Great St. Bernard Pass* (1801).
35. Yellow is the first color the human eye sees and can therefore be a visual irritant if used in large areas.
36. Robert Mapplethorpe, *The Black Book* (Boston: Bullfinch, 1986).
37. Kobena Mercer, "Just Looking for Trouble: Robert Mapplethorpe and Fantasies of Race," in *Black British Cultural Studies: A Reader*, ed. Houston A. Baker Jr. et al. (Chicago: University of Chicago Press, 1996), 283.
38. Ibid.
39. Kobena Mercer, "The Down Series," in Choi and Tsai, *Kehinde Wiley*, 81.
40. Robert Hobbs, "Kehinde Wiley's Conceptual Realism," *Kehinde Wiley* (New York: Rizzoli), 18.
41. Frederick Hartt, *Art: A History of Painting, Sculpture, and Architecture*, 4th ed. (New York: Prentice Hall, 1993), 1:292.
42. Ibid., 447.
43. *Kehinde Wiley: An Economy of Grace*, directed by Jeff Dupre (PBS, 2014).
44. This is something John Singer Sargent learned when he incorporated a small yet risqué innuendo (one gown strap hanging off the shoulder) in his portrait *Madame X*.
45. Hortense J. Spillers, "Mama's Baby, Papa's Maybe: An American Grammar Book," *Diacritics* 17, no. 2 (Summer 1987): 64–81, 65.

46. Karyn B. Collins, "Kehinde Wiley: Portraits in Black," http://fashion reverie.com/?p=10699.
47. I am disturbed by this model's absence in the exhibition book. Her visage is beautiful and offers a contrast to the hard expressions of the other models. The fact that in the documentary there is a discussion about haute couture not being designed for black bodies, and then to have a full-busted, fuller-figured model be excluded from the book, is problematic.

CHAPTER TWO

1. A version of this chapter was originally published as "'So I Decided to Quit It and Try Something Else for a While': Reading Agency in Nat Love," in *Fathers, Preachers, Rebels, Men: Black Masculinity in U.S. History and Literature, 1820–1945*, ed. Peter Caster and Timothy R. Buckner (Columbus: Ohio State University Press, 2011).
2. Elizabeth Alexander, *The Black Interior: Essays* (St. Paul, MN: Graywolf, 2004), x.
3. Athena Matua elucidates this point in the introduction to her edited collection *Progressive Black Masculinities*, when she describes how certain discriminatory acts experienced by black men are unique and specifically perpetrated because of both their blackness and maleness.
4. Alexander, *The Black Interior*, x.
5. The published title is *The Life and Adventures of Nat Love Better Known in the Cattle Country as Dead Wood Dick By Himself; A True History of Slavery Days, Life on the Great Cattle Ranges and the Plains of the "Wild and Woolly" West, Based on Facts, and Personal Experiences of the Author.*
6. Racial uplift is an ideology that emerged in black political discourse after emancipation. Black "race men" and "race women" worked to uplift the race, primarily through the adoption and performance of white middle-class values. Kevin K. Gaines, *Uplifting the Race: Black Leadership, Politics, and Culture in the Twentieth Century* (Chapel Hill: University of North Carolina Press, 1996), xiv, explains the purpose of racial uplift in the following terms: "Generally, black elites claimed class distinctions, indeed, the very existence of a "better class" of blacks, as evidence of what they called race progress. Believing that the improvement of African Americans' material and moral condition through self-help would diminish white racism, they sought to rehabilitate the race's image by embodying respectability, enacted through an ethos of service to the masses."
7. Drake, "'So I Decided to Quit It.'"
8. For an argument about the erasure of race, see Georgina Dodge, "Claiming Narrative, Disclaiming Race: Negotiating Black Masculinity in *The Life and Adventures of Nat Love*," *a/b: Auto/Biography Studies* 16, no. 1 (Summer 2001): 109–26.
9. Mark Twain's *Adventures of Huckleberry Finn* (1885) serves as an example,

with many textual parallels with Love, of how one creates a space for reimagination. A significant difference being Twain's departures are canonized and Love's are subordinated in a "field" so intent on constructing itself in specific ways that it ignores the "freedoms" Love's narrative might offer.

10. Nat Love, *The Life and Adventures of Nat Love, Better Known in the Cattle Country as "Deadwood Dick"* (Lincoln: University of Nebraska Press, 1995), 130.

11. Emmanuel Chukwudi Eze, *Race and the Enlightenment: A Reader* (New York: Wiley-Blackwell, 1997), 2–3.

12. Ibid., 5.

13. Michael Omi and Howard Winant, *Racial Formation in the United States: From the 1960s to the 1990s* (New York: Routledge, 1994), 61–62.

14. Ibid., 64.

15. Kimmel, *Manhood in America*, 13.

16. Ibid., 15.

17. See Stephen Jay Gould, *The Mismeasure of Man* (1981; New York: W.W. Norton, 1996).

18. Kimmel, *Manhood in America*, 68.

19. Shirley Ann Wilson Moore, "'We Feel the Want of Protection': The Politics of Law and Race in California, 1848–1878," *California History* 81, no. 3/4 (2003): 96–125, 103, http://www.jstor.org/stable/25161701.

20. Ibid., 109.

21. Ibid.

22. For full details of the court proceedings, see William E. Franklin's "The Archy Case: The California Supreme Court Refuses to Free a Slave." *Pacific Historical Review* 32, no. 2 (May 1963): 137–54.

23. California jurisprudence was often viciously discriminatory toward Chinese Americans, and much of the social progress afforded to African Americans during this time was not extended to Chinese Americans.

24. Lawrence B. de Graaf, "The City of Black Angels: Emergence of the Los Angeles Ghetto, 1890–1930," *Pacific Historical Review* 39, no. 3 (1970): 323–52, 326, http://www.jstor.org/stable/3637655.

25. Love appears in the US Census as residing in Salt Lake City, Utah, in 1890, and residing in California in 1900, 1910, and 1920.

26. De Graaf, "The City of Black Angels," 329.

27. Ibid., 332.

28. Ibid.

29. Quoted in Lonnie G. Bunch III, "'The Greatest State for the Negro': Jefferson L. Edmonds, Black Propagandist of the California Dream," in *Seeking El Dorado: African Americans in California*, ed. Lawrence B. de Graaf, Kevin Mulroy, and Quintard Taylor (Los Angeles: Autry Museum of Western Heritage/Seattle, University of Washington, 2001), 129–48, 129.

30. Quoted in de Graaf, "The City of Black Angels," 334; de Graaf quotes the passage as cited in Charlotta Bass's *Forty Years* (Los Angeles, 1960), 14.

31. The 1910 census lists Love as renting a home in Malibu, California.
32. Over time, and especially during the early twentieth century, which ethnic groups were granted the status of "white" varied and changed.
33. Love, *The Life and Adventures*, 153.
34. Jean Toomer, *Cane*, ed. Darwin T. Turner (1923: New York: W.W. Norton, 1988), 42.
35. Ibid.
36. Ibid.
37. Walter Mosley, *Devil in a Blue Dress* (1990; New York: Washington Square Press, 2002), 56–57.
38. *Devil in a Blue Dress* is set in Los Angeles in the late 1940s, a period when clearly defined slums emerged, and strong racial hostility was directed toward African Americans.
39. Mosley, *Devil in a Blue Dress*, 253.
40. See Cheryl I. Harris, "Whiteness as Property," *Harvard Law Review* 106, no. 8 (June 1993): 1707–91.
41. *Los Angeles Investment Company v. Gary*, 181 Cal. 680; *Title Guarantee and Trust Co. v. Garratt*; and *Jones and Guatier v. Berlin Realty Company*.
42. Bunch, "'The Greatest State for the Negro.'"
43. Wahneema Lubiano, "Black Nationalism and Black Common Sense: Policing Ourselves and Others," in *The House That Race Built: Black Americans, U.S. Terrains*, ed. Wahneema Lubiano (New York: Pantheon, 1997), 232–52, 232.
44. Ibid., 233.
45. Karen Odom, "Black Men in the Saddle," *Ebony Jr.*, January 1978, 12–14.
46. William Loren Katz, "Reprinting the Negro Past," *Crisis* 76, no. 3 (March 1969): 122–28, 123.
47. John Wideman, "West of the Rockies: The Brief Saga of Deadwood Dick, Aunt Clara Brown, and Today's Black Pioneers Who've Sought Greater Horizons and Found Them," *Black Enterprise*, June 1977, 159–66, 186–87, 159.
48. Ibid., 166.
49. "The Old West Heritage Revived," *Washington Afro-American* (Washington, DC), February 22, 1977, 8.
50. Gary Coleman was a child actor whose fame is attached to the television sitcom *Different Strokes*, which aired from 1978 through 1986 and featured Coleman and his television brother as orphaned Harlemites who are taken in by a wealthy white Park Avenue businessman who employed their mother prior to her death.
51. "White Heroes Replaced in Coleman's TV Movie," *Jet*, July 25, 1983, 55.
52. "Those Early-Day Cowboys Weren't All Nordic Types," *Lewiston Morning Tribune* (Lewiston, ID), February 21, 1965, 4.
53. Robert W. Peterson, "Black Cowboys," *Boys' Life: The Magazine for All Boys*, April 1994, 10.

54. *Billboard*, February 17, 1996, 70.
55. Raymond W. Lowry, "Nat 'Deadwood Dick' Love: 1854–c. 1910," *Virgin Islands Daily News* (St. Thomas, VI), June 30, 1970, 13.
56. A 1974 issue of *Crisis* includes a poem by Lee Bennett Hopkins that he most likely wrote when he was using the work of black poets to reach children he was teaching in Harlem; his style is not nearly as sophisticated as Alexander's, but it does demonstrate an earlier interest in memorializing Love through poetry.
57. hooks makes this statement in Marlon Riggs's documentary, *Black Is, Black Ain't*.
58. Ross, *Manning the Race*, 92–93.
59. Love, *The Life and Adventures*, 103.
60. Ibid., 18.
61. Ibid., 21.
62. Ibid., 30.
63. Ibid., 41.
64. Ibid., 42–43.
65. See Bederman, *Manliness and Civilization*.
66. Love, *The Life and Adventures*, 105.
67. "Director's Commentary," *Blazing Saddles*, directed by Mel Brooks (Warner Home Studio, 2007), DVD, 30th anniversary special edition.
68. Lyle mistakenly refers to "Camptown Races" as "The Camptown Lady."
69. Love, *The Life and Adventures*, 24.
70. Quoted in Eze, *Race and the Enlightenment*, 55.
71. Ibid., 38.
72. Love, *The Life and Adventures*, 130 (emphasis mine).
73. Ibid., 147.

CHAPTER THREE

1. My mother and her sister—my uncle kept out of it—had stopped speaking to one another the previous year when my grandmother died from cancer. My mother, aunt, and grandfather had ugly disagreements around money and the hospice care my mother provided for my grandmother—disagreements so shameful, they are best left unspoken.
2. My grandfather's surname was actually spelled Booth, with no *e* at the end. See introduction, note 21.
3. He enlisted August 9, 1940.
4. When my mother's sister learned I was writing about her father, she did share what she knew—some stories told by him and others that her older cousin, who also served in the armed forces, had told her.
5. Morrison, *Beloved*, 323 (emphasis mine).
6. Ibid., 324.

7. In his monograph *Freedom with Violence: Race, Sexuality, and the US State* (Durham, NC: Duke University Press, 2011) Chandan Reddy uses this term to address the contradictions inherent in the 2010 National Defense Authorization Act (NDAA). The Matthew Shepard and James Byrd, Jr., Hate Crimes Prevention Act was attached to the original bill by Congress. The NDAA is passed every year by Congress and establishes a budget for the Department of Defense. The inherent violence of warfare is counterintuitive to an amendment that protects US citizens from violence based upon their actual or perceived gender, sexual orientation, gender identity, or disability.

8. Morrison, *Beloved*, 317.

9. My grandfather was known for not liking clutter and throwing away items he deemed unneeded, sometimes even when they were needed.

10. Clarence Taylor, "Patriotism Crosses the Color Line: African Americans in World War II," *History Now: The Journal of the Gilda Lehrman Institute*, http://www.gilderlehrman.org/history-by-era/world-war-ii/essays/patriotism-crosses-color-line-african-americans-world-war-ii.

11. "The Beginnings of a New Era for African-Americans in the Armed Forces," *Fact Sheet*, http://www.nj.gov/military/korea/factsheets/afroamer.html.

12. In 1866 Congress created six segregated army units. African American soldiers eventually became called Buffalo Soldiers because of their participation in postbellum Indian wars. They were given their name by western Plains Indian tribes who thought the dark, woolly-texture hair of the black soldiers resembled the fur of buffaloes.

13. I am indebted to my good friend Captain Tiffany Cullens (US Army) for pointing out to me what a treasure I had and why it was a treasure.

14. Hondon B. Hargrove, *Buffalo Soldiers in Italy: Black Americans in World War II* (Jefferson, NC: McFarland, 1985), viii.

15. Ibid.

16. Randolph had successfully petitioned President Franklin Roosevelt to desegregate the defense industries on June 25, 1941, through Executive Order No. 8802, but it would take nearly a decade before military units would be desegregated, too.

17. I owe gratitude to my colleague Devin Fergus for pushing me to think about how the concept of crisis might shape how I tell and analyze my grandfather's story.

18. "Melting away" was a pejorative phrase commonly used by white commanding officers to describe black infantrymen and combat troops in an effort to depict them as incompetent, cowardly, and ultimately incapable of efficient combat service.

19. Quoted in Hargrove, *Buffalo Soldiers in Italy*, 128.

20. See Bederman, *Manliness and Civilization*, 1–2.

21. Hargrove, *Buffalo Soldiers in Italy*, 78, 139. Hargrove is particularly critical of General Almond for consistently failing to speak up in defense of his soldiers when Truscott and Clark would lambaste them.
22. There is a notation that it was a "temporary" assignment.
23. Hargrove, *Buffalo Soldiers in Italy*, 139.
24. Hargrove, "Author's Note," *Buffalo Soldiers in Italy*, iv.
25. Quoted in Hargrove, *Buffalo Soldiers in Italy*, 5.
26. Quoted in Hargrove, *Buffalo Soldiers in Italy*, 9.
27. Hargrove, *Buffalo Soldiers in Italy*, 9.
28. Lloyd French, "Comments of 366th Infantry Veterans Attending Their 41st Reunion at Fort Devens, Massachusetts and the Presentation of the Distinguished Service Cross to Mrs. Arlene Fox, Widow of Lieutenant John R. Fox," Black Military Oral History Project (transcription) 8, Howard University Archives, Moorland-Spingarn Research Center, Howard University, 4.
29. His first wife died.
30. Hondon Hargrove, "Il Corsaro: A Story of War and Friendship," *Michigan History* 64, no. 1 (Jan./Feb. 1980): 14–18, 18.
31. Daniel K. Inouye, *Journey to Washington* (Englewood Cliffs, NJ: Prentice Hall, 1967), 157.
32. Chester Himes, *If He Hollers Let Him Go* (1945; New York: Thunder's Mouth Press, 1986), 203.
33. Ibid.
34. Michael Kilian, "Army Removes Cloud over Black Korean War Unit," *Chicago Tribune*, April 30, 1996, http://articles.chicagotribune.com/1996 -04-30/news/9604300190_1_24th-infantry-regiment-white-units-official -army-report.
35. Fred L. Borch III, "The Largest Murder Trial in the History of the United States: The Houston Riots Courts-Martial of 1917," *Army Lawyer*, March 2012, 28.
36. Ibid.
37. Henry Louis Gates Jr., "Tarantino 'Unchained,' Part 1: 'Django' Trilogy?," *The Root*, December 23, 2012, http://www.theroot.com/articles/history/ 2012/12/django_unchained_trilogy_and_more_tarantino_talks_to_gates .html.
38. Ibid.
39. My grandfather and his cousins had watched the 1996 film adaptation of John Grisham's novel *A Time to Kill*, starring Samuel L. Jackson and Matthew McConaughey. The film chronicles the rape, beating, and attempted murder of a ten-year-old black girl in rural Mississippi. When the girl survives and identifies the two white assailants, they are arrested, but her father fears the jury will acquit them. Taking the law into his own hands, he shoots and kills both rapists outside of the courthouse and inadvertently shoots a court deputy in the leg. The district attorney seeks the

death penalty, and when a guilty verdict seems imminent, the defense attorney appeals to the jury's twisted moral codes by asking the jury to close its eyes, describing the lurid details of the girl's assault, and then, asking the jury to imagine it was a white girl. The film concludes with the white lawyer inviting himself and his family to a cookout at the black victim's home, explaining that he wants their children to play together.

40. Christopher Jordan Dorner was a real-life black man who did, in fact, exact revenge for real or imagined racist experiences with the Los Angeles Police Department. After writing a manifesto in which he declared he would take vengeance upon the LAPD, Dorner initiated a nine-day police manhunt as the LAPD and other law enforcement agencies tried to capture him and bring him to justice for murdering two civilians and two police officers, as well as injuring other police officers and civilians. Dorner reportedly died from a self-inflicted gunshot wound to the head when he was barricaded in a cabin engulfed in flames on February 12, 2013.

41. French, "Comments of 366th Infantry Veterans."

42. Robert A. Brown, "Interview," October 28, 1981, with Colonel John Thomas Martin, Black Military Oral History Project 5, Howard University Archives, Moorland-Spingarn Research Center, Howard University.

43. My grandmother died in September 1997 from cancer. My grandfather died in May 1998, when he had a heart attack on a golf course. My uncle died in November 1998 from a massive heart attack caused by a cocaine overdose. It was tragic.

44. My mother was not a good sister to her siblings in childhood or adulthood and because of what was probably undiagnosed bipolar disorder, growing up as her sibling and as her child was incredibly unpleasant. I would imagine my mother has no regret or sense of culpability for the beating my aunt received. In my mother's mind, she is not flawed; it is everyone else who has problems.

45. My grandfather is the very young man in the top right photo, sitting farthest to the left and looking over his shoulder. The caption to the left notes he is Sgt. Gilbert Booth of Forsythe, GA. http://www.history.army .mil/photos/WWII/maneuvers/maneuvers.htm.

46. I have no proof, but I do often wonder if my grandfather reserved so much disgust for his wife and children, and not his extended family, because his immediate family looked like his oppressor. My grandmother immigrated from Germany when my grandfather was assigned to a US base toward the end of his military career. My grandfather had a light complexion, and his children consequently did not look phenotypically black. He, thus, lived in a household in which only he would be subjected to racial prejudice.

47. I found the "list" separate from the military material, which was arranged in orderly folders. The list, however, was in his old briefcase. Other material included his college and graduate school transcripts, cards of appreciation from work, a letter he wrote to someone about chaperoning

my cousin's middle-school trip to Washington, DC, and numerous photo-copies of "dirty jokes," which I assume he had circulated at work.

CHAPTER FOUR

1. An earlier version of this chapter was published as "More than National-ism in Charles Burnett's *Killer of Sheep* and Kasi Lemmons's *Talk to Me*," *Spectrum* 1, no. 2 (2013): 29–54. © Reprinted with permission of Indiana University Press.
2. The acronym HBCU stands for Historically Black Colleges and Universities.
3. As an academic whose research engages popular culture, I am now well aware that *The Cosby Show* was a groundbreaking show, and I am also aware of the critics who ironically whined about the show not represent-ing all black families, as if all black families could ever be represented in one situational comedy, or as if *Good Times* or *The Jeffersons* represented all black families. *Good Times* aired on CBS from 1974 to 1979. It was created and produced by Norman Lear and set in the now-demolished, infamous Cabrini-Green housing projects in Chicago, Illinois. *The Jeffersons* also aired on CBS and ran from 1975 to 1985; it was one of the longest-airing sitcoms.
4. The full name of the case: *Hwesu S. Murray v. National Broadcasting Company, Inc., Brandon Tartikoff, The Carsey-Werner Company, a California Partnership, Marcia Carsey and Thomas Werner* (1987).
5. This program is administered by the US Department of Health and Human Services.
6. Gordon, *Ghostly Matters*, 166.
7. Spillers, "Mama's Baby, Papa's Maybe," 66.
8. *Murray v. National Broadcasting Co., Inc.*, S.D.N.Y., July 15, 1987, 671 F.Supp., 236.
9. Ibid., 239.
10. Ibid., 239–40.
11. Ibid., 239.
12. Ibid., 240.
13. Ibid., 241.
14. Deborah A. Levine has concluded that Murray's fusing was not as "sim-plistic" as the court suggests. Citing *McGhan v. Ebersol* (1985) and *Ed Graham Productions v. National Broadcasting Company* (1973), Levine dem-onstrates how previous New York jurisprudence supports Murray's claim. The test for novelty in these cases was not whether individual elements of an idea are "original," but whether the combination of multiple elements is novel. According to Levine, Murray easily passed this test, as well as the *Stanley* test by which a new twist on an old idea is understood to be an entirely new idea. She also finds that under the Nimmer Treatise on copy-

right law, and the "elaborated idea" test, Murray would prevail and hold an undeniable interest in the concept. Entertainment law attorney Richard J. Greenstone argues that if Murray had sued on a copyright cause of action, he would have prevailed because copyright law requires independent creation, not novelty. The conclusions reached by both legal scholars and a rather persuasive dissent, arguing that the defendant considered the idea novel when they described it as "unique intellectual property" in the remedies section of the contract, raise questions about why Murray's case was dismissed under summary judgment and was not tried by a jury. Deborah A. Levine, "*The Cosby Show*: Just Another Sitcom," *Loyola of Los Angeles Entertainment Law Review* 9, no. 1 (1989): 137–51; Richard J. Greenstone, "'It's Not Sufficiently Novel,' Held the Judge," *Entertainment and Sports Law* 6, no. 2 (Fall 1987): 5–7.

15. *Murray v. NBC*, 241.
16. Ibid., 245–46.
17. Ibid., 240.
18. Moynihan describes the black urban family as a "tangle of pathology." US Department of Labor, *The Negro Family: The Case for National Action* (Washington, DC: Department of Labor, Office of Policy Planning and Research, March 1965), 30.
19. Lisa Duggan, *The Twilight of Equality? Neoliberalism, Cultural Politics, and the Attack on Democracy* (Boston: Beacon Press, 2003), x.
20. Ibid.
21. Anthony B. Aktinson et al., "Top Incomes in the Long Run of History," *Journal of Economic Literature* 49, no. 1 (2011): 3–71, 6. http://eml.berkeley .edu/~saez/atkinson-piketty-saezJEL10.pdf.
22. Ibid.
23. Tim Koechlin, "The Rich Get Richer: Neoliberalism and Soaring Inequality in the United States," *Challenge* 56, no. 2 (March/April 2013): 5–30.
24. Ibid., 10–11.
25. Ibid., 11.
26. For more on income inequality, see Nobel Prize-winning economist Joseph E. Stiglitz's *The Price of Inequality: How Today's Divided Society Endangers Our Future* (New York: W.W. Norton, 2012).
27. Koechlin, "The Rich Get Richer," 4.
28. Duggan, *The Twilight of Equality?* xxii.
29. US Dept. of Labor, *The Negro Family*, 30.
30. Ibid., 16.
31. Ibid., 30.
32. Jessica Dixon Weaver, "The First Father: Perspectives on the President's Fatherhood Initiative," *Family Court Review* 50, no. 2 (2012): 297–309, 297.
33. Ibid., 299.
34. In February 2013, not long after his State of the Union address, President Obama spoke in Chicago. While some of what he said resonated with

people and was a repetition of national concerns he had addressed previously, in noting the unprecedented increase in gun violence over the past year he focused on families and proposed incentives to encourage people to get married. Perhaps more people should marry—there are clear-cut economic benefits and therefore social benefits for children in two-parent households, but Obama ignored the social factors, such as unemployment, a dysfunctional criminal justice system, and failing public schools that contribute to gun violence.

35. Weaver, "The First Father," 297.
36. Ibid., 302.
37. Stephen Baskerville, "The Politics of Fatherhood," *PS: Political Science & Politics* 4 (December 2002): 695–99, 695.
38. Kaaryn Gustafson, "Breaking Vows: Marriage Promotion, the New Patriarchy, and the Retreat from Egalitarianism," *Stanford Journal of Civil Rights & Civil Liberties* 5, no. 2 (October 2009): 269–308, 289.
39. Ibid., 281.
40. Quoted in Aly Parker, "Can't Buy Me Love: Funding Marriage Promotion versus Listening to Real Needs in Breaking the Cycle of Poverty," *Southern California Review of Law & Social Justice* 18, no.2 (Spring 2009): 493–536, 503.
41. Ibid., 503.
42. For more discussion on the politics surrounding responsible fatherhood legislation and movements, see Scott Coltrane, "Marketing the Marriage 'Solution': Misplaced Simplicity in the Politics of Fatherhood," *Sociological Perspectives* 44, no. 4 (Winter 2001): 387–418; and Maureen R. Waller, "Viewing Low-Income Fathers' Ties to Families through A Cultural Lens: Insights for Research and Policy," *Annals of the American Academy of Political and Social Science* 629, no. 1 (May 2010): 102, 24. For specific links between responsible fatherhood politics and marriage promotion geared toward black men and marriage restriction, see Sean Cahill, "Welfare Moms and the Two Grooms: The Concurrent Promotion and Restriction of Marriage in US Public Policy," *Sexualities* 8, no. 2 (2005): 169–87. For specific links between recent marriage promotion and postbellum use of marriage to "civilize" newly freed slaves, see Angela Onwuachi-Willig, "The Return of the Ring: Welfare Reform's Marriage Cure as the Revival of Post-Bellum Control," *California Law Review* 93 (December 2005): 1647–96.
43. See Katherine M. Franke, "Taking Care," *Chicago-Kent Law Review* 76 (2001): 1541–55; and Martha Albertson Fineman, "Contract and Care," *Chicago-Kent Law Review* 76, no. 3 (2001): 1403–40.
44. *Murray v. NBC*, 242.
45. Guerrero, "The Black Man on Our Screens," 398.
46. Duggan, *The Twilight of Equality?* 10 (emphasis mine).
47. *Murray v. NBC*, 242.
48. Guerrero, "The Black Man on Our Screens," 396.
49. Paula J. Massood, "An Aesthetic Appropriate to Conditions: *Killer of Sheep*,

(Neo)Realism, and the Documentary Impulse," *Wide Angle* 21, no. 4 (October 1999): 20–41, 36.

50. Armond White, introduction (on cover), *Killer of Sheep*, directed by Charles Burnett (Milestone Film & Video, 2007), DVD.

51. An example of a black man registering the kitchen as an intimate space can be found in Henry Louis Gates's autobiographical essay, "In the Kitchen," *New Yorker*, April 18, 1994, 82–86.

52. I refer to Stan's wife as "Stan's Wife," because that is the only form of identification she has in the film other than that of a mother.

53. Massood, "An Aesthetic Appropriate to Conditions," 32.

54. Ibid.

55. Ibid., 29.

56. White, introduction, *Killer of Sheep*.

57. Lolita Buckner Inniss, "A Domestic Right of Return? Race, Rights, and Residency in New Orleans in the Aftermath of Hurricane Katrina," *Boston College Third World Law Journal* 27, no. 2 (2007): 325–73, 328.

58. The real-life aurochs were large cattle-like animals, but for reasons of pragmatism, *Beasts* uses potbellied pigs as aurochs, since the choice of animals smart enough to train for the film was limited to pigs and dogs.

59. Deborah A. Salem et al., "Effects of Family Structure, Family Process, and Father Involvement on Psychosocial Outcomes among African American Adolescents," *Family Relations* 47, no. 4 (1998): 331–41, 338.

60. Sandra L. Hofferth, "Race/Ethnic Differences in Father Involvement in Two-Parent Families: Culture, Context, or Economy?," *Journal of Family Issues* 24, no. 2 (March 2003): 185–216, 187–91.

61. Noodling is when you use your bare fist as bait to catch fish from the side of a boat or in waders.

62. hooks, *We Real Cool*, xii.

63. bell hooks, "No Love in the Wild," *New Black Man (in Exile)*, September 5, 2012, http://newblackman.blogspot.com/2012/09/bell-hooks-no-love-in -wild.html.

64. Ibid.

65. Ibid.

66. Ibid.

CHAPTER FIVE

1. Patrick J. Egan and Kenneth Sherrill, "California's Proposition 8: What Happened, and What Does the Future Hold?" (National Gay and Lesbian Task Force Policy Institute, January 2009), http://www.thetaskforce.org/ downloads/reports/reports/pi_prop8_1_6_09.pdf.

2. Nelson George, a black popular culture author and critic, was the executive producer of the series.

3. Born Robert Moppins Jr. and later legally known as Robert Beck, but best known by his pen name, Iceberg Slim was a pimp, hustler, and ex-felon who launched a popular urban fiction series while incarcerated during the 1960s. Rappers like Ice Cube and Ice-T pay homage to Beck's legend through their own selected stage names.

4. John W. Roberts, *From Trickster to Badman: The Black Folk Hero in Slavery and Freedom* (Philadelphia: University of Pennsylvania Press, 1989), 1.

5. Roberts uses Stagger Lee or Stackolee as an example. Roberts, *From Trickster to Badman*, 185–212.

6. Snipes would play a similar role several years later in *Sugar Hill* (1994), which repeated the theme of admirable badman. A more contemporary version of the theme is the highly acclaimed HBO drama *The Wire*.

7. It is important to note that the types of heroes I am referencing are distinctly different from those in film series such as *Dirty Harry* and *Die Hard*, in which the good guys go rogue in order to infiltrate crime. The characters in these types of films are often framed by violence and a disregard for due process, but their actions are always to protect civilians and bring about some form of justice. The Frank Lucases and Nino Browns are involved in activities that are against the law and self-serving.

8. When I discuss the "black community," I am cognizant that desegregation dismantled what once was a literal black community. I continue to use the phrase as a means of describing a black collective experience or sensibility in general terms.

9. Mark Jacobson, "Lords of Dopetown," *New York*, October 25, 2007, http://nymag.com/guides/money/2007/39948/.

10. Roger Ebert, "Training Day," October 5, 2001, http://www.rogerebert.com/reviews/training-day-2001.

11. Frederick S. Barrett et al., "Music-Evoked Nostalgia: Affect, Memory, and Personality," *Emotion* 10, no. 3 (2010): 390–403, 401.

12. David R. Shumway, "Rock 'n' Roll Sound Tracks and the Production of Nostalgia," *Cinema Journal* 38, no. 2 (Winter 1999): 36–51, 37.

13. The interview can be viewed on YouTube and various hip-hop media websites.

14. George Lipsitz, *The Possessive Investment in Whiteness: How White People Profit from Identity Politics* (Philadelphia: Temple University Press, 1998), 1.

15. Darlene Clark Hine, William C. Hine, and Stanley Harrold, *African Americans: A Concise History*, 3rd ed. (Upper Saddle River, NJ: Pearson Prentice Hall, 2009), 560.

16. Cornelius Eady, *Brutal Imagination* (New York: G.P. Putnam's Sons, 2001), 62.

17. Ibid., 105.

18. Ibid.

19. Ibid., 106.

20. Ibid., 81.

21. Ibid., 88–89.
22. Ibid., 90.
23. The italicized words are interspersed in bold type in the front matter of the book—like a code for the reader to decipher.
24. In *Looking for Leroy,* Neal notes the challenges the series and its actors encountered with regard to recognition because of the un/believability of the storylines, as well as the criminal business ingenuity of the real-life Baltimore crew around which the writers framed the series.
25. Quoted in Neal, *Looking for Leroy,* 92–93.
26. "Antoine Dodson to Become a Hebrew Israelite," Huffpost Live, http://live .huffingtonpost.com/r/segment/antoine-dodson-renounces-homosexuality -to-become-a-hebrew-israelite/5182bb0dfe3444064200027e.
27. Dale Carpenter, *Flagrant Conduct: The Story of Lawrence v. Texas* (New York: W.W. Norton, 2012).
28. The use of "bisexual and transgender" or LGBT by Carpenter or others analyzing this case is not prevalent, but the case is celebrated widely as a LGBT civil rights victory.
29. Carpenter's investigation reveals that, in all likelihood, Garner and Lawrence were not engaged in any sexual act at the time of the deputies' arrival; in fact, the two never had any sexual relations before or after their arrest, explaining why they initially pleaded not guilty to the charges and changed their plea to no contest only after being contacted by gay civil rights legal counsel.
30. *Lawrence* overturned *Bowers v. Hardwick* (1986), which held that there was no constitutional protection for acts of sodomy, allowing states to outlaw those practices.
31. The March on Washington, the 16th Street Baptist Church bombing, *Brown v. Board of Education* (1954), the Civil Rights Act, the murders of Chaney, Goodman, and Schwerner, and Freedom Summer are some of the events memorialized in 2013 and 2014.
32. Manning Marable's biography of Malcolm X, *Malcolm X: A Life of Reinvention* (New York: Viking Penguin, 2011), complicates the latter attribute, as Marable reveals same-sex relationships during Malcolm's early life.
33. Carpenter, *Flagrant Conduct,* 277.
34. Garner died on September 11, 2006, from, as reported by his brother, complications caused by meningitis, although some believed the cause of death was tuberculosis, and Lawrence, who did not realize Garner was ill, thought pneumonia (Carpenter 280). Upon his death, his family was too poor to bury him. Executive director of Lambda Legal, Kevin Cathcart, tried unsuccessfully to raise money within the gay community, and in mid-October, Garner's family released his body to the state for a no-cost cremation.
35. In *Black Sexual Politics,* Patricia Hill Collins remembers the black community's silence around the hate-crime murder of a fifteen-year-old black

lesbian, Sakia Gunn, in Newark, New Jersey, on May 11, 2003. "Black leaders and national organizations," by Collins's account, "spoke volumes through their silence." Patricia Hill Collins, *Black Sexual Politics: African Americans, Gender, and the New Racism* (New York: Routledge, 2005), 116.

36. Collins, *Black Sexual Politics*, 88.

37. Athena D. Mutua, ed., *Progressive Black Masculinities* (New York: Routledge, 2006), 5.

CHAPTER SIX

1. Kanye West et al., *Late Registration* (Roc-A-Fella, Def Jam, 2005).

2. For a detailed history and explanation of how radical and unprecedented this order was, see Eric Foner, *Reconstruction: America's Unfinished Revolution, 1863–1877* (New York: Harper and Row, 1988).

3. "Forty Acres and a Mule" is memorialized in black public memory as the name of the African American filmmaker Spike Lee's film production company.

4. For brief overviews of the evolution of Sherman's order, see Henry Louis Gates Jr., "The Truth Behind '40 Acres and a Mule,'" http://www.theroot .com/print/69062; and Barton Myers's report online in the *New Georgia Encyclopedia* at http://www.georgiaencyclopedia.org/nge/Article.jsp?id=h -3353.

5. "The Freedmen in Georgia: Report of the Conference between Secretary Stanton, General Sherman, and the Colored People," *New-York Daily Tribune*, Monday, February 13, 1865, 5, http://chroniclingamerica.loc.gov/ lccn/sn83030213/1865-02-13/ed-1/.

6. Ibid.

7. Ibid.

8. Foner, *Reconstruction*, 243.

9. Ibid.

10. Ibid., 245.

11. The Fifteenth Amendment granted suffrage only to black men. Women of all races would have to wait until the Nineteenth Amendment was ratified in 1920 to be granted suffrage. This act of Congress created significant dissension between the white women's suffrage movement that had largely supported abolition and further efforts toward securing civil rights for African Americans.

12. Foner, *Reconstruction*, 247.

13. Ibid., 247 (emphasis mine).

14. Ibid., 250 (emphasis mine).

15. Michael J. Klarman, *From Jim Crow to Civil Rights: The Supreme Court and the Struggle for Racial Equality* (New York: Oxford University Press, 2004), 80.

16. Ibid., 19.

17. Quoted in Juliet E. K. Walker, *The History of Black Business in America: Capitalism, Race, Entrepreneurship* (New York: Macmillan Library Reference, 1998), 150.

18. Although Garvey rejected white political alliances and social interaction, his business mortgages were held by white-owned banks. Walker, *The History of Black Business*, 222.

19. Walker, *The History of Black Business*, 222.

20. Ibid., 221.

21. Wilson Jeremiah Moses, *Creative Conflict in African American Thought: Frederick Douglass, Alexander Crummell, Booker T. Washington, W. E. B. Du Bois, and Marcus Garvey* (New York: Cambridge University Press, 2004), 255.

22. Mark Christian Thompson, *Black Fascisms: African American Literature and Culture between the Wars* (Charlottesville: University of Virgina Press, 2007), 49–50.

23. Robert A. Hill, ed., *Marcus Garvey: Life and Lessons* (Berkeley: University of California Press, 1987), 208.

24. Quoted in Sigmund C. Shipp, "The Road Not Taken: Alternative Strategies for Black Economic Development in the United States," *Journal of Economic Issues* 30, no. 1 (March 1996): 79–95, 87.

25. Amy Jacques Garvey, ed., *Philosophy and Opinions of Marcus Garvey* (Dover, MA: Majority Press, 1986), 55.

26. Ibid.

27. Hill, *Marcus Garvey*, 290–93.

28. Thompson, *Black Fascisms*, 61.

29. Garvey, *Philosophy and Opinions of Marcus Garvey*, 72.

30. Hill, *Marcus Garvey*, 345.

31. Ibid., 210–11.

32. Moses, *Creative Conflict*, 247.

33. Shipp, "The Road Not Taken," 87.

34. Walker, *The History of Black Business*, 182.

35. William Muraskin, "The Harlem Boycott of 1934: Black Nationalism and the Rise of Labor-Union Consciousness," *Labor History* 13, no. 3 (1972): 361–73, 361.

36. Ibid., 363.

37. Moses, *Creative Conflict*, 251.

38. Walker, *The History of Black Business*, 222.

39. Moses, *Creative Conflict*, 251.

40. Hill, *Marcus Garvey*, 305.

41. For details of the vicissitudes of the Black Star Line, see Tony Martin, *Race First: The Ideological and Organizational Struggles of Marcus Garvey and the Universal Negro Improvement Association* (Westport, CT: Greenwood Press, 1976).

42. Martin, *Race First*, 154–60.

43. Edmund David Cronon, *Black Moses: The Story of Marcus Garvey and the Universal Negro Association* (Madison: University of Wisconsin Press, 1955), 100.

44. Quoted in Martin, *Race First*, 174.
45. Eason was expelled for ninety-nine years because of charges of financial "irregularities." See Martin, *Race First*, 318, for additional details.
46. Moses, *Creative Conflict*, 275.
47. Martin, *Race First*, 319.
48. Ibid., 321.
49. Ibid.
50. Ibid., 323; there are black men (and women) with red hair and fair skin, so I am not sure why the conclusion was so definitive, particularly considering the risks involved with gaining access to the white body parts of a white person, whether living or dead.
51. Judith Stein, *The World of Marcus Garvey: Race and Class in Modern Society* (Baton Rouge: Louisiana State University Press, 1986), 166.
52. Ibid.
53. Martin, *Race First*, 326–27.
54. See Stein, *The World of Marcus Garvey*, 167; Moses, *Creative Conflict*, 281; and Martin, *Race First*, 325.
55. For an empirical study of the trouble with criminal law, race, and drugs, see Michelle Alexander, *The New Jim Crow* (New York: New Press, 2010) and Paul Butler's *Let's Get Free: A Hip Hop Theory of Justice* (New York: New Press, 2009).
56. Richard Majors and Janet Mancini Bilson, *Cool Pose: The Dilemmas of Black Manhood in America* (New York: Lexington Books, 1992).
57. Two different approaches to lynching: the NAACP contributed to an antilynching fund, whereas a *Negro World* editorial promised the UNIA would fight lynching by physical means (Martin, *Race First*, 276). Once the Dyer Bill was presented, however, the UNIA supported it in spite of its opposition to the NAACP. The UNIA's "Declaration of the Rights of the Negro Peoples of the World" advocates self-protection in its twelfth and sixteenth declarations:

> 12. We believe that the Negro should adopt every means to protect himself against barbarous practices inflicted upon him because of color.
>
> 16. We believe all men should live in peace one with the other, but when races and nations provoke the ire of other races and nations by attempting to infringe upon their rights, war becomes inevitable, and the attempt in any way to free one's self or protect one's rights or heritage becomes justifiable.

58. Martin Summers, *Manliness and Its Discontents: The Black Middle Class and the Transformation of Masculinity, 1900–1930* (Chapel Hill: University of North Carolina Press, 2004), 1.
59. Kimmel, *Manhood in America*, 1.
60. Ibid., 13.
61. Hill, *Marcus Garvey*, 291.

62. Ibid., 125.
63. Garvey, *Philosophy and Opinions of Marcus Garvey*, 312.
64. Ibid., 315.
65. Ibid.
66. Ibid.
67. Ibid., 319.
68. Tom Brokaw, *Boom! Voices of the Sixties: Personal Reflections on the '60s and Today* (New York: Random House, 2007), 338.
69. Ibid., 271.
70. When Sam Cooke released "A Change Is Gonna Come" in 1964, the civil rights movement immediately adopted it as an anthem.
71. Klarman, *From Jim Crow to Civil Rights*, 18.
72. Simon Frith, Will Straw, and John Street, *The Cambridge Companion to Pop and Rock* (Cambridge: Cambridge University Press, 2001), 89.
73. Quoted in Suzanne E. Smith, *Dancing in the Street: Motown and the Cultural Politics of Detroit* (1999; Cambridge, MA.: Harvard University Press, 2003), 104.
74. Ibid., 17.
75. Ibid.
76. Berry Gordy, *To Be Loved: The Music, the Magic, the Memories of Motown* (New York: Warner Books, 1994), 306.
77. Ibid.
78. Mark Anthony Neal, "Rhythm and Protest: Motown's Forgotten Revolution," http://newblackman.blogspot.com/2010/06/rhythm-and-protest-motowns-forgotten.html.
79. Barrett Strong performed this hit, cowritten by Gordy and Janie Bradford. The Beatles, the Rolling Stones, and the Doors, among others, later covered the song.
80. Brokaw, *Boom!* 338.
81. Mark Anthony Neal, "Sold Out on Soul: The Corporate Annexation of Black Popular Music," *Popular Music and Society* 21, no. 3 (1997): 117–35, 117.
82. Gerald Posner, *Motown: Music, Money, Sex, and Power* (2002; New York: Random House, 2005), 3.
83. Gerald Lyn Early, *One Nation under a Groove: Motown and American Culture* (1995; Ann Arbor: University of Michigan Press, 2004), 91.
84. On April 3, 1968, King gave his "I've Been to the Mountaintop" speech in Memphis, Tennessee, where he was supporting the Memphis sanitation workers' strike.
85. Garveyism and the UNIA have always held a place in the consciousness of Pan-Africanists and black nationalists, and Garvey's influence on Malcolm X, whose father was a UNIA member, is well noted, but the following the UNIA had during Garvey's heyday in Harlem has significantly diminished. However, Brooklyn rappers Mos Def and Talib Kweli's release of their *Black Star* collaboration in August 1998 paid explicit homage to

Garvey through its title referencing Garvey's Black Star Line steamship company. The tracks on the CD are reminiscent of Garvey's critiques of Eurocentrism, social ills, black unity, and embracing blackness.

86. S. Craig Watkins, "'Black Is Back, and It's Bound to Sell!' Nationalist Desire and the Production of Black Popular Culture," in *Is It Nation Time? Contemporary Essays on Black Power and Black Nationalism*, ed. Eddie S. Glaude Jr. (Chicago: University of Chicago Press, 2002), 191.

87. Quoted in Walker, *The History of Black Business*, 269.

88. Walker, *The History of Black Business*, 269.

89. Shawn Carter, *Decoded* (New York: Spiegel and Grau, 2010), 56.

90. The incident occurred in 1993.

91. Carter, *Decoded*, 15.

92. Ibid., 17.

93. Ibid., 3.

94. Ibid., 7.

95. Ibid., 22.

96. Ibid.

97. Ibid., 27.

98. Ibid., 239.

99. It is worth noting that she replaces another black woman in that position, Oprah Winfrey, who was number one in 2013 and moved to number four for 2014 (Jay-Z is number six). Ellen DeGeneres also made the top five for 2014, making the top five predominantly women. It is also worth mentioning that Katy Perry and Robert Downey Jr. join DeGeneres as the only white celebrities on Forbes's 2014 list of most powerful celebrities.

100. Ula Taylor, *The Veiled Garvey: The Life and Times of Amy Jacques Garvey* (Chapel Hill: University of North Carolina Press, 2002), 23.

101. Ibid., 31.

102. Ibid., 37.

103. Ibid., 50.

104. Ibid., 60.

105. Ibid., 56.

106. Phillip Brian Harper, "Synesthesia, 'Crossover,' and Blacks in Popular Music," *Social Text* 23 (Autumn–Winter 1989): 102–21, 107–8.

Index

Abbott, Robert S., 184
Adams, Vivian Clark, 88
Adventures of Huckleberry Finn
(Twain), 218–19n9
Africa, 56, 75, 178, 182, 190
African American literature, 51,
54, 60–61; intertextuality
in, 52
African Americans, vii, 31–32,
59, 152, 192–93, 204, 206–9,
231n11; the badman, 153–54;
black people, haunting effect
on, 118; black property rights,
122; and black rage, 106, 109;
black rights, ix; in California,
219n23, 220n38; citizen-
ship, struggle for, 173–75;
and common sense, 64; crack
cocaine epidemic, 195, 197;
criminal behavior, excused
by, 151; and disremembrance,
82; "driving while black," 197;
folk heroes of, 153–54; heroin
epidemic, 195; home ownership, difficulty of, 61–63; and
homosexuality, 151; hoodies,
criminalization of, xi; informal
economies among, 194–95;
land ownership, 173; pain and
shame, collective suffering of,
82; Proposition 8, support of,
150; race-restrictive covenants, 63; as racialized group,
118; and segregation, 58,
63–64; and self-reliance, 176;
social and cultural capital, lack
of, 170; "stop and frisk" stops,
ix–x, 211n4; as suspects, vii–ix;
the trickster, 153–54; and
twisted criminality, 151; usable pasts, 167–68; and wealth
building, 171, 182–83
*Against Race: Imagining Political
Culture beyond the Color Line*
(Gilroy), x
agency, xi–xii, 39, 50, 52, 188
*Ain't I a Feminist? African American
Men Speak Out on Fatherhood,
Friendship, Forgiveness, and
Freedom* (White), 7
Alexander, Elizabeth, 53, 66–69,
221n56; and black interior,
51–52, 76
Alexander, Michelle, xi
Almond, Edward E., 97–100, 103,
111, 223n21
American Broadcasting Corpora-
tion (ABC), 125
American dream, 59, 106, 110, 138,
158, 170, 195
American Educational Research
Association, 215n26
American Gangster (film), 15,
17, 152, 155; soundtrack of,
156–57
American Negro Academy, 2
American West, 70–71; in public
imagination, 72; and race, 76
Anansi, 153
Angelou, Maya, 30–31
Anna Records, 192
anthropometrics, 57